Achieving World-Class Schools:

Mastering School Improvement

Using a Genetic Model

Achieving World-Class Schools: Mastering School Improvement Using a Genetic Model

Paul L. Kimmelman and David J. Kroeze

Christopher-Gordon Publishers, Inc.
Norwood, Massachusetts

Credits

Christopher-Gordon Publishers, Inc.
1502 Providence Highway, Suite 12
Norwood, MA 02062
800-934-8322

Printed in the United States of America

10 9 8 7 6 5 4 3 2   06 05 04 03

Library of Congress Catalog Card Number: 2002100023

ISBN: 1-929024-45-2

Acknowledgments

There are so many people who in the course of a career have in one way or another had an influence on our work. We could never mention all of them so we begin by saying thank you to them.

First, we would like to thank Elaine Aumiller and Jean McGrew. Without their support, critical questioning, and thoughtful input, this book would not have been written. Jean has synthesized his thoughts in the Foreword. We are indebted to Elaine for her invaluable contributions to this book and for the incredible time she devoted to its completion. She has been a true partner in our work. Her ideas, rewrites of the manuscript, and incredible graphics are sincerely appreciated.

Our guest writers deserve a debt of gratitude: Michael Barber, Marie Carbo, David Clarke, Christopher Cross and Rene Islas, Jan deLange, Denis Doyle, Ramesh Gangolli, Governor James Geringer, Richard Haynes, Paul Houston, Susan Loucks-Horsley, George Nelson, James Stigler and Jim Hiebert, Martin Ripley, Andrew Rotherham, Laura Singer, and Dennis Sparks. Their work on behalf of education is exemplary and we are proud to feature their thoughts and expertise in our book. (Their essays can be found interspersed throughout the book and in appendix A.)

We want to acknowledge the untimely death of Susan Loucks-Horsley who passed away shortly after writing her guest essay. Susan's passion for professional development and education was always evident in her work. We are fortunate to have her thoughts included with our book.

We want to thank our colleagues, in particular the leaders of the First in the World Consortium, for being our professional friends over the years. Education is a complex profession and whether it was a school board member, administrator, teacher, or a member of the support staff, their contributions to education have helped many children and young adults. We are indebted to Gina Burkhardt, Executive Director of the North Central Regional Education Laboratory, and members of her staff for providing perspective on the importance of education research and implementing it in classrooms.

We want to thank our families for enduring our countless hours of debate, discussion, and absence from family responsibilities. To the Kimmelmans, Marsha, Leah, Renee Roen and her husband Scott, Jim and his wife Sandy, Paul's mother Helen and her husband Sam, please know that I appreciate all that you have done to help me with my career. To the Kroezes, Linda, Steven, Erin, Ryan, David, and Kristin, I thank you for your patience and understanding as Paul and I wrote this book. Your sacrifice enabled us to achieve this work. Thank you for your support of my career.

Finally, a sincere thank you to Sue Canavan and Christopher-Gordon Publishing. You guided, remained patient, and took a chance. We hope we fulfilled your expectations.

Authors Comments: An Update

Two significant education events took place as this book was going to press in December 2001. The first event was the release of the results from PISA, Program for International Student Assessment sponsored by the Organization for Economic Cooperation and Development. A summary of those results and a Web site address for more information are included in chapter 2 in the section on PISA. The second event was Congress approving the Elementary and Secondary Education Act (ESEA). This legislation was expected to be signed by President Bush in January 2002. The new ESEA contains the most significant changes since it was written in 1965. Congressmen John Boehner and George Miller and Senators Judd Gregg and Edward Kennedy were the conferees who guided the final legislation through Congress. Their work was considered a bipartisan effort and a significant achievement given the different political views about education in Congress. Some highlights of the new legislation are:

- Beginning in 2005–2006, each state will be required to annually test students in grades 3–8 in reading and mathematics. Each state will also be required to add science exams the following year and students will be tested one time during grades 3–5, 6–8, and 10–12. Schools that fail to make adequate yearly progress toward all students meeting proficiency will face serious consequences.

- To ensure that states have acceptable standards, they will be required to randomly test their students using the National Assessment for Educational Progress (NAEP). The Act specifically prohibits a national test for all students.

- By 2006 all teachers will be expected to meet a new definition of highly qualified. States could require teachers to pass subject tests or have a major in their teaching assignment.

- Parents will have the option to obtain private tutoring for their children in schools that fail to make adequate progress for two consecutive years. In addition, parents could send their children to another public school if their children are in unsafe or failing schools.

- The number of programs in the ESEA was reduced. Some programs that duplicated services were combined.

- Students in bilingual education will be tested in reading in English after three consecutive years of school attendance in the United States. There will no longer be a requirement that bilingual students be taught in their native language.

- Public school districts will be required to issue reports that show how their students perform. The reports will include graduation rates and student achievement results must be categorized along racial, gender, and economic lines.

- Federal funds will be directed toward the most disadvantaged students. Title I programs in areas with disadvantaged students will receive increased funding.

The ESEA contains over 1,000 pages of legislation. As of this writing, it was too early to fully understand the implications for educators. To be sure, the federal role in education has taken on greater responsibility for ensuring that all American children receive a high-quality education and achieve proficiency according to their state standards. If they don't, the consequences could be severe and include parental choice for private tutoring or even sending their children to a different public school.

Foreword

It takes a village to raise a child.[i] The message is simple, that is, the core values of the child's community will relentlessly seep into the child's experience and shape the emerging adult. Does the child experience a compassionate community practicing daily acts of kindness and consideration? Does the child experience gangs, drugs and violence as the norm? Is the community excessively competitive—"We're number one"?

Whatever those core values, they will be absorbed by the community's children. Certainly, parents can play a major role in combating negative values as they steer their child to adulthood. However, most parents recognize this to be a daunting task knowing "It [does] take a [whole] community to raise a child.

The same could be said of schools—it takes a whole school community to educate a child. After all, schools are the most common community for America's children throughout their formative years. It doesn't take long for children to figure out what is valued and what is not. "It takes a whole school . . ."

Why, then, have American schools been under such criticism for the last several decades? Why, then, with U.S. income and productivity the envy of the world, do American students appear to show only mediocre achievement? Why, then, have billions of additive dollars not produced more substantive results?

The authors, veteran school administrators, forcefully argue that the schoolhouse design (or school district) is flawed and until those flaws are addressed, no amount of money or hand wringing will produce the "world class" results the authors believe attainable. Left unaddressed, "world class" will remain only political rhetoric passed on from one administration to the next.

While the flaws are many, they are neither incomprehensible nor so numerous as to be overwhelming. Each flaw considered separately probably could find a reasonable remedy among thoughtful educators. However, it is exactly "considering each flaw separately" that is, according to the authors, the single greatest flaw of all. To reach for the stars, schools must think and operate *holistically*. Simply stated, "The whole is larger than the sum of the parts."

Is the holistic design proposed by the authors achievable? Yes, but only if schools (school districts) are willing to devote more cerebral energy than has been evident so far. A journey to holistic thinking is not for the timid or the faint of heart, and even with the best holistic thinking and application, noticeable results will not emerge quickly.

To facilitate the journey to "holism" the authors proffer a metaphoric road map, the human genetic system. The human genetic system may well be the ultimate example of holistic design. Each subset of the human gene is designed to work in sync with other subsets. Working properly (holistically)—good health. Working improperly—poor health and even death. It is an apt metaphor for any school or social system.

The reader, however, must keep in mind that the genetic design is a metaphor. The purpose is to stimulate rethinking about how schools, which are dynamic and living entities similar to the human body, function holistically to generate optimal health. Neither schools nor the human genetic code can be truly understood by examining only separate components.

But in order to visualize the whole, one must sort out the parts for review, that is, examine the *relationship* of parts to other parts and to the whole. While the whole is indeed greater than the sum of its parts, the whole remains an abstraction that can only emerge from attending to the critical parts.

The authors provide the reader a picture of those parts/relationships (in school design) by drawing parallel examples from the human genetic system. The reader must keep in mind that this parallel genetic metaphor is designed to focus the mind on the *relationship* of parts to one another and to the whole.

And what *parts* may there be? While the authors will consider several parts-to-whole, the quintessential consideration is that of defining *core values*. Old hat? Been there, done that? Maybe. How many of us have rank-ordered a ten-question survey seeking to define our schools' core values? How many of us have spent an afternoon of staff development debating core values in order to establish our objectives for the year? Does anyone really believe that such minimal attention will drive the schools? Doubtful. Simply stated, is the establishment of core values really (in itself) a core value? Not very often.

Deciphering core values is an arduous and usually conflicting task. Many educators simply don't have the patience to dig deeply into the institutional psyche. Far too often, some low-level common denominator is found acceptable, thus allowing everyone to get back to the *real* work. This, of course, misses the point. The real work for those aspiring to world-class levels is first and foremost to define and operate from a clearly understood set of core values in every part of school operation. Without such understanding, holistic execution is nearly impossible.

Reflection? Certainly a positive in the educators' lexicon. Some individuals are more reflective concerning the school enterprise than others. But how often is there arduous collective reflection among school staffs? When was the last time you remember a staff collectively concluding "This isn't working and we must make a change"? Time consuming? Yes. Difficult? Yes. Impossible? No. Critical to those who aspire to "world class"? Absolutely.

Research? How many schools are driven by research? Not many. How many schools even pay much attention to whatever educational research that may exist? Not many. How many schools use collective standardized test scores and local assessment measures as an in-depth diagnostic tool? Not many.

Certainly it is arguable that there exists a disconnect between those who produce education research and practitioners. Many researchers don't see application as their responsibility, nor is it high on the priority toward promotion. Can research make a difference? Yes, or at least it should. Can the disconnect between researcher and practitioner be fixed? Yes, but it will take a lot of work. Is research critical to "world-class" performance—probably. Stated another way, schools are unlikely to achieve such status if they ignore the core research available.

Finally, staff development. Not much needs to be said here. Most readers can fill in the blanks—and they are mostly blanks. Unfortunately, most staff development is, at best, unfocused and occasional. An inspirational speaker supplemented with announcements and some handouts is a common format. Follow up? Hardly ever.

It takes a *whole* school to educate a child. It takes core values, reflection, research, staff development, plus other citations identified by the authors, all working systemically to make a *whole* school "world class." The genetic metaphor is apt. The human genetic system is designed to operate holistically, that is, each part operating purposefully with other parts. When not operating purposefully, the whole is negatively affected.

The authors do not offer an easy formula or "cookbook." Quite the contrary. Their challenge is daunting. Can a school/school district accomplish that which is proffered in the following pages? Only the reader can determine that. It is reasonable to consider, as the authors do, ". . . it does take a whole school to educate a child (to a world-class level)." If the reader agrees, let the journey begin. The next steps are . . .

> Jean B. McGrew
> Director, Off-Campus Graduate Programs
> Loyola University Chicago

Endnotes

i.   Hillary Rodham Clinton, *It takes a village: and other lessons children teach us* (New York: Simon & Schuster, 1996).

Preface

We began our work on the genetic model for education long before we became aware of The Human Genome Project, a public/private undertaking to identify all of the human genes to improve human health, and the publication of *Genome-The Autobiography of a Species in Twenty-three Chapters* by Matt Ridley.[ii] In his book, Matt Ridley writes about the 23 human chromosomes and how they work to make a human being. While we always believed our genetic model was a fundamentally sound concept for transforming schools to achieve world-class performance, Ridley's work and The Human Genome Project further convinced us that using the principles of genetics for school improvement made sense. First, it incorporates the concept of local control of schools. There are differences in the compositions of human beings just as there are in the governance of schools; yet, each is capable of world-class achievement. Second, just as it takes more than one chromosome to build a human system, improving a school system requires more than one approach. Organizations, like human beings, are complex and require complex strategies to improve. Finally, The Human Genome Project set out to identify every human DNA–gene strand that makes up a human being. A similar project in education could identify all of the research and practices that have been proven to help students learn and teachers teach more effectively. It takes just 30,000–40,000 genes to make a human being, far fewer than the 140,000 that were predicted prior to the Genome study. Educators do not need to use every practice to be successful—just enough to ensure that every student learns what is expected of him/her. Different combinations of genes make different human beings; likewise, different teaching strategies ensure success for different students.

We believe the concept of the genetic model can help take an organization out of the chaos of American education reform. We have identified six chromosomes (core areas) as the basis from which to start writing a plan to achieve world-class performance. Genetically there are two categories of chromosomes, X and Y. We have also developed two categories of chromosomes as well. Our first category is the capacity-building chromosomes: leadership, change, and professional development. Our second category is the teaching-learning process chromosomes: curriculum, instructional practice, and assessment. Our six chromosomes are not intended to be the only chromosomes for a genetic model; others can be selected or added later.

We delve deeper into the make-up of our chromosomes by identifying genes of research and practice to assist in the crafting of a genetic model. We offer examples of the potential genes you could use, but as we noted earlier, only 30,000–40,000 of over 3 billion possible genes are used to make a human being; likewise, a few effective educational practices could lead to world-class student achievement.

Imagine a project in education that identified the core areas of a world-class education system and cited all of the known research on each of them. It seems to us that a project of this type would about bring systemic thinking that is long overdue. In the end, educators would have the necessary information to make informed decisions regarding how their schools could become internationally competitive and world-class.

This book is divided into two parts. Part I, chapters 1-3 includes the background for using the genetic model, concepts of world-class education, and a description of the model itself. These chapters offer a backdrop for using the genetic model and should be considered the less complex portion of the book.

Part II is more complex and will require the reader to delve in to the complexities of using a genetic model. Like truly effective scientific work, the process of using the genetic model should be considered not only "hard work" but requiring a sustained oversight of the school improvement effort. This section of the book includes a thorough set of activities and examples to guide the reader through the process.

We believe the process of improving education goes beyond the simple adage, however, of it being just hard work. Real education improvement is organizationally complex, cerebral, and requires an incredible leadership effort. In that context, it is advisable to be forewarned that chapters 4 and 5 are not "light" reading. In all likelihood they will need to be read more than one time for a clear understanding of our work. Once understood we are confident that using the genetic model will lead to a conceptual understanding of the complexities of educational improvement based on sound research and practices.

In chapter 1, we explain why a genetic model can be used to improve school systems. We hope that by using a scientific analogy for school improvement that the wider American community, both supporters and critics of education, will better understand the complexities and challenges inherent in school systems and in the teaching-learning process. It is our hope that the reader will capture our vision of a more sophisticated conceptualization of school systems—a conceptualization that is necessary to meet the challenges of the 21st century society. A conceptualization we also see in both the business and medical professions.

In chapter 2, we articulate the critical components of a world-class school system. While there is no unanimous agreement on the definition of a world-class school system, we can safely say that our genetic model provides the structure to address the most critical factors leading to world-class performance and status. For example, topics such as leadership, change, collaboration, curriculum, benchmarking, teaching as a science, assessment, and professional development integrate systemically to provide a meaningful framework for a school district to begin the quest.

The genetic model is described in chapter 3. This chapter compares how DNA–gene strands, chromosomes, and organisms can be used to conceptualize the fundamental principles, research-based practices, and core areas that form a world-class school district. While we do not delve into great detail on the biological concept of genetics, we do discuss some scientific principles that we feel are pertinent to the theme of our book.

Chapters 4 and 5 discuss our two categories of chromosomes. The capacity-building chromosomes comprise chapter 4. The chapter is divided into three sections, one for each chromosome: leadership, change, and professional development. Chapter 5 discusses the teaching-learning process chromosomes: curriculum, instructional practice, and assessment.

Finally, we provide a set of activities for each chromosome at the end of chapters 4 and 5 to assist you as you begin building your genetic model. These activities are intended as a guide and include worksheets that will focus your thinking and lead you through the development of each chromosome.

Striving to become world-class means that a district is capable of articulating and demonstrating the ability to compete and perform with the highest achieving countries in the world. To do so requires a local commitment to benchmark all aspects of the education system with those of high-achieving countries. However, it does not mean wholesale importing of their "best practices" into the local setting. World-class performance must be accomplished within an American culture of beliefs and practices. There are no "silver bullets."[iii] World-class benchmarking, although not a new concept, is just now becoming part of the local school district vocabulary and operation. It is the concept of comparing oneself against broader standards. It is no longer realistic to rely on state and nationally-normed achievement measures as the primary criteria for analyzing competitive student performance. In addition to these benchmarks, there is sufficient international data in mathematics, science, and reading to guide knowledgeable educators on a path toward world-class standards in their own school districts.

We hope our work helps you look at your schools with an eye toward world-class student achievement while recognizing that local control is the basis for the governance of American schools. It is unlikely that a federal mandate is going to impose a single solution that will improve the achievement of American students. Instead, the decision about how to improve will be left to the states and local school districts. The genetic model allows for local control but utilizes research-based, data-driven decision-making with a qualitative review of education practices in schools and countries that have high student achievement and effective teaching practices.

Finally, the goal of developing the genetic model is to focus on those values, beliefs, and practices that will bring about higher student achievement and improved teaching. The ultimate outcome is to improve performance that results in the students becoming members of a WORLDWIDE COMMUNITY OF EXCELLENCE. This process is not designed to create a horse race to be number one; rather, its purpose is to develop a learning community of high-performers who can compete with the highest-achieving students in the world.

Endnotes

ii. Matt Ridley, *Genome-the autobiography of a species in twenty-three chapters* (New York: Harper-Collins, 1999).

iii. Paul Kimmelman, "Looking for the education Lone Ranger-six silver bullets that could save our schools," *American School Board Journal* (November 1998).

Part I

Theoretical Underpinnings

Setting the Context for Using
the Genetic Model

World-Class Education Concepts

The Genetic Model

Chapter 1

Setting the Context
for Using a Genetic Model

Overview of Key Concepts

- *Leading school systems to world-class performance is a complex task involving many interrelated concepts, beliefs, relationships, and structures.*

- *School districts often lack the systemic capacity to develop, implement, and extend new ideas about teaching and learning to most teachers and students.*

- *Organizations face natural obstacles that deter school improvement efforts. These obstacles are categorized into three groups: organizational, practical, and political.*

- *The genetic model provides a conceptual process to develop a comprehensive relationship among essential components in schools.*

- *The genetic model can be used to begin the process toward scaling up to world-class performance.*

Introduction

One must wonder why two school superintendents would use a genetic metaphor to organize schools that could lead to world-class performance. Actually, the idea of utilizing DNA, genes, and chromosomes grew out of the authors' sensitivity to America's deep-seated belief in local control of schools. The science of genetics is about the manifestation of individual, distinct characteristics and traits of living organisms. Schools are living organizations, that we call social systems, whose function is to facilitate human development and learning. These organizations possess unique, individual characteristics that have a direct impact on the teaching-learning process and, ultimately, on students. The genetic model is a conceptual paradigm for schools and school districts to define and communicate their unique organizational characteristics that can lead to world-class performance.

After a number of years of working with policymakers, researchers, the U.S. Department of Education staff, our communities, administrators, teachers, and students, we have concluded that leading a school system to world-class performance is a complex task involving many interrelated concepts, beliefs, relationships, and structures. The extent to which these factors are developed and implemented will determine if a school district is achieving its desired outcomes or not. If poorly defined, they will not lead to world-class performance. If they are clear, based on high-quality research and practices, and well understood by district staff, they will lead to higher student achievement. Therefore, the fundamental task for a school district is to define, communicate, and implement concepts, relationships, beliefs, and structures that create a learning environment that leads to world-class performance.

In this book, we delve into essential areas of school improvement, believing that there are ways to define a school or district's own future and achieve its desired outcomes. It is through grappling with these areas that school districts will discover what they can truly achieve.

The Educator's Paradox

In U.S. education, practitioners have worked for years to scale up practice and provide a more effective learning environment. Yet, their best efforts seem to have had little impact on achieving long-term, significant improvement. Richard Elmore, a Harvard University professor, describes the problem of scaling up as follows:

> Innovations that require large changes in the core of educational practice seldom penetrate more than a small fraction of

U.S. schools and classrooms, and seldom last for very long when they do. By "core of educational practice", I mean how teachers understand the nature of knowledge and the student's role in learning, and how these ideas about knowledge and learning are manifested in teaching and classwork.[1]

Dr. Elmore contends that there is a deep, systemic incapacity of U.S. schools, and the practitioners who work in them, to develop, incorporate, and extend new ideas about teaching and learning in anything but a small fraction of schools and classrooms.[2] The paradox is that teachers and administrators all over the United States are working tirelessly to implement new practices and bring about improvements in American education. However, they experience frustration because these improvements do not materialize to their own satisfaction or those of their communities. Frequently, the promising ideas of today become fads or bandwagons. It is common for educators to resist implementing new programs when criticism of them and their practices becomes a public issue. School districts, however, boast of their institutional changes (changes in structures—for example, textbooks, tests, schedules, and so forth); yet, the core teaching-learning practices usually remain the same.

Efforts to move to scale are notable but often incomplete. New initiatives are typically developed with identifiable components in place for success, but the action plans are not thorough. Staff members do not fully understand the expectations placed on them or the implementation processes; yet, they do their best to implement the initiative. Sometimes they are not adequately trained for the initiative, resulting in implementation that is only partially effective, if at all. Time to refine practices and assimilate them effectively into the classroom is usually inadequate. Often, administrators and teachers do not wait a sufficient amount of time for positive results to be realized before passing judgment on the new initiative. In addition, the teachers are rarely recognized for their efforts.

The result is that dedicated professionals become discouraged; the programs are not adequately designed to achieve the desired results; the organization remains status quo, but with another failed effort that becomes part of the district's culture. Once again the promise of moving to scale is not realized.

A new way of planning is needed if districts want to success-fully scale-up the quality of their programs and instruction. The genetic model may be the answer for those districts.

Why Use a Genetic Model?

Well-designed organizational frameworks and sound research are readily available to practitioners, so why should educators use a biological model for school improvement? The answer is simple— a biological model offers school districts a comprehensive frame-work to develop successful school improvement efforts. The central thesis of the genetic model is this: World-class schools can only be realized when there is a comprehensive interrelationship of essen-tial core areas in schools. The model helps educators weave the es-sential pieces of effective schools together in the educational context. The theories of genetics explain how and why a living organism looks and functions the way it does. In the case of schools, sound theories of leadership, change, adult learning, and the teaching-learning process provide the basis to help educators understand the complex, structural connections necessary to provide quality education for students. The genetic model guides district leaders and staff members through a process to develop structures that strengthen the district's capacity to improve education for its stu-dents. The model helps the district to keep at the forefront of its work the notion that every major function of a school has a distinct relationship with and impact on other functions in the school.

School districts already devote countless hours to developing major core areas such as curriculum, instructional practice, and pro-fessional development to help them operate effectively. Yet, we ob-serve that the core areas are incomplete; they may include some effective components, while lacking others. The development of one core area may not clearly align with another. The result is that some areas are incomplete and ultimately insufficient to accomplish the intended outcomes.

A set of core areas must be connected for an efficient education system to function. If these areas are not connected, counter-productivity and dysfunctionality result. For example, a district has a rigorous curriculum with high standards. The curriculum is based on sound research and articulates effective instructional practice. If, however, the staff is not provided with the necessary professional development to implement the curriculum the way it was intended, it will not lead to high-quality instruction or learning. In addition, if companion assessment measures are not developed to determine whether students are actually learning what is expected of them, then no data exist to verify that they are acquiring the content and cognitive skills that were anticipated. Consequently, the school district will not be able to determine how well the students are learning the curriculum. What is frequently missing in districts is a method to integrate these core areas with each other to maximize their impact in the organization.

The genetic model is the catalyst to initiate a thorough development of all the areas and can serve as the agent of their integration. It provides the scaffolding for an organization to accomplish what should matter most in schools—students achieving at high levels of performance in all disciplines. The genetic model provides a process for educators to focus on quality research and make decisions that will lead to a plan for success. The model helps educators build the capacity to implement the teaching-learning process that leads to world-class performance.

Finally, the genetic model requires commitment and time to implement it effectively. Too often practitioners seek simple solutions to complex problems. There are no simple solutions for improving schools. A comprehensive set of well-developed core areas takes time to evolve. That time and commitment will yield results for those who are willing to seek world-class performance from their students and teachers.

Obstacles to Sustained Reform

For decades educators have wrestled with the dilemma of why reform efforts cannot be successfully developed and sustained in school districts. Many initiatives begin with district-wide excitement and show great promise. Soon, however, these promising programs are yesterday's failures. Occasionally, there are isolated reports of success; yet, those initiatives are not replicated on a widespread basis benefiting others. Why is it so difficult to replicate these programs? Our investigation has led us to a harsh conclusion about the inability of sustaining reform: School districts have a difficult time conceptualizing change and building capacity to improve within a political environment.

Educators confront obstacles that are both internal and external. These obstacles present significant realities, and if they are not addressed, there is little hope of realizing sustained improvement. We have identified three categories of obstacles: organizational, practical, and political.

Organizational Obstacles

- Event-driven change occurs instead of value-driven change.
- There is a lack of systemic foundation for improvement.
- There is a lack of organizational and personal capacity–building for change.
- Undervaluing the need for professional development is commonplace.
- Stakeholders are not engaged in the development of new initiatives.

Practical Obstacles

- Research is generally too complex to be applied in schools.
- A simplistic view of reform is typically used (such as jumping on the current fad or bandwagon).
- The "winds of change" move too quickly for teachers and administrators to adequately adapt to new reforms.

Political Obstacles

- Educators work in a political environment, which provides pressure that often results in nonrational decision-making.
- Parents want change to look the same as what they experienced in school.

The following section describes the obstacles in more detail. In doing so, we believe some remedies will be identified and will contribute to successfully overcoming the obstacles.

Organizational Obstacles

Event-Driven Change Occurs Instead of Value-Driven Change

School improvement initiatives are frequently implemented as separate events. Rarely are they connected to or derived from a value-driven mindset and long-term action plan. In his book *Coming Clean About Organizational Change: Leadership in the Real World*, Jerry Patterson contends that most attempts at systemic change result only in "event change."[3] He contends that this level of change has no lasting impact on the norms, values, or power relationships in any part of the system. It is simply an event in the life of the school or district with little connection to the history or future of the organization. He writes:

> Organizations move through their organizational life in an event-driven fashion, not anchored to a set of organizational principles that focus the organization's energy and direction. . . . Event-driven means that change is characterized by a series of episodes, unconnected to each other, unconnected to a core set of principles, and occurring for a short time before being relegated to the proverbial last-year's-new-thing shelf.[4]

Patterson argues that many topics possess a foundation of core educational principles and have the potential of contributing to a value-based school district. Three such topics could be cognitive neuroscience research, performance-based assessment, and cooperative learning However, topics are not usually well developed in the district, are not implemented appropriately, and ultimately, have minimal impact on achievement. Contrary to the hope that these initiatives will transform the learning environment and have a lasting impact, they are short-lived. The initial momentum and excitement from staff members dissipates, their enthusiasm wanes, and they lose commitment.

Members of an organization do not intend to be event-driven. Leaders work with consultants to develop and prepare for change in their districts. They launch the initiative with high interest and genuine excitement. Yet, as they try to implement the plan over time, staff members voice concerns that the program was an additional burden, another "add-on" that did not make sense. The staff could not make the connection between the new program and what they believed was a sound practice they were already using in their classrooms. Sound familiar?

Superintendents then find themselves asking why their teachers cannot capture their vision? Why do they not want to embrace a new program? It makes so much sense. The teachers' best efforts cannot overcome the fact that they see no link between the new program and their basic beliefs about the program it replaced. In the end, the program was not part of their value system for effective practice. As a result, the staff reacts to the components of the program rather than embracing the overall direction as something to be protected and nurtured. They do not believe that it was a critical part of their teaching-learning process but rather an event for a moment in time. If districts ever hope to achieve success in scaling up, educators must start by defining their basic values, beliefs, and principles.

The Lack of Systemic Foundation for Improvement

A systemic foundation for improvement is needed for any new initiative to be successful. In his book, *The Fifth Discipline*, Peter Senge outlines a systems-thinking approach to organizations.[5] A fundamental proposition of his book is the notion that the organization must be viewed as a whole. He notes the importance of interrelationships among key functions rather than individual stand-alones and encourages the reader to look for the patterns of change, not merely static snapshots. Changes in one part of the system must be implemented with thought given to how those changes influence other parts of the system. If not, improvements in one area may produce unintended negative results elsewhere within the system.

A critical aspect of systems thinking is that change within the system is continuous; the system is always in a state of flux, sometimes evident, sometimes not. Educational leaders typically have not thought systemically; therefore, reform has most often been approached in a fragmented manner.

If improvement efforts are to have a lasting impact, they must be considered within a systemic framework. According to Patterson, systemic change seeks to affect the norms, values, and power relationships throughout the organization.[6] People must examine their fundamental organizational beliefs and change their practices to fit their revised beliefs. This examination requires collaboration throughout the organization, recognizing that change will have an impact on every aspect of it.

The whole is greater than the sum of its parts. This concept points to the fact that the parts do not function independently. Rather, they are integrated in a way that the whole is uniquely of greater value or utility than the individual pieces. The function of one part can have an impact, positive or negative, on other parts. As leaders implement a new initiative, they must be cognizant that the program will have an impact on other parts of the organization and at the same time be affected itself by other parts of the organization. This is the interactive nature of organizations. It is imperative that leaders consider the impact of interaction and plan for how to address that impact.

The Lack of Organizational and Personal Capacity-Building for Change

Building capacity for change means building a culture for continuous improvement. This culture is necessary to successfully implement proposed improvements. In its absence, sustained reform is unlikely. It is a common scenario for teachers to exhibit high motivation at the beginning of a project, but lose their enthusiasm when they are faced with the inevitable challenges that arise during its implementation. They and frequently the leaders of the initiatives feel unprepared to address the challenges. This lack of capacity to resolve issues and generate solutions is discouraging to everyone.

Sustained change can occur when an organization builds the capacity of its staff for that change. Building capacity for continuous improvement means providing an environment for people to embrace change and to seek and gain knowledge. It is developing communities of learners who work together on common problems and issues with the goal of gaining insights and creating solutions. It is using technology to open new avenues for ensuring ongoing access to the most current knowledge, providing new strategies for all staff members to use research productively, building a repertoire of teaching skills, knowing how students learn, and learning how to self-analyze for the purpose of raising standards. This process requires time and cannot be accomplished through "short cuts."

The concept of capacity-building for change is critical for successful reform. It is a requirement for school improvement and one of the cornerstones of the genetic model. We will address it further in chapter 4.

Undervaluing the Need for Professional Development Is Commonplace

More than at any other time in history, educators are being called upon to learn new strategies to meet the demands of a changing society. Knowledge and information about the teaching-learning process, as well as various subject areas, is expanding with emerging research. Technology is providing access to research and facilitating the creation of new learning opportunities for teachers and students.

Change in the area of professional development is being driven by a variety of forces. Dennis Sparks and Stephanie Hirsh in their book, *A New Vision for Staff Development*, identify three driving forces that are changing professional development: a focus on results-driven education; the need for systems thinking within school organizations; and the expectation for teachers to make sense out of their practice in classrooms.[7]

The National Commission on Teaching in America published a report identifying what matters most in the learning process. The Commission identified teaching as the most important factor in making a difference in student learning. In the report, the Commission calls for restructuring professional development and creating high standards for teachers. The National Commission on Mathematics and Science Teaching for the 21st Century, more commonly known as the Glenn Commission, calls for an emphasis on professional development and the need for highly trained and qualified teachers.[8]

National education movements have also placed new demands on educators as well. The standards movement and new emphasis on assessment of student learning and accountability are sweeping the country as part of the reform movement. The U.S. Congress in the reauthorization of the Elementary and Secondary Education Act (ESEA Senate and House Proposals HR1 and SB1, 2001) has called for testing in Grades 3–8 in mathematics and reading to ensure students are making adequate yearly progress.

Despite the increased emphasis on these critical initiatives, school districts across America continue to view professional development as a frill to be cut when expenditures must be reduced. It is not viewed as a fundamental necessity to prepare teachers to meet the needs of their students. The time has arrived for school districts to recognize the value and need of professional development for staff members to build their professional capacity to meet the challenges of 21st century teaching.

Stakeholders Are Not Sufficiently Engaged in the Development of New Initiatives

Frequently, the critical stakeholders are not part of the reform initiatives at the developmental stage yet they are expected to accept ownership of them. As a practical matter, without ownership, there is no compelling reason for teachers or parents to ensure the success of new initiatives.

How often have teachers said, "This change (program) is being forced on us"? When new initiatives are launched without the involvement of those who must implement them, they are doomed to failure. Teachers need to be involved in the planning, development, and decision-making surrounding new programs. Absent this engagement, there is little motivation for them to invest in the reform initiative. They often ask, "Why is this program being implemented and how will it affect us?" Understandably, they react with a protective attitude, concerned about how the new program will require them to change their practice.

If they are involved in the planning of the new initiative, they will gain a clear understanding of the desired change and why it is better than what is currently in place. It is within this formative and developmental context that people acquire information, skills, knowledge, and ownership. Further development of this concept will be addressed in chapter 4.

Parents also need to understand and embrace new initiatives. If they believe the current practices are effective, then changing them will raise questions about their validity. When parents are engaged in dialogue at the developmental stage, they gain a clearer understanding and appreciation for what is proposed and how it will improve their child's education. They will then be more inclined to support the new direction.

Practical Obstacles

Research Is Generally Too Complex to Apply in Schools

Considerable attention is being given to the difficulty classroom teachers and administrators have using educational research effectively. There is a serious gap between understanding what research findings can offer practitioners and actual implementation of those findings. Peter McWalters and Dennis Cheek, Commissioner and Director of Information Services and Research of the Rhode Island Department of Elementary and Secondary Education, write that practitioners have protested for years that the research community continues to ignore the most pressing issues in educational practice and presents practitioners with research that is too narrowly focused, too prescriptive, too complex, and too remote from the real world of schools.[9] They also suggest that when research is funded it should meet four criteria:

1. Relevance (Does it address issues as perceived by classroom teachers?)

2. Quality (How good is it in terms of methods and rigor as judged independently by an expert panel using systematically derived and applied criteria?)

3. Usefulness (Can it be efficiently integrated into the real world of schools?)

4. Cost effectiveness (How does it compare to other research-validated approaches in terms of benefits versus costs?)[10]

Mary Kennedy, professor at Michigan State University, writes that many educators do not see a connection between the activities of researchers and the day-to-day demands in school leadership and instructional practices. The establishment or improvement of connections between research and practice will require that research be more persuasive and authoritative, more relevant, and more accessible.[11]

Douglas Christiansen, Commission of Education for the State of Nebraska, concurs that a major obstacle to reform is the limited capacity of educators and schools to access the research findings, interpret them appropriately, and plan systemic implementation strategies.[12] These capacities include time, training and coaching, and sustainable support resources. McWalters supports Christiansen's points by suggesting that the education community lacks a culture regarding the study of educational research. In this culture practitioners read, analyze, and interpret educational research. He states that the research community must do a better job of synthesizing educational research. These syntheses must involve teachers and administrators as both users and co-shapers of research questions and designs so that the resultant summaries are viewed as relevant, timely, and well focused.

This disconnect between research and practice raises the need for an important connection—the concept of collaborative research. It is the idea that a partnership should exist between the researcher and practitioner. The researcher-practitioner partnership must address distinct priorities to assist each other's understanding of their different work environments, thereby bridging the gap between them. It will necessitate identifying clear priorities by gaining a mutual understanding between the partners and their different environments and working approaches.

Educational research provides insights and information on topics that have the greatest impact on student achievement. The capacity to use research must be developed so that classroom teachers can use it effectively. They need time to become familiar with the findings and professional development to implement them.

The use of research is another cornerstone of the genetic model. Too often, leaders seek answers without the benefit of sound research to guide them. World-class performance cannot be achieved without it. Throughout this book, research is a fundamental underpinning for developing core values and principles upon which actions and plans will be based.

A Simplistic View of Reform

With so many issues confronting school leaders today, they tend to look for the packaged solution to improve student achievement. Using this approach is a simplistic view of reform. No single factor by itself can have an impact on improving student achievement. There are no quick fixes. Long-term reform requires an action plan for improvement, professional development, and a commitment to devote the necessary time for the program to succeed.

Too often, leaders search for a program that works elsewhere and can be imported into their districts. Single programs or practices rarely produce dramatic, long-term improvement. Moreover, implementing a new program must be viewed within the context, culture, and conditions of the school and classroom. In other words, a program that works in one setting is not guaranteed to work in another.

If educational leaders continue to view scaling-up as singularly focused efforts absent a context of variables, such as implementing a new program without sufficient professional development, potentially good initiatives will continue to fail. Reform is hard work. It requires leadership, commitment, time (years), professional development and most of all, persistence.

Rapid Winds of Change

Change is a recurring theme in this book. As a practical matter, there is more change going on than anyone can fathom. In school districts, teachers must work in collaboration with each other to learn new curricula and instructional strategies. They want to do an excellent job; yet, too much is expected of them within a short amount of time. Just when teachers begin to gain a comfort level with a new program or teaching strategy, another unrelated program is added. In essence, the horizon keeps moving, always slightly out of reach.

Teachers need time to learn new practices, reflect on the impact they have on learning, and refine them as they assimilate these practices into their teaching strategies. When teachers collaborate, it takes a great deal of time and energy. Results from the new programs are often expected too quickly. Because teachers are not given the needed support and time, many collaborations fail. Accountability measures are warranted but they must be applied reasonably. This problem must be rectified if schools are going to achieve world-class performance.

Teachers need time to learn the new practices and curriculum and to implement the changes effectively. Doing a partial job of implementing new programs and then moving on to other "reforms" leaves teachers with a host of mediocre, incomplete efforts to implement them. Leaders have to set priorities, remain patient, and persevere.

Political Obstacles

Political Pressure for Nonrational Decisions

Many education initiatives start out with great promise but soon fail. Why does this happen? Often it is because of inadequate training (undervaluing professional development) and poor implementation. Other times the district has not adequately communicated information about the new program to parents (no support building) and they are left to conjure up their own understanding and perceptions of it. The media can also stifle a potentially positive effort through inaccurate and incomplete reporting.

Regardless of the reasons, these new initiatives are then labeled fads and bandwagons. Groups rise up in opposition to them while others are supportive. The result is generally a confrontation between them. Sometimes it is local or regional. Other times the dispute can be national, for example, whole language versus phonics.

Ultimately, teachers and administrators are caught in the crossfire with their boards of education, teachers, and the parent community. Each group tries to defend the merits of its own position. In reality, most new initiatives are attempted to address the gaps or inadequacies of current practice. In doing so, they may inadvertently be sending a message that the strengths of current practices are also inadequate when, in fact, they are not. What begins as a credible attempt to resolve deficiencies in current practice soon becomes a political issue. Quality endeavors become tarnished in the ensuing battles. Educators are forced to make politically expedient decisions to quell the dissent. The programs are diluted to the point of not being able to accomplish their intended objectives. These piecemeal efforts result in mediocre curriculum with little improvement in the instruction of students.

Parents Want Change to Look Familiar

Parents purport to want changes in their schools that lead to improved student performance; yet, they become uncomfortable when new programs look different than what they have experienced. Parents are looking for improved student achievement but resist changes they perceive as a radical departure from past practices. People, in general, desire the status quo. If change looks different, they believe their children are not getting the crucial basics that they need. This perception was seen vividly when many school districts began to use the writing process as a means for students to hone their grammar and spelling skills. Teachers taught spelling rules and procedures using students' actual writing. When parents saw their children were not bringing home the Friday spelling test of twenty words, they assumed that the schools were not teaching spelling. It made no difference that, while students could spell words independently on a list test, they could not use them appropriately in their writing. When composition "drafts" with spelling errors were sent home, parents became incensed that teachers appeared not to care whether students could spell correctly. This situation resulted in a public outcry for reinstating spelling books. Boards of education had to confront the political issue of a parent protest and decide whether to support the new program or the parents. Of equal concern is that sometimes a parent protest reflects the concerns of an active minority and not the majority of parents.

This illustration points out the critical need to educate parents on what the expectations are for new programs. It is equally important to explain to them why some aspects of the new program will not look the same as the old program and to reassure them that the fundamental basics will still be taught.

It is important to bear in mind that all adults went through an educational system and, therefore, believe they have a familiarity with it. Schools must strike a reasonable balance with their communities over their proposed changes in education and the parents' familiarity with current programs. Parent and community education is critical. Informed, proactive strategies are essential to avoid, or at the very least minimize, political confrontation.

It is critical to be aware of these obstacles that block effective reform. By recognizing them, leaders can plan for future activities with built-in safeguards. The genetic model provides for these safeguards.

Schools and School Districts as Living, Dynamic Organizations

Schools and school districts are living, dynamic organizations that have a specific culture and life of their own. They are social systems operating by the bonds of shared values and goals, defined roles and responsibilities, and social interactions of individuals who have their own unique views and beliefs about their place in the organization. The district is a product of its own experiences (successes, failures, defining moments, and tragedies), which forge relationships and galvanize perceptions and practices within the organization. Finally, schools and school districts mirror, respond to, and adapt to their environment and must function within it. It is within that environment that change and improvement must occur. In order to be effective, any improvement efforts must address the values and beliefs that drive the behaviors of the staff and functions in that school.

These organizations as living systems take on a character of their own that distinguish them from other similar organizations. School District A can be very different from School District B. This phenomenon mirrors the biological world of living organisms whether plant or animal. As noted earlier, organizations can be different, use different strategies, subscribe to different philosophies, and still achieve world-class performance. This notion is the message of the book. World-class performance can be achieved!

Summary

- Leading school systems to world-class performance involves developing many interrelated concepts, beliefs, relationships, and structures. The fundamental questions to ask are "How can the school district define, communicate, and implement these fundamental underpinnings in a manner that provides the best learning environment for students?" and "What does it take to create an environment that leads to world class performance?"
- Educators struggle with a paradox of working diligently to improve but rarely meeting their expectation.
- Organizations face natural obstacles that block meaningful school improvement efforts.
    - Organizational obstacles include a lack of value-driven change, no systemic foundation for improvement, a lack of organizational and personal capacity to change, undervaluing professional development, and not engaging stakeholders in the development of improvement efforts.
    - Practical obstacles include research being too difficult to apply in schools, a simplistic view of reform by educators, and change happening too quickly.
    - Political obstacles include working in a political environment and parents wanting change to look like structures of the past.
- Schools and school districts are living, dynamic organizations that have a specific culture and life of their own.

- The genetic model provides a process to develop a comprehensive relationship of the core areas in schools.
- The genetic model is the catalyst to initiate a thorough development of the core areas of schooling and serve as the agent of their integration.
- The genetic model leads practitioners through a process of analyzing quality research and making decisions that will create a framework for success—world-class performance.

Endnotes

1. Richard Elmore, "Getting to scale with good educational practice," *Harvard Educational Review* (Spring 1996) 66: 1–2.
2. Elmore, "Getting to scale with good educational practice," pp.1–3.
3. Jerry Patterson,–*Coming clean about organizational change: leadership in the real world* (American Association of School Administrators: Arlington, VA, 1997), pp. 34–36.
4. Patterson, *Coming clean about organizational change*, p. 34.
5. Peter Senge, *The fifth discipline* (New York: Doubleday, 1990).
6. Patterson, *Coming clean about organizational change*, pp. 3–4.
7. Sparks and Hirsh, *A new vision for staff development* (National Staff Development Council and Association for Supervision and Curriculum Development, July 1997), pp. 4–11.
8. *Before it's too late*, A report to the nation from the National Commission on Mathematics and Science Teaching for the 21st Century (Washington, DC: The U.S. Department of Education, 2000)
9. McWalters and Cheek, "A collaborative approach to educational research: what will it take?" Policy paper by the National Education Research Policy and Priorities Board Forum (Washington, DC: U.S. Department of Education, September 1999), pp. 1–3.
10. McWalters and Cheek, "A collaborative approach to educational research: what will it take?", p. 1.
11. Mary Kennedy, "The connection between research and practice" Educational Researcher (October 1997), pp. 4–14.
12. Douglas Christiansen, *Research to practice: a framework for closing the gap* (policy paper) (Fall 2000), pp. 1–4.

Chapter 2

World-Class Education Concepts

Overview of Key Concepts

- International comparisons provide a benchmark for a definition of world-class performance.
- International assessments are essential to identify world-class academic achievement.
- High academic standards are critical to achieve world-class performance.
- Some useful concepts for analyzing world-class education are discussed in this chapter.

Introduction

Chapter 1 set a context and provided an overview for using a genetic model to achieve world-class performance. Arguably, one could contend that the use of a genetic model is not necessary, but we believe it provides a more scientific, understandable, and, most important, a "user-friendly" framework for organizing world-class schools. Further, why shouldn't educators use scientific principles for their action planning? Perhaps on too many occasions it is the absence of the relationship between science and education that has resulted in a lack of respect from business leaders, policymakers, and scientists toward educators. Former President William Clinton even referenced genetics in a speech to the National Board of Professional Teaching Standards when he said, "We couldn't be unlocking the mysteries of the gene if it weren't for computer advances because that's really what enables us to map out the gene ..."[13] His reference to genetics in a speech on teaching only reinforced our notion that a genetic model is a good idea for writing a plan to organize world-class schools.

We believe genetics is a good metaphor for our book because it is science, uses data, and does not necessarily have a ready answer for every complex question. Just because individuals are different genetically does not mean they are not capable of world-class performance. When runners line up for the 100-meter run in the Olympics, their genetic composition, while very different, does not preclude their world-class performances. Tiger Woods, a 150-pound golfer hits a world-class 300+ yard drive while other golfers who are much larger physically cannot match his performance. Like Olympic runners and professional golfers, educators can use different strategies to achieve world-class performance. The genetic model offers education decision-makers flexibility in selecting how they want to reach their objectives and enables them to achieve successful outcomes.

With approximately 15,000 public school districts in the United States governed by independent boards of education, it is unlikely that each district would use similar strategies or identify the same educational concepts to achieve its world-class goals. The genetic model addresses the American passion for local control of its schools by recognizing that each independent school district can pursue the concept of world-class performance in its own way. One thing is clear; school districts in the future need to use data-driven, research-based information and a qualitative review of literature on education practices in high-achieving countries to organize a world-class education program. We recognize that there are a variety of strategies to achieve world-class status as long as that status is measured and based on the highest achievement in the world.

This chapter provides an overview of world-class education concepts and practices. We discuss a broad array of ideas that have been proffered by others and offer six chromosomes, or core areas, we believe are essential to develop a world-class program. We would suggest that as all organisms have a determined number of chromosomes, there are six essential chromosomes for a school system that are within the control of the district. To get started, we have organized the six chromosomes into two categories in a manner similar to how chromosomes are classified as X or Y. The capacity-building category includes leadership, change, and professional development chromosomes. The second category, the teaching-learning process, is comprised of curriculum, instructional practice, and assessment chromosomes. This chapter will provide the reader with far more than six potential education chromosomes. All teachers, administrators, and/or districts will need to clone their own world-class system. However, we believe our six chromosomes are the basis to get started and, if used systemically, will lead to high achievement.

What does it mean to be world-class? According to *Random House Webster's Concise Dictionary*,[14] world-class means being among the world's best and of the highest caliber. Using this definition, it is clear that international comparisons are essential if educators and representatives from school communities want to proclaim their schools are world-class. We find the term world-class is used far too often and in most instances without supportive evidence to uphold the claim. The time has come for those who want to say their programs are world-class to support those claims with evidence based on international comparisons.

Why International Comparisons

There was a time when "Made in America" meant quality was assured. This is no longer the case. The market share of American cars, for example, has diminished over the last decade. A casual observation of any shopping center parking lot in the United States provides evidence that an eclectic array of makes and models of cars from England, Germany, Japan, Korea, and Sweden have been purchased by American consumers. This was hardly the case in the 1960s or 1970s. Americans no longer watch programs on television sets made in this country; electronics has virtually disappeared from the U.S. manufacturing base.

What does it mean to lose the ability to compete with the other countries? For one thing it means the United States has moved from a high level of self-sufficiency to dependency on other countries to produce goods that American consumers use daily. That reliance also suggests that other countries are able to produce those goods more cheaply and, therefore, enhance their economies to the detriment of U.S. consumers, who must pay higher prices or see their jobs eliminated.

While these facts may not be of significant immediate concern, trends do evolve over periods of time, and these trends should serve as a wake-up call to American educators to carefully evaluate how they are preparing the future workforce. Are U.S. school programs designed to meet the needs of America's future workforce? Is it important for U.S. students to be literate in order for the workforce to maintain an economic self-sufficiency in the United States? Business and political leaders in the United States have been speaking out on these issues. They are telling anyone who will listen that the answer is "yes" to those questions, and the answers reinforce the need for American students to rank high on the international comparison chart.

A Definition of World-Class Education

We have noted that *Random House Webster's Concise Dictionary* said world-class means being among the world's best and of the highest caliber. We believe that international comparisons are essential if school leaders want to proclaim that their schools or programs are world-class. Second, we believe that school districts must use benchmarks, that is those measurable and definable comparisons that demonstrate their students' academic achievement is comparable to those countries that are recognized as the best in the world.

It is no longer appropriate for American school districts to rely only on commercially prepared nationally-normed tests or intrastate comparisons of their students' achievements. How well one district does in comparison to neighboring districts will be irrelevant if its students cannot compete with the highest achieving students in the world. Educators must begin to think in global terms because their students are actually competing in a global society that has been reduced to worldwide access through the Internet. Students are going to compete globally with their peers for jobs and educational opportunities, not just with friends in their school or in neighboring school districts.

While we have used a dictionary definition of world-class, we have come to recognize there is no universally accepted agreement on what specifically constitutes a world-class education. To develop one is a daunting task. On the other hand, the Third International Mathematics and Science Study, a consensus among 41 countries, does identify countries that have high-achieving students on specific mathematics and science concepts and allows for further research of their curricula and educational practices. The Progress in International Reading Literacy Study and Performance on International Student Assessment will also provide information on student achievement using international comparisons. These assessments can provide the basis for determining what constitutes world-class achievement.

The process of establishing world-class standards in education would be much easier if there were an "Education Olympics." Just imagine, representatives from each country could line up and race to set the standards. All of the rules would be the same and no special circumstances would be necessary to account for the many internationally different approaches to schooling. Unfortunately, this concept is not realistic. Comparing educational achievement internationally is a highly complex and sophisticated process.

We suggest that world-class schools in the United States be developed with careful use of credible education research and an intense review of educational practices in countries recognized for their high achievement. This process, if implemented in local school districts, would ultimately result in identifying curriculum standards and educational practices that would enable their students to compete globally. The discussions would be based on credible information rather than unsupported suppositions often spoken to impress or convince constituents that their schools are actually better than they really are.

Careful consideration should be given to education practices in other countries that appear to work for them and are considered by other educators to be world-class. For example, high-achieving countries tend to have a national curriculum that is understood and taught by their teachers. While the cause-effect relationship of a national curriculum and high achievement should be accepted with a degree of skepticism, there is clearly ample evidence that a rigorous, intended curriculum taught by competent teachers understanding what they teach leads to successful outcomes. The caveat in this claim is that some low-achieving countries also have national curricula. The implication for educators in the United States is that the world-class standard is a *rigorous* curriculum taught by *well-trained* teachers. The national curriculum is one example of how to define world-class standards.

International Assessment

Embodied in the concept of world-class schools is the use of international benchmarks, that is those measurable and definable criteria that demonstrate students' academic achievement or teacher practices in one country compared to those of countries with the highest student achievement in the world. It is now becoming increasingly more possible to make such comparisons. For three decades there have been international studies in mathematics and science, (First, Second, and Third International Mathematics and Science Studies—FIMSS, SIMSS, TIMSS) and now two more comprehensive international studies are in place that will become significant achievement benchmarks. Those studies are Progress in International Reading Literacy Study and Program for International Student Assessment. These three international studies will enable educators to better understand their students' performance data on an international basis. Using these international assessments for comparisons is essential for determining world-class achievement. They are the best available data to use and are described in the following sections.

Third International Math and Science Study (TIMSS)

TIMSS is the third generation of international comparisons of student achievement in mathematics and science. TIMSS examined student achievement at grade equivalents of 3 and 4 (population 1), 7 and 8 (population 2), and students enrolled in their final year of secondary school (population 3). It included performance assessments in populations 1 and 2, questionnaires related to achievement for students to complete, and their opinions about mathematics and science. Teachers were asked to complete questionnaires about their lessons as well as their beliefs about teaching mathematics and science. Administrators responded to questions about staffing levels, availability of resources, in-service education, and retention rates.

Another component of TIMSS was a comprehensive curriculum analysis of textbooks and curriculum guides from the participating countries. The textbooks and guides were analyzed for their topic content, sequencing, and emphasis. Dr. William Schmidt from Michigan State University was responsible for the curriculum analysis (*http://ustimss.msu.edu*)

One of the chromosomes discussed in this book is *curriculum*. TIMSS data provides insight as to why mathematics and science curricula in the United States have resulted in the disappointing achievement of American students. Schmidt discovered that the U.S. mathematics and science curricula lacked coherence, focus, and rigor. In what has become the best-known sound bite from TIMSS, Schmidt said, "The American curriculum is a mile wide and an inch deep." TIMSS analysis was quite clear in the findings that American textbooks contain too many topics and repeat them in too many grades.

TIMSS also included videotaping of teachers in grade 8 mathematics classes in Germany, Japan, and the United States. Observations from those videotapes were analyzed and a database was created for comparative analysis. Dr. James Stigler from University of California-Los Angeles directed the video study (*http:// www.lessonlab.com*). Differences in instructional practice from high student achievement countries demonstrate that they have very distinct teaching strategies and support our notion that instructional practice is an essential chromosome for world-class achievement.

The purpose of the video study was to compare actual mathematics teaching methods in eighth grade classes in Germany, Japan, and the United States. The key findings from the video study were:

- The content of U.S. mathematics classes requires less high-level thought than classes in Germany and Japan.
- The U.S. teacher's typical goal is to teach students how to perform a task while Japanese teachers want their students to understand mathematical concepts.
- While American teachers claim they are familiar with reform recommendations, few apply the recommendations in their classrooms.

Case studies made up the final component of TIMSS. Researchers observed and conducted in-depth interviews with a sample of students, teachers, and administrators from Germany, Japan, and the United States. Topics in the case studies included implementation of national standards, methods of dealing with ability differences, adolescents' attitudes toward school, and the daily lives and working environments of teachers. Dr. Harold Stevenson from the University of Michigan directed the case studies project (*http:// www.ed.gov/pubs/SumItUp*). The case studies led to our belief that a capacity-building category of chromosomes was essential for systemic or large-scale educational improvement. High-performing countries on international assessments had focused on *leadership* and high quality *professional development* programs. For the United States to improve student achievement, changes in educational practices would be essential; therefore, we have included a chromosome on *change* to build a world-class education system.

Since TIMSS 1995, a retesting of some of the original TIMSS countries, some new countries, and 27 U.S. educational jurisdictions took place in 1999. TIMSS-Repeat (TIMSS 1999) was administered to only eighth grade students. Table 2.1 includes the countries that participated in TIMSS and TIMSS 1999 in the eighth grade.

TABLE 2.1—COUNTRIES PARTICIPATING IN TIMSS (POPULATION 2) AND TIMSS 1999		
Countries taking both TIMSS and TIMSS 1999 appear in **BOLD CAPS** Countries taking only TIMSS appear in regular print Countries taking only TIMSS 1999 appear in italics		
Albania	Iceland	**NEW ZEALAND**
AUSTRALIA	*Indonesia*	**NORWAY**
Austria	**IRAN,**	*Philippines*
BELGIUM-FLEMISH	**ISLAMIC REPUBLIC**	Portugal
Belgium-French	Ireland	Romania
BULGARIA	Israel	**RUSSIAN FEDERATION**
CANADA	*Italy*	Scotland
Chile	**JAPAN**	**SINGAPORE**
Chinese Taipei	*Jordan*	**SLOVAK REPUBLIC**
Colombia	**REP. OF KOREA**	**SLOVENIA**
CYPRUS	Kuwait	**SOUTH AFRICA**
CZECH REPUBLIC	**LATVIA (LSS)**	Spain
Denmark	**LITHUANIA**	Sweden
ENGLAND	Republic of Macedonia	Switzerland
Finland	*Malaysia*	**THAILAND**
France	*Moldova*	*Tunisia*
Germany	*Morocco*	*Turkey*
Greece	**NETHERLANDS**	**UNITED STATES**
HONG KONG		
HUNGARY		

Progress in International Reading Literacy Study (PIRLS)

PIRLS was administered in 2001. PIRLS is a study of fourth grade students (ages 9 and 10) that is designed to measure their reading literacy and achievement. It focuses on the reading literacy achievement of young children and their experiences at home and school in learning to read. PIRLS is intended to provide valuable comparative information about children's levels of reading literacy that can be used to improve reading instruction and learning. Some of the information researchers hope to obtain from PIRLS is as follows:

Reading Literacy Achievement
- How well do fourth grade students read?
- How does this compare with that of students in other countries?

Habits and Attitude
- Do fourth grade students value and enjoy reading?
- How do the reading habits and attitudes of students compare with those of students in other countries?

Instructional Experiences
- How is early reading instruction organized in each country's schools?
- How do the instructional practices of each country's teachers compare with those of teachers in other countries?

Reform
- Where should effort and resources be directed to improve reading literacy of young children in each of the countries?

PIRLS will be administered every four years. The first assessment was conducted in 2001 and followup administrations are scheduled for 2005 and 2009 (http://www.pirls.org/pirils2001.html).

TABLE 2.2—COUNTRIES PARTICIPATING IN **PIRLS**		
Argentina	Hungary	New Zealand
Belize	Iceland	Norway
Bulgaria	Iran	Philippines
Canada	Israel	Romania
Colombia	Italy	Russian Federation
Cyprus	Kuwait	Scotland
Czech Republic	Latvia	Singapore
England	Lithuania	Slovak Republic
France	Macedonia	Slovenia
Germany	Moldova	Sweden
Greece	Morocco	Turkey
Hong Kong	Netherlands	United States

Program for International Student Assessment (PISA)

PISA is designed to monitor on a regular basis the achievement levels of 15-year-old students as they approach the end of secondary school. The purpose of PISA is to measure the extent to which students are acquiring the skills and knowledge necessary to participate fully in society and meet the challenges of the future. PISA is designed to answer several questions for the governments of the participating countries. Some of those questions are:

- Are our schools preparing children for full participation in society?
- What educational structures and practices maximize the opportunities of students from disadvantaged backgrounds?
- How much influence does the quality of school resources have on student outcomes?

PISA includes three primary subject domains, reading literacy, mathematical literacy, and scientific literacy. Two-thirds of the testing time in each cycle is devoted to an in-depth assessment of one of the major domains. The major domain in the Year 2000 was reading, in 2003, mathematics, and in 2006, science.

PISA is intended to assess knowledge and skills that will enable students to participate fully in society and the economy and to become life-long learners. It will look at students' ability to reflect actively on their knowledge and experiences and to address issues that will be relevant to their future lives.

The term literacy is used as the basis for determining the skill levels and was chosen to reflect the breadth of the knowledge, skills, and competencies that are being assessed. There will be no single cut-off line between literate and illiterate; however, student performance will be defined between a series of successive levels of proficiency. Performance levels of individuals in each domain are represented by a distribution of scale scores. The three literacy categories are:

1. Reading literacy—Students perform a range of tasks with different kinds of text. Those tasks range from retrieving specific information to demonstrating broad understanding, interpreting text, and reflecting on the text's concepts and features.

2. Mathematical literacy—Students demonstrate the use of mathematical competencies at several levels, ranging from performance of standard mathematical operations to mathematical thinking and insight. The three dimensions that are assessed by PISA are content, process, and situational use of mathematics.

3. Scientific literacy—Students demonstrate the use of key scientific concepts in order to understand and help make decisions about the natural world. Dimensions assessed include concepts, processes, and situational use of science.

PISA was developed jointly by the Organization for Economic Cooperation and Development (OECD) member countries.

TABLE 2.3—COUNTRIES PARTICIPATING IN **PISA**		
Australia	Hungary	New Zealand
Austria	Iceland	Norway
Belgium	Ireland	Poland
Brazil	Italy	Portugal
Canada	Japan	Russian Federation
Czech Republic	Korea, Republic of	Spain
Denmark	Latvia	Sweden
Finland	Liechtenstein	Switzerland
France	Luxembourg	United Kingdom
Germany	Mexico	United States
Greece	Netherlands	

The countries that are not members of OECD, but participating in the study are Brazil, Leichtenstein, Latvia, and the Russian Federation. It is important to note that, although these countries are not members of OECD, they still chose to participate in an international secondary school analysis of student achievement. These countries consider international comparison of their students' achievement important. The PISA consortium is led by the Australian Council for Education Research and includes the Netherlands National Institute for Educational Measurement, Westat from the United States, and the Service de Pédagogie Expérimentale Université de Liége, Belgium.

The first PISA assessment took place in Spring 2000 and results were reported in 2001. Assessment thereafter will occur every three years. In 2003, PISA will also specifically assess student ability to solve problems (http://www.pisa/oecd.org).

PISA UPDATE-DECEMBER 2001

As this book was going to press the first results from PISA were being released. The emphasis in the first PISA assessment was reading literacy. Scores were categorized for countries scoring significantly higher than the OECD average, significantly lower than the average, or no significant difference from the average. Students from the United States scored in the middle of the participating countries on the reading, science, and mathematics portions of the assessment. Of interest is the fact that the gap between the best and worst readers in the United Stateswas wider than in any of the other countries.

In reading, the highest scoring countries were Finland, Canada, New Zealand, Australia, Ireland, Korea, United Kingdom, Japan, Sweden, Australia, Belgium, and Iceland. In the middle category were Norway, France, United States, Denmark, and Switzerland. Scoring in the lowest category were Spain, Czech Republic, Italy, Germany, Liechtenstein, Hungary, Poland, Greece, Portugal, Russia, Latvia, Luxembourg, Mexico, and Brazil.

Preliminary analysis of the results from all three assessments indicate the best performing students in the United States are comparable to the highest performing students in the top achieving countries. The poor performance of a significant minority of American schools lowers the overall U.S. performance. This finding is consistent with the results from the TIMSS-R where suburban schools did very well and urban schools had very low scores.

More detailed and updated information is available on the OECD Web site (*www.sourceoecd.org*).

Summary of International Assessment

TIMSS was the largest, most comprehensive, international comparative study of educational achievement ever undertaken. The findings from TIMSS demonstrated that U.S. students have a long road to travel to become world-class in mathematics and science.

As a footnote, there were some students in the United States who did perform at a world-class level in mathematics and science. The First in the World Consortium, a consortium of eighteen Illinois school districts of which your authors served as leaders, participated in the original TIMSS in all three of the populations tested. The First in the World Consortium was the only identifiable local group of students in the world at all three grade levels that ever participated in a study of this type. The results from the First in the World Consortium's participation demonstrated that overall, its students were at or very close to the highest student achievement in the world in both mathematics and science.

The First in the World Consortium participated in TIMSS 1999 with other U.S. education jurisdictions including cities, states, and other consortia. The results confirmed that the students in the First in the World Consortium were still world-class achievers in both subjects. The Consortium's claim of being world-class achievers is supported with data and research and thus is a justifiable claim.

TABLE 2.4—TIMSS 1999 BENCHMARK GROUPS	
States	**School Districts/ Consortia**
Connecticut	Academy of School District No. 20, Colorado Springs, CO
Idaho	Chicago Public Schools, IL
Illinois	Delaware Science Coalition, DE
Indiana	First in the World Consortium, IL
Maryland	Fremont/Lincoln/Westside Public Schools, NE
Massachusetts	Guilford County School, NC
Michigan	Jersey City Public Schools, NJ
Missouri	Miami-Dade County Public Schools, FL
North Carolina	Michigan Invitational Group, MI
Oregon	Montgomery County Public Schools, MD
Pennsylvania	Naperville Community Unit School District No. 203, IL
South Carolina	Project Smart Consortium, OH
Texas	Rochester City School District, NY
	Southwest Pennsylvania Regional Math and Science Collaborative, PA

As the newer international assessments PISA and PIRLS begin to evolve, a more specific definition of world-class educational standards will emerge. These assessments will make it possible to more clearly define what is world-class educational performance. Our chromosome on *assessment* is an essential component to determine if a school district is performing at a world-class level. We would caution our readers to recognize that while attempting to achieve world-class education standards, international comparisons are not always an exact science. For now, our discussion of world-class education will address what has been done to date, and we will offer suggestions for designing your world-class education plan using the genetic model. We believe the genetic model offers the essential categories to achieve world-class performance when used holistically, integrating all six chromosomes in a systemic plan to achieve your intended goals.

High Standards

Three educational summits, organized by politicians and business leaders, have been held in the last decade. President George Bush and the National Governors' Association sponsored the first summit in 1989. At that summit, six performance goals for the nation's schools were written and later expanded to eight goals.

Those goals were:

1. All children will start school ready to learn.
2. The high school graduation rate will increase to at least 90%.
3. All students will become competent in challenging subject matter.
4. Teachers will have the knowledge and skills that they need.
5. U.S. students will be first in the world in mathematics and science achievement.
6. Every adult American will be literate.
7. Schools will be safe, disciplined, and free of guns, drugs, and alcohol.
8. Schools will promote parental involvement and participation.

In 1996, the National Governors' Association and the IBM Corporation sponsored a summit that was attended by 40 governors, business leaders, and 40 education experts. At the second summit, there was a commitment to creating standards-based education in every state.

Finally, in 1999 Project Achieve, Business Roundtable, Council of Great City Schools, Learning First Alliance, National Alliance of Business, National Education Goals Panel, and the National Governors' Association conducted a third summit. On the agenda was improving teaching quality, increasing students' opportunities to learn the content and the standards, promoting choice and diversity of schools, strengthening accountability systems, and building public support for implementation of a standards system. These summits along with the increased involvement of business leaders and politicians in education matters are proof positive that America's educational system is going to have to look at becoming world-class or continue to see proposals for alternative solutions to improve educational performance of U.S. students.

Of further interest should be the comments made by Professor Michael Barber in a paper for the Skol Tema Conference in Stockholm in 1999. Dr. Barber, a professor at the Institute of Education at The University of London, was appointed to head the new standards and effectiveness unit in the Department of Education and Employment in England and is currently an education advisor to Prime Minister Tony Blair. England has pursued a course of high standards and assessments to improve its education system. Dr. Barber is one of his country's prominent educational leaders and has written numerous books on the topic of education reform. (Dr. Barber's guest essay can be found on page 52.)

Dr. Barber noted that the day Prime Minister Tony Blair was elected he said, "Our goal is the creation of a world-class education system in which education is not the privilege of the few but the right of the many." Barber continued by saying that 30 or 40 years ago, developed countries could tolerate substantial underachievement in their education systems because there was a plentiful supply of unskilled or semiskilled jobs in the economy. Changes in the global economy mean that observation is no longer true. The task, therefore, is not merely to improve the existing education system but to transform it so that it can achieve a dramatically more demanding goal—to become capable of providing high standards for all children.

International comparisons of student achievement are acknowledging that U.S. students are far from the best in the world. This fact alone should be of concern to American educators and policymakers and a reason to insist on high academic standards. The economic well being of the United States and the fact that it should have the best education system in the world are reasons enough to encourage international comparisons with countries emphasizing rigorous education standards.

World-Class Concepts

The remainder of this chapter will be devoted to a discussion of concepts that should be considered when organizing a world-class school system, what others have to say about world-class schools, and the six chromosomes (core areas) recommended to get started. Using these examples should enable you to begin the process of scaling up your school system.

As noted earlier, the definition of world-class standards will evolve as more international tests are administered. We have suggested that TIMSS and at least two new assessments, PIRLS and PISA, will offer additional opportunities to make international comparisons of student achievement. For now, the process to articulate a definition of world-class is challenging but must include an intense review of the literature on international education and research on high student achievement. Our six chromosomes (core areas) are leadership, change, professional development, curriculum, instructional practice, and assessment. Applying research on international student achievement and a qualitative review of the education practices in high-achieving countries along with our genetic model can lead to a locally defined world-class school district organized with valid, definable data and information. The lack of a specific definition of world-class education is no longer an excuse for not pursuing a world-class agenda for schools.

As stated earlier, there is no single definition of world-class schools. In fact, what is considered world-class to one educator is usually debated to the contrary by another. It is possible, however, to review quantitative research and what appear to be effective educational practices to support an interpretation of world-class achievement for any school or school district. Benchmarking using international testing can lead to world-class outcomes and should be the basis for local school district decision-making.

Two authorities on world-class education are Richard Haynes and Donald Chalker, professors at Western Carolina University; they have written two books on world-class schools, *World Class Schools*[15] and *World Class Elementary Schools*.[16]

Haynes and Chalker have discussed world-class education practices in their books rather than delineating a single definition of world-class performance. They emphasize that although an education practice works in one country, it does not mean that U.S. schools will want to implement it; and vice versa, an American education practice does not automatically mean it is world-class.

In the opinion of Haynes and Chalker, the ten nations representing the finest education systems in the world are identified in Table 2.5.

TABLE 2.5—COUNTRIES WITH WORLD-CLASS SCHOOLS AS IDENTIFIED BY HAYNES AND CHALKER	
Canada	Taiwan
France	State of Israel
Federal Republic of Germany (former West Germany)	Japan
	Republic of Korea (South Korea)
Great Britain	United States
New Zealand	

Haynes and Chalker created an agenda for educators who want to incorporate elements of world-class schools in their particular setting. They suggested the agenda be carefully reviewed in order to eliminate those elements that might not be feasible or desirable. Proper implementation of the Haynes-Chalker agenda can take up to three years. For that reason, the elements need to be coded (1, 2, or 3) with an action plan incorporating them according to the first, second, or third year scheduled for implementation. The elements are as follows:

- Curriculum
- Teachers
- School governance

- Student assessment
- Students
- Parents, home, community

The following is a brief overview of the criteria they identify in each element. A more comprehensive review of their books provides additional detail as to how each selected country implements those elements in its world-class structure. It is also important to emphasize that new developments in the elements occur each year, making it important to review each country's educational activities annually.

Curriculum

Haynes and Chalker believe it is essential to have a national curriculum framework. That curriculum should be disseminated widely and articulated for teachers, parents, students, and the community-at-large. The curriculum determines what is taught at each grade level and has an established pace with guidance on minimum teaching time per subject. They advocate a preschool curriculum for children starting around age 2 or 3. France is identified as a world-class country for its recognition of early childhood education.

Teachers

Element two recognizes the importance of teachers planning together in a "teachers' room." Teachers are provided time to reflect together on their lessons and carefully review the curriculum to be taught. Cooperation and sharing of materials are two components of their world-class teacher element. They recommend an increase in the number of years of preparation required for teacher certification and a 220-day work year.

Teachers are also accorded respect in their world-class culture. While it may seem trivial, they talk about teachers displaying their degrees and certificates in their classrooms, being provided with business cards, and removing as many nonteaching responsibilities from their duties as possible.

Governance

Although Haynes and Chalker tend to favor a national ministry of education, they acknowledge that the concept is not feasible in the United States. However, they do emphasize that the United

States cannot afford to continue with a fragmented and decentralized system of governance if it is to achieve world-class performance. The United States needs rigorous national goals to guide its approximately 15,000 school districts toward high-achievement.

Assessment

Student assessment is an important aspect of the Haynes-Chalker world-class plan. All assessment is aligned with the articulated curriculum and multiple-choice/true-false tests are discouraged. There are identified benchmarks for student mastery of curriculum, starting at kindergarten, and final benchmarks at the end of elementary and high school. National testing of students is necessary to implement their assessment plan.

Students

Students are taught the characteristics of successful students and encouraged to replicate that success. There are peer mediation programs to reduce school distractions and the need for advisory programs, character education, and alternative programs for disruptive students.

Parents, Home, and Community

Parents, home, and community are all integral to a world-class school system. Preschool parents actively participate in school activities even before their children attend school. They are also provided with developmentally appropriate materials to assist their children in school preparedness. Local school districts develop a parents' charter that clearly delineates the responsibility of the school to the parents and the responsibility of the parents to the school.

Community businesses are encouraged to make it possible for parents to be involved in their children's school. That involvement includes allowing parents to attend conferences and volunteer in school activities.

Summary of World-Class Concepts

Haynes and Chalker have taken what they believe to be world-class practices from their selected countries and offered suggestions to develop a world-class education system. Their work to date is the most comprehensive information on the concept of world-class education.

Betty Steffy and Fenwick English in their book, *Curriculum and Assessment for World-Class Schools*, referenced the seven components recommended by the Business Roundtable as the basis for world-class education. The seven components are:

1. Standards that set high academic expectations linked to a system of school-based sanctions and rewards documenting accountability
2. School autonomy that provides the resources and decision-making flexibility to hold schools accountable for student learning
3. Professional development leading to continuous improvement for teachers and administrators
4. Parent involvement that supports choice and active involvement in the creation of the learning environment
5. Learning readiness that focuses on preschool skill development for children identified as at risk for school failure
6. Technology to access knowledge
7. Safety and discipline in the learning environment[17]

The Business Roundtable has been very active in promoting education reform in U.S. schools. Many business leaders are concerned about the educational preparation of American students for the workforce.

Alan Greenspan, Chairman of the Federal Reserve System, spoke before the Committee on Education and the Workforce of the U.S. House of Representatives. In his speech, Greenspan said,

> The pressures we face today are not unlike those of a century ago, when our education system successfully responded to the multiplying needs brought about by a marked acceleration in technological innovation. As those advances put new demands on workers interacting with an increasingly more complex stock of productive capital, high school education proliferated—enabling students to read manuals, manipulate numbers, and understand formulae. Students were thus accorded the skills necessary to staff the newly developing as-

sembly lines in factories and the rapidly expanding transportation systems whose mechanical and automotive jobs required a widening array of cognitive skills. For those who sought education beyond high school, land grant colleges sprang up, as states reacted to the increased skills required by industry and especially agriculture, the dominant occupation a century ago.

By today's standard, the required share of "intellectual workers" in our labor force was then still small. But the technological innovations of the latter part of the nineteenth century began to bring an increasing conceptualization of our gross domestic product—that is, a greater emphasis on value added stemming from new ideas and concepts as distinct from material inputs and demanding physical labor. The proportion of our workforce that created value through intellectual endeavors, rather than predominantly through manual labor, began a century-long climb. In 1900, only one out of every ten workers was in a professional, technical, or managerial occupation. By 1970, that proportion had doubled, and today those types of jobs account for nearly one-third of our workforce.

Moreover, this simple statistic undoubtedly understates the ongoing increase in the analytic content of work, because there also seems to have been a marked increase in the need for conceptual skills in jobs that a decade or so ago would have been easily characterized as fully manual labor. Indeed, the proliferation of information technologies throughout the economy in recent years has likely accelerated this shift in the skill requirements of many occupations away from routine work and toward nonroutine interactive and analytical tasks.[18]

The Charlotte Mecklenburg school system in North Carolina embarked on a world-class schools project that was chronicled by Denis Doyle and Susan Pimentel. (Mr. Doyle's guest article can be found in appendix A.) Ten notable individuals including former Secretary of Education William Bennett, James Comer from Yale University, and Patricia Graham, former Dean of the Harvard Graduate School of Education, served on the district's world-class schools panel. Of interest was their conviction that change was necessary, but the panel members held widely divergent views about what that change would involve. The panel's deliberations, according to the authors, could be captured in a single sentence, "For 150 years American schools kept the pedagogy constant and let the results vary; for the future we must vary the pedagogy and produce high levels of accomplishment for all." In other words, raise standards.[19]

The world-class schools panel concluded the following:

- Leadership matters and it does not matter a little or even a lot. Leadership is everything.
- Substance matters. Contrary to popular opinion education is not content-free. What you teach makes a difference.
- A few things make all the difference. Requiring mastery and focusing on measured outcomes is a transforming insight that affects everything that goes on in schools.
- Set measurable goals and hold yourself to them.
- Everything affects everything else. A substantive change in one area of schooling necessitates changes in other areas.
- Edicts from on high must stop except for the edict that ends all edicts. That is because those individuals at the heart of the system, the teachers and principals, have had little say-so.
- Build community support and work on it all the time.
- The process never ends, there is no finish line; there is only the race.
- Understand technology because modern information technologies are not simply mechanical or electromechanical means to do old things faster. Technology transforms everything it touches.
- Restructuring means big change and it is not a matter of rearranging the deck chairs.
- Communicate, communicate, communicate.

What Will It Take to Have World-Class Achievement in Mathematics and Science?

by George D. Nelson, Ph.D

Former Director of Project 2061 of the American Association for the Advancement of Science and former Shuttle astronaut

First, just what do we mean by "world-class achievement in mathematics and science"? There are at least two notions, and they are often confused. One is the traditional school report card approach of doing relatively better than everyone else does—placing at the top of the curve, winning the contest. The other is the idea of achieving standards that describe an absolute level of learning. In the standards-based approach, the measurement is against a widely agreed upon set of learning goals that define important skills and conceptual knowledge. As an example, imagine an international golf match. Is the winning team "world-class" with an average score of 32 strokes over par? Or does "world-class" status demand scores closer to par no matter what the other teams' score? We are familiar with setting absolute goals in education—everyone should read at or above grade level, for example—but have not yet taken this approach in mathematics and science.

Project 2061's goal is the achievement of universal literacy in science, mathematics, and technology. Literacy is measured against a set of benchmarks that have been carefully assembled by the nation's scientific and education research communities and supported by the best teachers. This absolute goal is not necessarily inconsistent with the relative goal of placing first on an international test. Indeed, placing first could be one milestone along the way. With a test designed to be a reliable and valid indicator of achievement of the literacy goals, the two notions would be fully compatible. "World-class" would imply both placing high in the contest and achieving absolute standards. For golfers, it is winning the Ryder Cup with a score close to par; for school districts, it is having the highest relative reading scores with all students reading above grade level.

Can we get to "world class" from here? In principle, we know what is needed:

- A coherent set of literacy benchmarks—clear learning goals for mathematics and science that all students are expected to achieve. Most students should eventually achieve at levels well beyond the benchmarks, which is not the case today.
- Curriculum materials that align with the benchmark's content and pedagogically support student learning
- A K–12 curriculum, coherent across the grade levels and disciplines, that targets the benchmarks and is uniquely designed to work for individual states, districts, or schools
- Reliable and valid assessments that measure student progress towards the benchmarks and provide feedback to improve instruction
- Teachers who have deep knowledge of children, content, and instruction, the skills to choose and use excellent curriculum materials, and the support they need to work as professionals in their classrooms and with their peers
- Students who are ready and expected to learn and who have the support they need to succeed
- A community of administrators, school boards, parents, businesses, and government agencies that understands the learning goals and is willing to support and reform with time, resources, and policies

Developing and assembling these elements is the reform challenge, whether it is in traditional public schools, charter schools, private schools, or for-profit schools. (The school descriptor does not guarantee that any particular element is in place. Real competition that could drive change must come from what a school does, no matter what it is labeled.) Some elements are already in place. We have excellent sets of learning goals in mathematics and science from the American Association for the Advancement of Science, the National Research Council, and the National Council of Teachers of Mathematics. States and districts should consider taking advantage of these national efforts rather than constructing their own goals with insufficient resources, expertise, and time. New analysis tools are providing insights into alignment and instructional quality of curriculum materials and assessments. Based on this new information, the demand for better materials and tests should lead to continuous improvement in these areas. Solid empirical research to verify the effectiveness of the materials and assessments is sorely needed. With effective curriculum materials and assessments available at each grade level, coherent K–12 curricula can be designed, assembled, tested, and improved by states, districts, or schools.

Higher education, professional organizations, and school districts must take responsibility for substantially reforming undergraduate mathematics and science education, teacher preparation, and staff development programs. Right now, the culture tolerates—and often promotes—activities that are irrelevant, redundant, and too short-term to be effective. Local districts and communities must find a way to create and support a cadre of education leaders and professional teachers. (A 12-month appointment for teachers with well planned and executed professional development is an interesting idea currently on the table.) Federal, state, and local governments must play appropriate roles by formulating coherent policy and providing the resources necessary for significant reforms. And they must stay the course long enough for improvement in student performance to occur. Ten years might be long enough to get a good start. The business community can affirm how long it takes to retool a company and its culture. The same is true for schools. School reform requires both urgency and patience— urgency because we cannot wait to get started, patience because real progress will take a long time.

Finally, the nation and its communities must take on the social issues of poverty and crime that inequitably stack the deck against so many of our children, denying them the opportunities that a good education can provide. While these issues are outside the scope of Project 2061 or any single school or agency, we must recognize and acknowledge their importance and contribute as citizens to finding and implementing solutions.

Can we get to "world-class" in mathematics and science? Yes, for the future of our planet, our nation, and our children, we must. It is possible; it won't be easy; and it will take time.

There is an evolving concept of what may be models for American world-class schools. The models emanated from a Comprehensive School Reform Demonstration Program that was sponsored by Congressmen David Obey, (WI) and John Porter, (IL), members of the U.S. House of Representatives at the time. The Comprehensive School Reform Demonstration Program assists public schools in implementing effective comprehensive school designs. Of note is that in FY 98, Congress appropriated $145,000,000 to state education agencies to provide competitive incentive grants to school districts that elected to pursue comprehensive reform. Congress does not tend to fund new programs that it does not believe will work.

There were nine criteria used for choosing the models that were selected as guides for comprehensive school reform. School districts were encouraged to use the models that were recommended but were free to choose other models, develop their own, or combine models as long as they adhered to an approach using the following nine criteria.

1. Comprehensive design with aligned components
2. Support within the school
3. Measurable goals and benchmarks
4. Effective research-based methods and strategies
5. Professional development
6. External technical support and assistance
7. Parental and community involvement
8. Coordination of resources
9. Evaluation of strategies

There were 17 comprehensive models named in the Comprehensive School Reform Demonstration Program legislation. The models are:

1. Accelerated Schools
2. America's Choice
3. Atlas Communities
4. Audrey Cohen College
5. Coalition of Essential Schools
6. Community for Learning
7. Co – NECT

8.   Direct Instruction
9.   Expeditionary Learning Outward Bound
10. High Schools that Work
11. Modern Red Schoolhouse
12. Paideia
13. Roots and Wings
14. School Development Program
15. Success for All
16. Talent Development High School
17. Urban Learning Centers

You can learn more about these programs by contacting:

- The U.S. Department of Education, at
  http://www.ed.gov/offices/OESE/compreform
- North Central Regional Education Laboratory, at
  http://www.ncrel.org/info/improve

Comprehensive school reform programs include the following eight basic components:

1.   Effective, research-based instructional methods and strategies
2.   High quality and continuous teacher and staff professional development
3.   Measurable goals for student performance and benchmarks for assessing progress which are aligned with state and local content standards and benchmarks
4.   A clearly articulated vision and direction whose goals are met through strong leadership and support within the school
5.   Meaningful involvement of parents and the local community
6.   Implementation of a plan for the evaluation of school reforms and student results achieved
7.   Coordination of available resources and efforts to seek external support as needed
8.   A comprehensive design that assures that all aspects of these components are aligned

A comprehensive school reform model has considerable potential to help American schools become world-class. The concept recognizes that for schools to improve, the entire organization needs to be considered. No more *silver bullet* attempts can be used to improve schools; improvement efforts must be systemic. The caveat is the need for more research on these programs to be certain they are effective and where they are most applicable. (See *Better by Design, A Consumer's Guide to Schoolwide Reform*[20])

England's Education Reform

We would be remiss if we did not discuss the educational reform to achieve world-class schools taking place in England. It is similar to the American comprehensive school reform model—but worthy of its own description.

It seems appropriate to describe how one country has chosen to make its schools world-class. Earlier in this chapter we noted that Great Britain's Prime Minister Tony Blair said his goal was to create a world-class education system in which education was not the privilege of the few, but the right of the many.[21] When Blair took office, fewer than 60% of 11-year-olds achieved the expected standard for their age level in numeracy and literacy. Thus began a massive effort on his part to build more rigor and accountability into the plan of the previous government.

Secretary of State for Education and Employment David Blunkett outlined his plan for England to achieve world-class schools. "In a world of rapid change, every pupil will need to be literate, numerate, well-informed, and prepared for the citizenship of tomorrow" according to Blunkett. In the 1997 Green Paper, a policy paper, the government set a goal of a world-class education system where every school is excellent or improving or both. The plan is based on the following objectives:

- To promote excellent school leadership by rewarding our leading professionals properly
- To recruit, retain, and motivate high quality classroom teachers by paying them more
- To provide better support to all teachers and to deploy teaching resources in a more flexible way

In order to develop effective leaders, it is essential to reward them well and give them freedom to manage without losing accountability. To support the plan, better pay for successful heads, performance-related pay for heads with fixed-term contracts, an appraisal system for heads, and a national framework for headship training were recommended. The recommendation included a proposal for a new National College for School Leadership. All of these recommendations are being implemented as part of the massive education reform underway in England.

The Green Paper noted that all the evidence shows that heads are the key to a school's success. The leader creates a sense of purpose and direction, sets high expectations for learning, monitors performance, and motivates the staff to give their best effort. The challenge is to create the rewards, training, and support to attract, retain, and develop many more heads of this caliber to lead their schools.

Better rewards for teaching are an essential ingredient of the plan. There would be higher pay for good teachers with assessment at a new performance threshold that would lead to the higher pay range. The premise behind this recommendation is a closer link between pay and appraisal than was previously the case.

In order to improve teaching, the government set a demanding agenda for high standards. The emphasis was to give teachers the training and support they need to do their jobs well and to progress in their careers. To accomplish this objective, new national tests for all trainee teachers to guarantee high-level skills in numeracy, literacy, and information and communication technology were proposed. In addition, the plan includes a new national fast-track scheme to recruit from the best graduates and move outstanding teachers quickly into the profession.

Continuing teachers will have a contractual duty to keep their skills up-to-date. There will be a new focus on professional development bringing together national, school, and individual priorities. Training would be outside of school hours to minimize disruptions to the students' education.

There are also student performance expectations that are outlined in the National Literacy Strategy. In 2002, 80% of 11-year-olds are expected to reach Level 4 or above in English tests. There is a detailed framework for their literacy that ranges from designating the number of minutes for whole class instruction and for group and independent work to specifying required curricular concepts.

Similar recommendations are in place for numeracy with a goal of at least four out of five 11-year-olds reaching the standards expected of them. It is noted that all primary schools should teach a daily mathematics lesson lasting 45–60 minutes. Consultants are employed to provide effective professional development to ensure high quality instruction.

Class sizes of 30 and under for 5-, 6-, and 7-year-olds are stipulated. There will be a network of excellence centers to spread good practice in teaching and learning. Also, opportunities for early childhood education are offered to parents who want them for their children.

England's plan is similar to America's Comprehensive School Reform Demonstration Model and Haynes and Chalker's world-class schools' elements. Although different, each plan emphasizes essentially the same components to achieve high quality education. The common themes are a rigorous curriculum, assessment of student achievement, improved teaching through high-quality professional development programs, effective leadership, and parental support for schools.

The following is a guest essay by Michael Barber, one of the key participants in England's education reform movement. Also, see Martin Ripley's guest essay on world-class tests in appendix A, page 297.

World-Class Education Concepts
Achieving High Standards in England:
A Summary of the Strategy

by Michael Barber
Head of Prime Minister's Delivery Unit

The English school reform has, at its core, a framework for continuous improvement. It has six elements, all built around the core idea of each school rising to a high challenge while benefiting from high support.

THE FRAMEWORK FOR CONTINUOUS IMPROVEMENT

The policies for each segment (starting at 12 o'clock) are set out in the following chart.

AMBITIOUS STANDARDS	• High standards set out in the National Curriculum
	• National Tests at age 7, 11, 14, 16
	• Detailed teaching programmes based on best practice
	• Optional World Class Tests based on the best 10 per cent in the 1995 TIMSS

DEVOLVED RESPONSIBILITY	• School as unit of accountability • Devolution of resources and employment powers to schools • Pupil-led formula funding • Open enrolment
GOOD DATA/CLEAR TARGETS	• Individual pupil level data collected nationally • Analysis of performance in national tests • Benchmark data annually for every school • Comparisons to all other schools with similar intake • Statutory target-setting at district and school level
ACCESS TO BEST PRACTICE AND QUALITY PROFESSIONAL DEVELOPMENT	• Universal professional development in national priorities (literacy, numeracy, ICT) • Leadership development as an entitlement • Standards Site [http://www.standards.dfee.gov.uk] • Beacon Schools • LEA (district) responsibility • Devolved funding for professional development at school level • Reform of education research
ACCOUNTABILITY	• National inspection system for schools and LEAs (districts) • Every school inspected every 4-6 years • All inspection reports published • Publication annually of school/district level performance data and targets
INTERVENTION IN INVERSE PROPORTION TO SUCCESS (Rewards, Assistance, Consequences)	For successful schools • beacon status • celebration events • recognition • school achievement awards scheme • greater autonomy

For all schools

- post-inspection action plan
- school improvement grant to assist implementation of action plan
- monitoring of performance by LEA (district)

For underperforming schools

- more prescriptive action plan
- possible withdrawal of devolved budget and responsibility
- national and LEA monitoring of performance
- additional funding to assist turnround (but only for practical improvement measures)

For failing schools
(as for underperforming schools plus)

- early consideration of closure
- district plan for school with target date for completing turnround (maximum 2 years)
- national monitoring three times a year
- possible fresh start or city academy

For failing LEAs (districts)
- intervention from central government
- possible contracting out of functions to the private sector

Over and above this framework, the government has invested in early years education, promoted high standards of literacy and numeracy at primary level by providing materials guidance and best practice in professional development for every single primary teacher, by introducing reforms of teachers' pay which link pay to performance and by beginning to strengthen secondary education in urban areas.

The results so far are promising at all levels, with particularly impressive gains in pupil outcomes at primary level, as illustrated below.

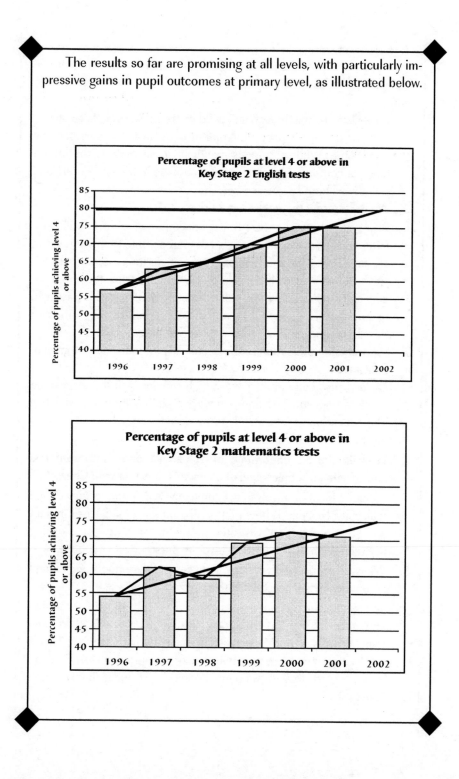

For the next phase of reform, the government recently set out seven strategic intentions on which it would base policy in future years. These are:

1. **We will see things through and build on the achievements so far**

   The first task is to ensure the reforms of the last few years become irreversible. While the focus may shift to secondary, the importance of continued investment and support in the early years and primary will not be missed.

2. **We will narrow the achievement gap**

   Rising standards are vital but if education is to contribute to a fairer society as well as a more prosperous one, then we need to see faster progress in areas of disadvantage than elsewhere. Policies that focus on such areas or on particular groups, for whom the education service has not delivered successfully in the past, will be pursued. The aim will be to build on the narrowing of the gap that the literacy and numeracy strategies have begun.

3. **We will tailor education to the talents, aspirations and potential of individuals**

   Once virtually all pupils achieve high standards in the basics, the range of opportunities and pathways available should be diverse. The education service needs to be flexible enough to respond to diverse talents and aspirations.

4. **We will offer the opportunity of high standards in both academic and vocational subjects and encourage "Education with Character"**

   A good education involves academic and vocational achievement. It also involves pupils becoming well rounded, creative, self-reliant and good at working with others. It is not a matter of choosing between these two goals: each young person deserves both.

5. **We will encourage diversity among secondary schools and extend autonomy for successful schools**

   To enable every secondary school to develop the distinct mission and ethos we need to encourage diversity. That is why the Green Paper promises more specialist, Beacon and faith schools. This is nothing to do with creating two tiers or encouraging selection and everything to do with meeting diverse need and achieving high standards.

6. **We will demonstrate trust in the informed professional judgment of teachers**

   There is a powerful new can-do culture among teachers. They are focused on outcomes, data and evidence more than ever before.

   Government needs to disseminate best practice effectively, encourage its adoption through professional development and trust teachers to use informed professional judgment.

7. **We will encourage partnerships**

   Everyone has a stake in the success of publicly provided education. We need to encourage partnerships between schools, local authorities, faith groups, community groups and business, so that society as a whole shares the ambition and contributes to the creation of a world-class service.

   The important role local authorities can play in taking forward this education strategy will be readily apparent. As they consider the future, they can examine their role in the light of these seven factors. Above all, their role is one of creating the capacity for successful change at local level. The success of cities like Nottingham and Liverpool and counties like Hertfordshire point the way forward. They can play an enabling role in building partnerships, creating a culture of success and intervening where necessary. Local authorities have played an important part in the success of recent years; their role in the future will be no less crucial.

Conclusion

As the emphasis shifts to bringing the same kind of step-change in performance at secondary level that has already occurred at primary level, schools at both primary and secondary level can be assured of increasing funding and investment in building and technology. Growth in excess of five percent—in real terms—is already budgeted through 2004. The English school system has therefore an opportunity to become world class. Its primary schools have already shown that rapid, system-wide improvement can be achieved.

More information on the reform effort in England can be found at *http://www.dfes.gov.uk/index.htm.*

Summary

The objective of achieving world-class schools is an international theme. Although there is no specific definition of world-class education, new international assessments are making it possible to compare student achievement around the world. Those assessments include TIMSS, PISA, and PIRLS.

World-class education concepts are also becoming more evident. Regardless of who is promoting world-class education, there is consistency in the concepts mentioned: effective leadership, a call for change of past education practices that have proven to be ineffective, focused professional development, articulated curriculum that is rigorous and taught for student understanding, high-quality instructional practice, and assessment of the intended curriculum. These concepts align with our six chromosomes (core areas).

Embedded in the recognition of our genetic model is acceptance of the fact that the chromosomes must be viewed as a process for school improvement and not treated as separate and distinct activities. To achieve world-class school status, it will be necessary to align a plan that integrates all of the chromosomes. How the plan is approached can remain flexible as long as the strategies are based on data-driven, research-based information and a qualitative review of literature on education practices in countries with high student achievement.

Key Concepts
- World-class education concepts are being explored through international cooperation on assessment and comparative studies.
- World-class education can only be achieved through international comparisons using a data-driven, research-based process with a review of quantitative and qualitative literature on education practices of high-achieving countries.
- International assessments are useful for identifying potential world-class academic achievement. Three of those assessments were addressed in detail: the Third International Mathematics and Science Study (TIMSS), Progress in International Literacy Study (PIRLS), and Program for International Student Assessment (PISA).

- High standards are a critical expectation for achieving world-class performance. Three education summits identified high standards as a significant aspect of performance goals for the nation's schools.
- Comprehensive School Reform Demonstration Program models and their basic components, the reform program in England, and world-class education books provide useful tools for analyzing world-class education.

Endnotes

13. White House Press Release (October 22, 1999). Remarks by the President of the United States to the National Board for Professional Teaching Standards, Hyatt Regency: Washington, DC.
14. WORLD-CLASS—being among the world's best and of the highest caliber. *Random House Webster's Concise Dictionary* (1998).
15. Donald M. Chalker and Richard M. Haynes, *World class elementary schools: agenda for action* (Lancaster, PA: Technomic Publishing, 1994).
16. Donald M. Chalker and Richard M. Haynes, *World class schools: new standards for education* (Lancaster, PA: Technomic Publishing, 1997).
17. Betty E. Steffy and Fenwick W. English, *Curriculum and assessment for world-class schools* (Lancaster, PA: Corwin Press, 1997).
18. Alan Greenspan, Statement before the Committee on Education and the Workforce, U.S. House of Representatives (September 21, 2000).
19. Denis Doyle and Susan Pimentel, *Kappan* (March 1993).
20. James Traub, *Better by design, a consumer's guide to schoolwide reform*, Thomas B. Fordham Foundation (December 1999).
21. Citation drawn from a Michael Barber speech delivered at the Skol Tema Conference Stockholm, Sweden (September 27, 1999).

Chapter 3

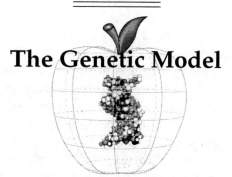

The Genetic Model

Overview of Key Concepts

- *Schools and school districts are living, dynamic organizations where interactions of systems produce specific district functions and outcomes.*

- *The genetic model is a framework to build well-articulated core areas and functions of the school district that can lead to world-class performance.*

- *The genetic model contains three distinct components: the DNA-Gene component, the Chromosome component, and the Organism component.*

- *There are six fundamental chromosomes that work interactively leading to high performance: leadership, change, professional development, curriculum, instructional practice, and assessment.*

Introduction

In this chapter we examine the biological connection between living organisms and school districts as living organizations. We will summarize the fundamental concepts in the sub-microscopic world of genetics. We will present only the basic genetic concepts in order to provide a general understanding of those biological principles that relate to the genetic model and guide the development of the six core areas of school district work related to teaching and student achievement.

It is important for the readers to understand these genetic concepts in relation to the development of the district's genetic framework. If that is accomplished, a new understanding of systemic planning will be in place. Using the genetic framework will enable educators to see how their school district can build the chromosomes that define their organization and lead to world-class performance.

Values, beliefs, principles, and practices play a fundamental role in successful school districts. It is critical to recognize this relationship. School districts are living systems that possess unique characteristics; these characteristics define their particular identity as well as distinguish them from all other similar organizations. Together we will explore the process for school districts to determine their organization's unique traits. As we progress through the book, the readers will apply the genetic concepts to their school district context and seek relationships among the six core areas. By doing so readers will gain greater insight into the impact of these areas on student achievement.

The Biological Context

Genetics illustrates the key interactions of biological life itself. We have chosen the genetic model as a metaphoric conceptualization for schools because it most closely represents the key interactions of social systems and the behavior that lies therein. Within any living being there is an interaction of systems that defines what it looks like and enables it to produce some function or product. This is precisely what occurs in schools in order to bring about desired results. When these systemic interactions occur, they lead to desired outcomes. The primary issue we want to address is how schools can structure various organizational components of work to bring about desired improvements. The genetic model is the framework by which school improvement can systemically be viewed, planned, and implemented.

The interaction of organizational core areas occurs, regardless of whether school districts consciously try to connect them. The question is: Are the results of that interaction productive and effective in achieving the district's desired results, high levels of performance? The answer rests in the degree to which the core areas are based on fundamental core principles that the district will live by and the extent to which these areas are planned to intentionally seek specific interactions. We contend that if school districts develop and guide the interaction of these six core areas, they will achieve their desired results.

In biology scientists study life in laboratories to closely examine how living organisms work. Biology utilizes the microscopic world of fundamental units of organisms, known as cells, and the sub-microscopic realm of the molecules that make up those cells. The organism we recognize as an animal or plant is not a random collection of individual cells but a multi-cellular cooperative. Though there are a multitude of biological concepts that frame our understanding about organisms, three will be identified in conjunction with our genetic model. These three biological concepts help to explain the function and structure of organizations. They also serve as an integral thread woven through the development of our model:

Concept 1
Within each cell, life's order is coded at the molecular level. The continuity of life is on DNA molecules. These molecules of DNA comprise genes that determine the characteristics and traits of the organism. These characteristics and traits (genes) are then passed on from one generation to the next.

Concept 2
Structure and function are correlated at all levels of the biological organism. Each cell has a specific structure and a specific function. For example, a blood cell has a specific structure and make-up and it serves a specific function in the body, specifically to carry oxygen and waste products.

Concept 3
Organisms are open systems that interact continuously with their environment, exchanging materials and energy with their surroundings. They adapt to the environment in which they exist. This environment includes other organisms as well as nonliving factors.

We believe there are powerful conceptual and real connections among these three biological concepts shaping the structure and function of living organisms and those of school districts. When educators gain an understanding of these critical connections, they are in a better position to skillfully develop the core areas of their district.

What Is the Genetic Model?

Biology is closely connected to the social sciences. All living things are the composition of a hierarchy of structures with specific functions interacting to create the uniqueness of the organism. In social systems such as school districts, there are a number of structures that function together to define what the organization looks like and how it functions. Throughout the book we will refer to these core areas as chromosomes. The genetic model is the biological framework to define those core areas and functions of the school or district that can lead to world-class performance. The value of using a genetic metaphor is that it emphasizes the concept that school districts are dynamic, interactive, and social in nature, just as living organisms are. As such, leaders will benefit by keeping these connections at the forefront of their planning and implementation.

Components of the Genetic Model

The genetic model is comprised of three distinct, yet interactive, components that school districts can develop to define what they want to be and how they can function. These three components include the DNA-Gene, the Chromosome, and the Organism itself. Figure 3.1 depicts these fundamental components and their integrated relationship.

The DNA-Gene component is the most fundamental level of the model where the genetic blueprint for the form and function of living organisms and districts is determined. The Chromosome component is the larger structure on which each of the related genes is located and interacts. It is this interaction that determines how the chromosomes will operate in living organisms and how districts will function. The organism component is the manifestation of the first two components, which are the DNA-gene strands and chromosomes. To the extent that these components are well defined and designed to work together will determine what organisms and districts will look like and how well they will function.

FIGURE 3.1—THE GENETIC CONNECTION TO ORGANIZATIONS

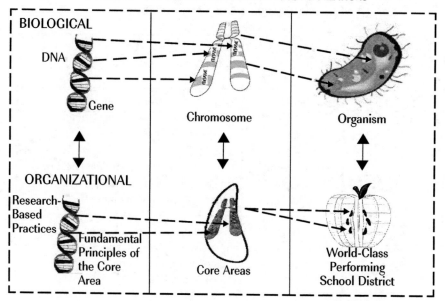

As we begin our description of the model, we will define and align the fundamental concepts. The alignment of these concepts will draw important connections between the biological and organizational domains. We will then describe each of the three components of the model both biologically and organizationally.

As a district develops its framework, it will be important to understand these genetic and organizational concepts and their alignment. Chart 3.1 defines four genetic concepts and four organizational concepts used in the model. These concepts will be the basis upon which a district develops it genetic framework for world-class performance. It then aligns these concepts to demonstrate their relationship to each other.

Chart 3.2 illustrates a very important distinction between when the seeds of world-class success are determined and when they are manifested. An organism only looks and acts in response to its genetic make up. Schools, likewise, will only look and function in response to the agreed upon collective values, principles, and practices of the individuals that work in them and the established structures that operate therein. Without this agreement, a school will demonstrate a disconnected set of random activities that do not lead to collective success.

CHART 3.1—ALIGNMENT OF BIOLOGICAL (GENETIC) CONCEPTS AND MEANINGS
WITH ORGANIZATIONAL CONCEPTS AND MEANINGS

BIOLOGICAL COMPONENT	CONCEPTS	MEANINGS
Gene  / DNA	**Gene** parallels **Fundamental Principle**	A discrete unit of hereditary information consisting of a specific nucleotide sequence in DNA The basic tenets (core values) held by a group and upon which that area of the organization is supported
	DNA parallels **Research-Based Practices**	A double-stranded, helical nucleic acid molecule capable of replicating and determining the inherited structure of a cell's proteins The substantive practices supporting the fundamental principles of operation
Chromosome 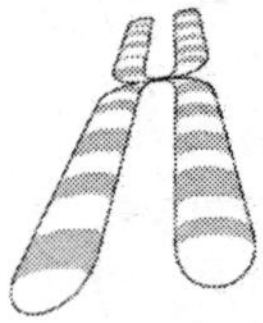	**Chromosome** parallels **Core Area**	A threadlike, gene-carrying structure found in the nucleus consisting of one very long DNA molecule and associated proteins The organizational area that includes the aggregate of fundamental principles and practices and that interact with other core areas in systemic functioning
Organism 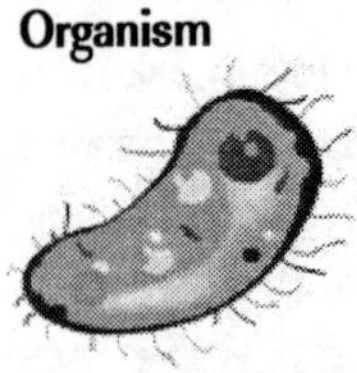	**Organism** parallels **World-Class Performing School District**	A living person, animal, or plant The regular interacting of interdependent groups of core areas forming a unified functional structure

CHART 3.2 —POINTS WHERE BIOLOGICAL (GENETIC) AND ORGANIZATIONAL CONCEPTS ARE DETERMINED AND MANIFESTED

BIOLOGICAL COMPONENT	CONCEPTS	DETERMINATION AND MANIFESTATION OF CHARACTERISTICS
Gene	**Gene** parallels **Fundamental Principles**	
DNA	**DNA** parallels **Research-Based Practices**	Points at which the function, form, and product of an organism or organization are DETERMINED
Chromosome 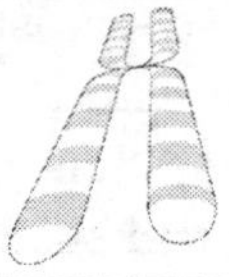	**Chromosome** parallels **Core Area**	
Organism 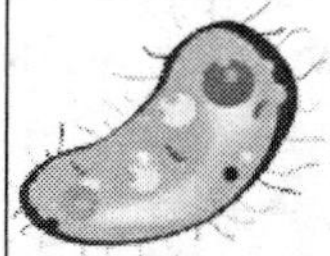	**Organism** parallels **World-Class Performing School District**	Point at which the function, form, and product of an organism or organization is MANIFESTED

DNA-Gene Component

Biological Concept. In biology, DNA molecules and genes are the most fundamental sub-microscopic components of all living cells. The DNA-gene strands are the genetic blueprints that define specific characteristics and traits of an organism. In Figure 3.2 we depict the DNA-gene relationship as the beginning point to determine a characteristic of an organism. It is at this point that the organism's structure and function are determined. Whatever is defined here will ultimately be manifested in the organism, as it exists.

At the sub-microscopic level of the DNA molecules and genes, characteristics and traits of plants and animals are determined. DNA material makes up a gene, and we call this the DNA-gene strand. People commonly refer to a person's genes when they talk about their physical attributes (for example, hair color, height, eye color, physical build, and so forth.)

The DNA molecules determine the specific characteristics (inheritable features) and traits (the variation of the features) of the organism. For example, the characteristic of eye color is determined by the DNA molecule and gene for color. The trait is the actual color of eyes—brown, blue, green, and so forth. The characteristic of height is determined by another DNA-gene strand. All features of organisms are determined at this level and the organism will have only those features that are defined by the DNA-gene strands. The genes can combine together to provide further variations of the different features.

This basic principle defines how people, plants, and animals will look and how they will function. In the study of genetics there are variations of this principle and much greater complexity with regard to how genes interact to form the characteristics of living organisms, but the fundamental idea remains simple; the characteristics and traits of living organisms are determined at the DNA-gene level. It is only at this level the appearance and function of the organism will be identified. This fundamental relationship holds true for organizations as leaders make decisions regarding what they value and how those values ultimately affect district-wide practices. Next we look at the organizational concept of this theory.

Organizational Concept. Organizations parallel this biological foundation. In the case of school districts, they operate on fundamental principles, shared values and beliefs. In the genetic model, we refer to these organizational counterparts of genes and DNA molecules as fundamental principles and research-based practices. Figure 3.2 illustrates this biological connection.

In some school districts values and beliefs are well articulated and communicated at all levels of the organization. Staff members can clearly articulate the practices that are implemented and can converse fluently about the reasons they exist. They know the purposes and the desired outcomes that these practices seek to accomplish. In other districts these research-based practices are not well articulated at the district or school level; yet, individuals engage in practices that they believe are worthwhile and productive.

FIGURE 3.2—THE GENETIC CONNECTION TO ORGANIZATIONS: DNA-GENE COMPONENT

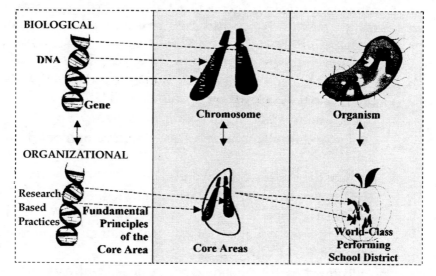

This lack of clarity about the practices prevents a district from making fundamental improvements despite people's perceptions that the practices seem relevant and effective.

There are two basic parts to this component of the DNA-gene strand in organizations: Fundamental Principles (gene) and Research-based Practices (DNA). As we describe these two parts, we will use examples from the Professional Development Chromosome for illustrative purposes. We will draw direct connections to their biological counterparts. We will provide examples of how principles and practices can be developed, accepted, and communicated in order to create a coherent, effective professional development program.

The first part of the DNA-gene component is Fundamental Principles (genes). These are the broad values that make up the core area of operation. They consist of the basic tenets (core values and beliefs) or body of tenets held by a group in a core area of the organization's operation. It is upon these tenets that the behavior in each core area of the organization is supported. A school district must determine the body of principles that it wants to develop.

Fundamental Principles parallel the gene component on the biological side. They are the tenets a school district believes must be in place to enable that core area to be world-class in its structure and function. In the core area of professional development, we suggest six fundamental principles (genes) that a district should consider when creating an effective, world-class professional development program. Figure 3.3 illustrates how all six genes are situated on the professional development chromosome (core area). They include

1. Create a philosophy statement, purpose, and goals of what professional development should do and be
2. Deepen understanding of content knowledge
3. Design and implement a professional development framework
4. Change the organizational culture
5. Implement professional learning strategies that support adult learner needs
6. Assess the effectiveness of the professional development program

Once identified, each gene should be articulated with a value statement that describes the overall commitment of the district to this part of the chromosome. To illustrate this concept, we have taken Gene 5 and written a value statement to which a district would commit.

FIGURE 3.3—SIX FUNDAMENTAL PRINCIPLES (GENES) TO DEVELOP IN THE PROFESSIONAL DEVELOPMENT CORE AREA (CHROMOSOME)

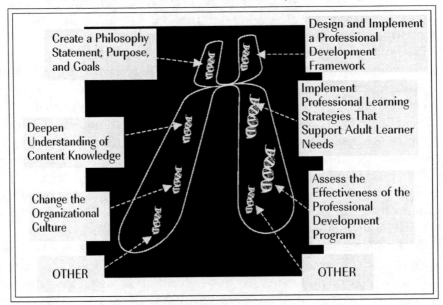

Professional Development Gene 5 (fundamental principle)
Implement specific professional learning strategies that
support adult learner needs.

Value Statement
The district will engage in a variety of professional learning strategies to support adult learner needs. These strategies will serve specific purposes in developing teacher
knowledge and skill levels for effective instruction.

This value statement for professional development Gene 5 articulates the tenet by which the district commits to live. It communicates the message to all staff members that their learning needs
will be supported in a variety of ways, and the district will be proactive to explore the strategies that best meet the teachers' identified needs. The district should develop a value statement for all of
the genes (fundamental principles) in each chromosome (core area).
In the case of professional development, there are six genes. A district would have six value statements if it accepted the six genes we
present. If it elected to delete some and develop others, a value statement would be written for each of the identified genes. We stress
that a district must ultimately select the genes it will commit to
implement. These genes can be of their own choosing, the ones we
present, or some combination of the two.

The second part of the DNA-Gene component is the Research-
based Practices. Research-based Practices parallel the DNA or genetic code of organisms. They are the cognitive, substantive pieces
that define the gene itself. These are the content particulars (the
what) that will determine what the gene will look like. They provide the specific focus of the gene. In other words, one could complete this statement using the research-based practices (DNA):

"What we mean by Gene X (fundamental principle) is that the
district will engage in DNA X (research-based practices . . . "

These content particulars provide the basis upon which specific actions will be developed. They represent the most important
directions that the district is committed to pursue in the quest for
world-class performance in that core area. They are at the heart of
how the district will function.

With these values and practices firmly in place, the district has
a plan for what it must do. It has an end in mind and a clear under-

standing of the impact this focus will have on the staff, the organization, and the teaching-learning process. Staff members' energy and effort can be directed in productive ways to accomplish the desired outcomes.

Gene 5 of the professional development chromosome is committed to using a variety of professional learning strategies to support adult learning. The DNA of that gene are the types of learning strategies the district will explore and implement. The task now is to define the DNA. The district must determine what professional learning strategies will be most effective in helping the teachers improve their skills and approaches to teaching. To approach this task, the district should answer some fundamental questions to guide its thinking.

- What professional learning strategies are proven to help staff members address the needs of the students and improve instruction?
- Does the district believe these strategies will help teachers achieve their professional development goals?
- What is the most effective combination of strategies for teachers to use given the goals they want to accomplish?
- Is the district capable of investing the financial resources over time to ensure that teachers have sufficient opportunity to learn and implement new instructional approaches?

Having given thought to these questions, the district may identify the following professional learning strategies: study groups, curriculum analysis, analysis of student data, videotape analysis, workshops, conferences, college coursework, and partnerships. If a district takes the time to develop these strategies to support this gene, it will have clarified a very important part of its professional development program. The task is to do this activity for every one of the professional development genes (fundamental principles). By doing so, the district will shape how it expects professional development to look and function.

In many school districts a variety of learning activities are offered as part of the professional development program. These activities may include a collection of high interest but disconnected activities, such as motivational speakers, in-district classes, and conference attendance by teachers and administrators. On the surface, these approaches may appear to be effective. After all, they can be very useful in meeting a teacher's or administrator's identified personal or professional interest. Participants may even find the activities energizing. However, the fundamental question is: Are these activities directed toward accomplishing the professional development goals of the individual teacher and the educational goals of the school or district? Even though the district was well intentioned and may have spent considerable funds providing these activities, more often than not there is little change in teachers' instructional practice.

At this juncture the reader may be thinking, "We have a good professional development program. Look at the activities we provide for our teachers and the resources we devote to these activities." This, in fact, may be the case. We would encourage you to examine the programs to see if they truly are achieving what you think they are accomplishing. It is important to recognize that teachers will engage in professional development activities regardless of whether there is a well-developed set of research-based practices or not. The difference, however, is that in the former situation they are working toward similar outcomes with a common philosophy and approach. In the organization where everyone approaches an area of need from individual perspectives, there will be different outcomes, lack of coordination, conflicting philosophical and organizational approaches, and ultimately, mediocre results. In short, the organization has engaged in potentially meaningful events but they have no lasting impact on the organization, the students, or colleagues. In this scenario, people have not grown to the extent they could; values, beliefs, and relationships have not been influenced for the better; and good practices have not permeated the system.

The district may believe that it is offering a quality professional development program, when in reality it is not providing the leadership that would produce higher student achievement. Frequently the cause of this is that the district did not have an articulated set of practices about what professional development should be or what it should accomplish.

Bear in mind, each district must make its own decisions about the genes to which it will commit. You may decide that six professional development genes are too many while another district may use more.

RESEARCH AS A NECESSARY INGREDIENT
IN EACH CHROMOSOME

While each district must decide on its own set of DNA-gene strands, we contend that sound research must be a fundamental part of every core area that is developed. We are convinced beyond any doubt that school districts must begin to ground their beliefs and practices in research. They must develop ways to better understand what research contributes to the practices that teachers and administrators engage in on a daily basis. In essence, if leaders understand the research and apply it with integrity, their practices will likely yield better results.

While research does not necessarily need to be a separate gene, it should permeate the chromosome and ultimately be the justification for districts to make their decisions. Research data and findings provide the evidence to support the actions school districts take. They are better positioned to develop coherent, rigorous programs that will support world-class initiatives and help them frame their future. In a time when school districts face multiple publics and agendas, they must rely on sound evidence for their leadership actions.

As districts work on their six chromosomes, they will be given the opportunity to incorporate research into their genes. To illustrate how this might be done, in Figure 3.3 we have taken Gene 3 from the list of six professional development genes and written a value statement and research-based practices for it. We then give some examples of research concepts and authors that can shape the district's views of professional development.

Professional Development Gene 3

Design and implement a professional development framework

Value Statement

The district will design and implement a professional development plan that represents the most current literature on effective professional development and includes fundamental components necessary to meet staff and district needs resulting in improved teaching and student achievement.

DNA 3

The professional development plan will include the following components:

- A research base to guide the development of each aspect of the framework

- A philosophy statement, program goals, and purposes
- Specific education and professional development goals
- A needs assessment
- An implementation component addressing content, professional learning strategies and outcomes
- A professional development evaluation instrument

This DNA-gene strand for a professional development plan includes six specific components that the district will commit to develop. As the reader will note, one of the components is the study and use of professional development research. A district would then need to build this research base for the professional development plan. Several concepts and research sources (and their related authors/organizations) could be explored to help shape the district's views of an effective professional development plan. Examples are provided below in Table 3.1.

TABLE 3.1 RESEARCH CONCEPTS FOR PROFESSIONAL DEVELOPMENT	
Research Concepts That Underpin the Professional Development Plan	**Primary Authors/Organizations**
Forces that are Shaping Professional Development	Sparks/Hirsh
Systems Thinking	Senge
The Change Process and Professional Development	Fullan/Hargreaves/Quinn
Research on Teaching Practices	Porter
Major Shifts in Professional Development	Sparks/Hirsh
Adult Learning Theory	Joyce/Showers
Specific Learning Strategies and Their Purposes	Loucks-Horsley
Theoretical Models for Professional Development	Sparks/Loucks-Horsley Corcoran/National Staff Development Council North Central Regional Educational Laboratory

Each of these research concepts and sources provides rich information to help districts clarify their beliefs about professional development. With this clarification, districts are better able to develop a focus and articulate practices that will be implemented. By taking this fundamental step, a clear path for the creation of a professional development plan will be provided.

In this section we have described the most fundamental and important component of the genetic model, the DNA-gene strand. The genetic code for district action is formulated at this level of development. It is at this level that districts must identify those principles they believe in and value. Districts make decisions here that determine what practices they will implement and what outcomes they expect of themselves. They decide what type of organization they want to be, how they want to educate children, and if they truly want to achieve world-class performance.

At this juncture it is important to introduce one additional concept with respect to the development of the DNA-gene strand and the function of the organism. The district does not function in a vacuum. It is affected by its environment. As the district determines its core values and practices, it must be cognizant of the environmental factors to which it must respond and adapt. The district may determine that some practices cannot be implemented because of the local district environment. For example, there may be little community support for pullout reading programs. Therefore, in-class grouping and differentiated instruction may be a more acceptable approach. This phenomenon reflects the biological Theory of Integrated View of Variability. Simply stated, the theory purports that an organism's physical traits reflect its overall genetic code and unique environmental history. Experiences and historical events play a powerful role in defining the perceptions and practices within a school district. As you determine what your principles and practices will be, the environment will be an important part of the discussions. What is important is to articulate what you believe and then determine how it can be implemented in your local environment.

It is at this point that we move to the second component of the genetic model: The Chromosome. Here we identify specific chromosomes for study and development. Unlike other factors such as revenue sources, socio-economic status, ethnicity, mobility, and individual family factors, these chromosomes are within the control of the school district and can be created and implemented solely by the district.

What, then, are the actual chromosomes that work interactively with each other to bring about an organization that produces high-quality outcomes? We develop this concept in this next section.

Chromosome Component

Biological Concept. The chromosome is a threadlike structure that carries the various genes and makes it possible for them to interact with each other. Chromosomes also interact with other chromosomes to create the traits we see in an organism. Walter S. Sutton, Theodor Boveri, and others were primarily responsible for the beginning development of the Chromosome Theory of Inheritance that describes this relationship. Early in the twentieth century, Thomas Hunt Morgan, an embryologist at Columbia University was the first scientist to discover that specific genes can be traced to specific chromosomes. He determined that genes have very specific locations on a chromosome, and they are passed along together as a unit on the chromosome.

Morgan's work also verified that all organisms have a certain number of chromosomes. On these chromosomes are a number of genes that carry the genetic code for various characteristics and traits. These genes as well as the chromosomes themselves interact with each other to create the traits we see in the organism. This same concept occurs in organizations.

As such, this vital interaction illustrates that the total organism is not merely the sum of individually isolated genes and chromosomes that have no connection. Rather it is the product of an intricate and complex blending of genetic codes within and across chromosomes. The organism is the manifestation of the DNA-gene and chromosome components working skillfully together to create its own uniqueness. These chromosome theories are significant to educators because they apply to the very essence of what occurs in organizations.

Organizational Concept. In the genetic model, chromosomes are linked to each other by their interaction. One chromosome's function affects the specific operation of other chromosomes. The Chromosome Theory of Inheritance illustrates that all chromosomes have specific DNA-gene strands located on them and they interact with each other. In the organization, therefore, the specific fundamental principles and practices (gene and DNA) will be determined for their specific chromosomes. These chromosomes will interact together to affect the function of the organization. This theory advances our thinking one step further in that it promotes the concept that the interacting of chromosomes produce the behavior exhibited by individuals in the organization. Figure 3.4 illustrates the location of genes on the organizational chromosomes. Just as there are chromosomes for characteristics including color, shape, size, and sex of organisms, there are chromosomes for the various characteristics and traits of the school district that contribute to improved student learning.

FIGURE 3.4—THE GENETIC CONNECTION TO ORGANIZATIONS:
CHROMOSOME COMPONENT

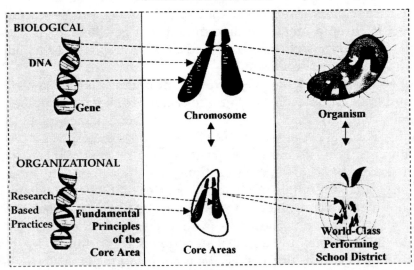

What then are the chromosomes or core areas that lead districts to world-class performance? We identify six chromosomes that are organized into two distinct categories: Capacity-Building Chromosomes and Teaching-Learning Process Chromosomes. The three Capacity-Building Chromosomes are Leadership, Change, and Professional Development. The Teaching-Learning Process Chromosomes are Curriculum, Instructional Practice, and Assessment.

As we have stated, these six chromosomes are within the control of the school district. They can be developed, integrated, and implemented primarily through the decisions made in the district. They are, for the most part, not determined outside the district and then forced upon the organization.

The development and interaction of the chromosomes must be thorough and rigorous. The district must recognize that each chromosome interacts with the others to produce specific outcomes. For example, what is expected in the curriculum will have an impact on the instructional practices teachers use and on what and how the curriculum is assessed. Their integration will define how the district's teaching-learning process operates. As we develop the six chromosomes in the next two chapters, we will stress their interactive nature and impact on achieving world-class performance.

Organism Component

Biological Concept. Having defined the DNA-gene and Chromosome components of an organism, we now look at the entire organism. Biologically, the organism is the product of its genetic blueprint and interrelated function of its chromosomes. We have also established that organisms function within the environment and must adapt to it.

All organisms reflect their genetic makeup. As human beings, we have a genetic map, which determines our physical, mental, social, and emotional characteristics and traits. These characteristics work together and are manifested in humans in their entirety, meaning all aspects of their physical appearance, internal anatomy, physiology, and behavior.

The overall genetic map for the organism includes its entire genetic makeup, not just its individual genes on a specific location of a chromosome. This genetic map represents all of the genes in the organism that are on the chromosomes and are working in an interactive relationship to determine the organism's appearance and behavior. An organism will reflect, therefore, its overall genetic map and unique environmental history.

Organizational Concept. Similarly, a school district's function and outcomes are the result of the fundamental principles and research-based practices (genes and DNA) in specific core areas (chromosomes), working closely in a systemic or integrated structure (the organism). When sound decisions are made about the most fundamental principles and beliefs and when they are working together optimally, the organization will operate effectively and produce high quality outcomes. Figure 3.5 illustrates the complete functioning organism and the school district that can achieve world-class performance.

FIGURE 3.5—THE GENETIC CONNECTION TO ORGANIZATIONS: ORGANISM COMPONENT

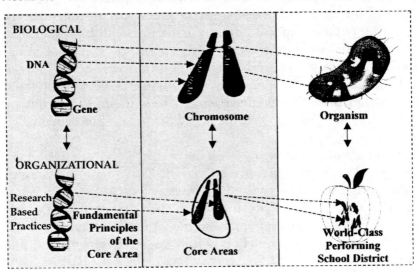

An organization manifests its overall integrated belief system and its unique environmental history. Organizations reflect the environment in which they operate. Community and other nonschool factors play a role in how students learn and how the school district functions. This is why socio-economic status, cultural factors, and mores of the community must not be ignored in the decision-making and value-building processes. By the same token, they should not be viewed as deterrents to striving for world-class performance.

While all factors of a district's functioning are not within the control of the school system, leaders must change those factors that can improve quality. They must proactively enhance those factors that are within their control. By doing so they can offer students the best opportunities to achieve.

Determining one's principles and practices sounds so simple and logical, yet why does it not happen more regularly in schools? We contend that a simplistic improvement approach is at the heart of this failure. There seems to be a lack of understanding how to skillfully develop and integrate the various chromosomes in the existing system.

The genetic model clarifies and guides this process. It focuses the leader's attention on the most important areas affecting student learning that are within the district's control. At the same time, the genetic model enhances understanding and awareness of the systemic nature of districts and the impact initiatives have on the whole organization. The extent to which districts make sound decisions about their fundamental principles is the degree to which the organization will bring about high quality learning outcomes.

Summary

- Schools and school districts are not a random collection of events and activities but a multifaceted cooperative.
- There are three components to the genetic model: the DNA-Gene, the Chromosome, and the Organism. In organizational terms these three components are defined as follows:
  o The DNA-gene component defines fundamental principles, values and research-based practices about how a district chooses to operate. The continuity and world-class of organizational behaviors are determined at this level.
  o The chromosome component determines the core areas that the district must develop to provide a quality education program. These core areas interact and are influenced by each other.
  o The organism component is the total manifestation of the DNA-gene and chromosome components. It is the school district's operation leading to world-class performance.
- The environment will have an impact on how the organization defines its beliefs, practices, and programs.
- The genetic model provides a systemic, integrated approach to the development of six chromosomes and this is required to bring about high-quality outcomes and world-class performance.

Part II

Implementing the Genetic Model

The Capacity-Building Chromosomes

The Teaching-Learning Process Chromosomes

Chapter 4

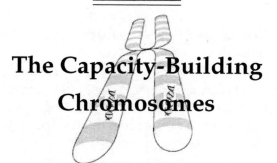

The Capacity-Building Chromosomes

Overview of Key Concepts

- *Each district must determine its own set of organizational "genes" and "DNA." These genetic components define how the district will operate and what outcomes it will produce.*

- *High student achievement is the result of an interactive system of the six core areas identified as chromosomes. These chromosomes are divided into two categories: Capacity-Building Chromosomes and Teaching-Learning Process Chromosomes.*

- *The Capacity-Building Chromosomes (Leadership, Change, and Professional Development) create and sustain an environment to be a learning organization.*

- *The Teaching-Learning Process Chromosomes articulate the educational program and define the system by which optimal learning will occur.*

Leadership Chromosome
- Effective leadership is essential to implement the genetic model and achieve world-class performance.
- Leadership is not specific to traditional roles in a school district such as superintendent or principal. Teachers can be very effective leaders and should be encouraged to accept responsibility for developing the chromosomes.
- Business executives and writers provide substantive ex-

amples for achieving successful practices that are applicable
to education settings.
- Communicating vision/philosophy, establishing an organizational culture for world-class operation, creating a process for participatory decision-making, and organizing a
guiding coalition are practices that effective leaders use to
provide world-class leadership.

Change Chromosome
- Change is a reality of life for organizations in the 21st century, and educators must become learners engaging in inquiry about new areas of learning.
- The change process must be nurtured and various challenges
of change must be addressed.
- Change must be implemented within the context of the
district's preferred future.
- Leaders must build the capacity of staff throughout the organization to implement change.
- Sustaining momentum for change initiatives requires proactive steps.

Professional Development Chromosome
- High-quality professional development programs include
activities that are specifically intended to improve teaching
and student achievement.
- To be effective, professional development must be sustained
over time, aligned with district, school, or teacher/admin-
istrator goals, benchmarked, and assessed.
- Planning professional development programs should be a
collaborative process and include relevant activities for the
participants.
- There are a variety of professional learning strategies that
can be used to meet the identified needs of teachers and the
district and can lead to high student achievement.

Introduction

In this book we propose that there is a fundamental interrelationship among six core areas contributing to high student achievement. We identify these core areas as *chromosomes*, consistent with our genetic metaphor. While these chromosomes should be developed individually, the reader must always remember that one core area plays an interactive role in the function of the others. No one core area alone is independently responsible for increasing student achievement; rather, their systemic interaction creates the capacity, the context, and the substance leading to higher student achievement.

These chromosomes are divided into two categories: Capacity-Building Chromosomes and the Teaching-Learning Process Chromosomes. The Capacity-Building Chromosomes are comprised of Leadership, Change, and Professional Development. The Teaching-Learning Process Chromosomes consist of Curriculum, Instructional Practice, and Assessment.

Chapters 4 and 5 are divided into two distinct sections. Section I of each chapter will develop and discuss three chromosomes by identifying the DNA-gene strands that comprise them. We will describe why the genes are so important to the development of the area and provide examples throughout. Chapter 4 will address the Capacity-Building Chromosomes and their related DNA-gene strands. Chapter 5 will present the Teaching-Learning Process Chromosomes and related DNA-gene strands.

Section II of each chapter will provide you with the opportunity to build your district's chromosomes based on those practices currently existing in your district or your district's preferred future. From that profile, we will ask the reader to project where there may be some gaps between what could be developed and what currently exists. Guiding questions are provided to stimulate the readers' thinking about various aspects of their chromosomes. Worksheets are supplied to begin building these chromosomes. For each worksheet you will articulate your district's fundamental principles and practices related to each DNA-gene strand on each chromosome. Finally, you will be encouraged to develop other genes as they pertain to the district's operation.

The Capacity-Building Chromosomes serve to create and sustain the environment for a district to be a learning organization. They define the district's overarching vision and its focus and process of continuous improvement in the organization. They articulate how and by whom decisions in the organization will be made. They also define how the organization adapts and responds to its environment. Finally, they address the structure for growth and learning opportunities for all of the people in the organization.

The Teaching–Learning Process Chromosomes articulate the substance of teaching and learning. They define the content and skills to be learned and how they are delivered and assessed. In the teaching-learning process, there must be clear alignment among curriculum, instructional practices, and assessment. This alignment represents the very nature of the teaching-learning process as it is designed to produce higher student achievement. In essence, the district must be clear about what it expects students to learn. Teachers must then teach the curriculum to students using age-appropriate and varied instructional methods recognizing all modalities of learning. Finally, teachers must assess what learning has taken place. Assessment serves to measure ongoing student progress, inform instructional practice, evaluate programs, guide student placement decisions, and provide summative information regarding student achievement. This important interactive process will be discussed in depth in chapter 5.

Without the Capacity-Building Chromosomes (creation and sustaining of the environment), the school district lacks the direction and the ability to meet the challenges of offering a rigorous academic program. In the absence of the Teaching-Learning Chromosomes (the rigorous academic program), a school district cannot provide or demonstrate that students are achieving at world-class levels; nor can the district determine where and how to improve the programs it offers to students. Therefore, all six chromosomes become integral parts in the quest for higher student achievement.

As the reader begins to explore each of these six chromosomes, we encourage you to reflect on your own district and ask yourself: In these areas what are the most important principles a school district needs to include that would lead to higher student achievement?

The reader will notice that some concepts are revisited across the chromosomes. This overlap was by design because it illustrates the significant interrelationship of concepts among the core areas and the need to consciously plan with that in mind. It also views the concepts from slightly different perspectives giving the reader a more comprehensive understanding of their dynamics in school operation.

It is our expectation that when the readers finish this book, they will have defined all six chromosomes for their district and will be in a position to identify those areas that need further development. We offer one final suggestion to consider as you develop your chromosomes. While you may start with the specific genes presented in this book, it may be apparent that you want to alter, eliminate, or include other gene areas. You may want to reconfigure some of the principles or adjust them in a way that is more suited to your culture and environment. We encourage you to do this! There is no single best grouping or identification of fundamental principles (genes) that is a "one size fits all" paradigm. You may even want to create your own unique chromosomes (core areas) with accompanying genes. Our one caution is that you base them on sound research and thorough study. Keep your benchmarks and indicators of world-class practices at the forefront.

Remember, the purpose for developing your genetic framework is to focus on those values, beliefs, and practices that will bring about higher student achievement. The outcome is to improve performance. The ultimate goal is to develop students who will be productive members of a WORLDWIDE COMMUNITY OF EXCELLENCE. The genetic model is not designed to create a horserace to be number one in the world; rather, its purpose is to help educators develop a community of high performers who can function with the best students in the world.

Section I

Leadership Chromosome

Introduction

It is important to remember that just as DNA-gene strands and chromosomes work together to form a human being, leadership, professional development, change, curriculum, instructional practice, and assessment enable a school system to achieve world–class performance. They work simultaneously and in conjunction with each other. It is counter-productive to emphasize professional development this year, curriculum the next, and another chromosome the following year. All six chromosomes must be effectively implemented simultaneously to achieve successful outcomes. Without effective leadership, however, it is unlikely that any of the chromosomes can be implemented successfully. Effective leaders know how to bring results to challenging situations. Achieving world-class performance in American public schools is not an easy undertaking. While some American schools may already be world-class, our goal is for America's education leaders to make all of them world-class.

We view leading school district activities in a different context than the traditional hierarchical model of school leadership. In most school districts, superintendents and principals are perceived as the leaders by virtue of their positions. Other staff members are normally not placed in leadership roles. Our concept of leadership for world-class schools means skillfully delegating responsibility and creating teams to accomplish important tasks. In the genetic model, the leader is the individual designated to be responsible for this activity. Thus, teachers and administrators play a partnering role in leading activities organized to improve the quality of teaching and learning. For example, a superintendent could organize a genetic model leadership team. The team would be comprised of a leader for each of the six chromosomes. It would meet regularly to coordinate the comprehensive plan that integrates the chromosomes to achieve world-class performance. This plan is systemic and large-scale. The premise behind this concept of leadership is that the individual entrusted with the leadership responsibilities needs to possess the necessary qualities that will achieve the intended goals.

There is an abundance of literature and research on leadership, much of it offering conflicting findings. Researchers find that although certain behaviors work in one setting they do not always work in a different setting. Our goal is to provide an overview of leadership for your planning process. We are deliberately not providing complex, leadership theories because they would not be relevant to the people we are encouraging to accept responsibility for guiding projects that yield world-class results. The leadership chromosome can be developed using theorists, researchers, and practices that align with the core beliefs and culture of your organization. It is most important to recognize that leadership is crucial to accomplish challenging goals; and, it takes a person or group of people who are willing to take risks, make the time commitment, and accept the consequences as they lead a sustained effort.

Effective leadership, regardless of whether it comes from a teacher, principal, or superintendent, is necessary to sustain the momentum to bring about substantive improvement in an organization. It is not situational or short-term, as often portrayed by someone performing a heroic act. Rather, it is sustained and focused, requiring an intense commitment to achieving a specific goal.

There also can be more than one leader working in a school district on different projects. It should be assumed that the superintendent and principal have leadership responsibilities as a result of their positions, but there are a number of other leadership roles to fulfill. For this reason we want to begin by providing a brief case study describing what we think is necessary to be an effective leader of organizations that must be able to adapt quickly to changing circumstances. We will then develop the four genes for the leadership chromosome. They are: communicate a vision/philosophy within a context of continuous improvement, establish an organizational culture for world-class operation, empower teachers through participatory decision-making, and organize a guiding coalition.

We begin with a case study recounting recent years at Motorola, arguably one of America's finest companies. We describe the trials and tribulations of Motorola's CEO, Chris Galvin.

Chris Galvin's tenure at Motorola provides a good context for understanding the difficult decisions leaders must make. His leadership transcends the phenomenal success of his company in the early 1990s to what has been a nearly 180 degree turn in a brief period of time. We use a business executive for our example because school leaders are often classified in a multitude of categories by district, that is, small, large, urban, suburban, rural, affluent, poor, K–12, elementary, and so on. The issues Galvin confronted are applicable to any one of these types of school districts. Because we are focusing on the role of leadership and not just superintendents and principals, we believe Galvin's story has significant implications for teachers who choose to accept leadership responsibilities. When overseeing the work of colleagues, teachers must understand that there can be consequences for their decisions. There will be times when leaders must make difficult decisions that affect how people work. We know that leaders must be prepared to alienate some people when they seek to achieve lofty goals. For those people, that quid pro quo is unacceptable and precludes them from accepting leadership roles. Leaders can be liked but their personal and professional relationships may be affected when they make difficult decisions. Colin Powell, United States Secretary of State, in a presentation on leadership says, "Good leadership involves responsibility to the welfare of the group, which means that some people will get angry at your actions and decisions. Trying to get everyone to like you is a sign of mediocrity, you'll avoid the tough decisions, you'll avoid confronting the people who need to be confronted and you'll avoid offering differential rewards based on differential performance because some people might get upset."[22] Such was the case for Chris Galvin.

Motorola was a Baldridge award-winning company. The Baldridge award is one of the most prestigious awards a company can receive. Its stock was doing very well and the company's products had good market share. In 1997, Galvin became CEO taking over the position from his father, Robert Galvin. By 1999, Motorola was experiencing serious problems and advisors were telling Galvin that he needed to terminate some close friends. The company's stock price was declining and it was losing its cellular telephone market to Nokia and Ericsson. Of significance to educators should be the fact that both companies are international and they became dominant sellers in the United States over Motorola despite their smaller size. Further, Nokia and Ericsson became dominant because they produced digital technology while Motorola failed to recognize the newer digital trend and was trying to sell analog technology. That one "small" mistake changed the fortunes of one of America's premier companies.

In light of Motorola's situation, it is important to recognize emerging trends that may be affecting education. Some of those trends are charter schools, vouchers, standards-based curriculums, international assessment, distance learning, performance-based pay for teachers, and alternative certification paths for teachers and administrators. For many years American public education has survived using traditional practices with little significant change or arguably successful outcomes. The academic achievement of America's minority children is very low. Some of the traditional practices that have not changed much are length of school year for students and work year for teachers, structure of school day, fixed salary schedules, textbook dominated curriculums, teachers pre-service programs, and ongoing professional development activities within school districts. While we are not actually going through scenario planning (a process that should be considered important for school officials who believe the Motorola experience is relevant for their setting), we are suggesting that the newer trends in education are beginning to take hold. We believe there should be serious concern for those who think the traditional education practices of the past will continue to work.

Analysts told Galvin his leadership style contributed to the company's problems because he was indecisive and took a hand's-off approach to management in an industry that demands speed and conviction. Galvin responded to his critics by reflecting on his approach to management and made some personal changes. First, he began meeting with his management team regularly, four times as often as in the past, and has become more involved in key decisions that affect the company.

Galvin is striving to find a satisfactory balance between delegating authority to his staff and being involved with their work. The closer working relationship builds trust between Galvin and his staff who can now work with the assurance they are doing what he wants them to do. The result: a more confident staff empowered to take responsibility for reaching their identified goals. The same principle would work for school leaders who want to engage their staffs in leadership roles without becoming too involved in their work. We call this practice "guided professionalism" and discuss it in more detail in the professional development and instructional practice chromosomes.

Galvin's thoughts on leadership are important for those who want the responsibility. "You have to live with the downside. You can be subject to all sorts of criticism. But, I understand that all problems are solvable, and there's no sense wasting energy worrying or fretting about it."[23]

The story of Motorola and its CEO is applicable to schools. A school district can operate successfully while declining conditions are evolving gradually, and they may not be obvious. These conditions may be setting trends that could lead to a significant decline in performance. Effective leaders must understand their role in the organization and carefully monitor both qualitative and quantitative information to ensure that there is always continuous improvement in important categories.

For many years, school success has been largely determined by student achievement measured by state and national assessment data. These assessments usually compare the achievement of students from one district to those in other districts of the state. Newer assessments are emerging that make comparisons more relevant. These assessments provide data showing how student achievement compares to their peers in other countries. This information is important. The international community is working more closely than ever which requires people to acquire competitive skills to be productive. American student achievement needs to be measured on an international scale.

These trends have implications for school leaders. They necessitate leadership at all levels of the organization, not just "top down". Motorola could be any school district. Society is experiencing rapidly changing technology. These changing conditions are an important warning to school leaders regarding complacency. Motorola's rapid decline from a Baldridge award-winning company to one that needed to revise its business strategy is serious; it demonstrates how quickly trends can affect successful companies, and its competition came from smaller companies in other countries.

There are four genes on the leadership chromosome. As we develop this chromosome, we ask the question: What are the most important principles that need to be implemented to realize effective leadership? The genes identify the fundamental principles we feel are general and applicable to teachers, as well as superintendents and principals, who are leading an activity. We believe effective leaders must exhibit these four gene areas:

1. Communicate Vision/Philosophy in a Context of Continuous Improvement.
2. Establish an Organizational Culture for World-class Operation.
3. Empower Teachers Through Participatory Decision-making.
4. Organize a Guiding Coalition.

We have identified theorists, researchers, and processes for the genes based on those people and practices we believe can inform effective leadership planning. We encourage you to use this information and other leadership literature for building your leadership chromosome.

Leadership Chromosome: Four Genes

Communicate a Vision/Philosophy in a Context of Continuous Improvement

Achieving world-class performance can only be accomplished when leaders articulate a clear and focused vision that is philosophically embedded in the beliefs and expectations of the organization. That vision must energize the staff and gain their acceptance as the essence of what the district seeks to be. True visionaries attempt to "push the envelope" in their organizations and offer challenging, high-quality goals for the staff. In sports, for example, the ultimate reward is winning a championship. Coaches and managers push their teams to achieve the championship goal. Educators need to strive for their students to achieve world-class performance measured in quantifiable ways. The function of the leader is to articulate that vision by providing opportunities for the staff to continuously improve teaching and student achievement.

The leader needs to set a context for that vision. It begins with the issue of what the organization must achieve to be successful. For schools, the leader develops a comprehensive improvement plan that is written with the involvement of the staff and incorporates specific, measurable goals. The other five chromosomes of the genetic model transform leadership into action, namely: nurturing a process of change, improving the quality of the workforce by providing professional development opportunities, using effective instructional practices, research-based curriculum materials, and measuring growth through assessment of student achievement.

Warren Bennis, highly regarded author and business administration professor, writes, "Effective leaders put words to the formless longings and deeply felt needs of others. They create communities out of words."[24] Bennis' comment supports the notion that effective leaders communicate their vision in a manner that is meaningful to the staff. It means focusing attention specifically on the goals of the organization and providing direction to achieve them. We believe education leaders should articulate a vision of world-class student performance and continuous improvement. They must believe it is the philosophical essence of the organization as they seek to lead others to embrace their high-stakes vision.

Establish an Organizational Culture for World-Class Operation

Leaders establish an organizational culture for world-class performance. It necessitates leading the staff to embrace it and make it part of their fundamental values, beliefs, and practices. Culture is the working environment of the organization. It emphasizes what is important and how the organization operates. Organizational culture is created through practices that become routine. Yet, cultures need to be nurtured over time with constant attention to the vision. We offer five DNA that are essential for creating an organizational culture that seeks to achieve world-class performance. These DNA must exist regardless of who is in the leadership capacity. The DNA are focus, innovation, sense of purpose, passion, and trust.

First, the leader must be *focused*. The goals must be very specific and the activities of the organization must work to achieve them. If, for example, the district goal is for students to achieve comparably with the highest achieving students in other nations in mathematics on the Third International Mathematics and Science Study (TIMSS) then activities must be planned to achieve that goal. It would send a confusing message if the district goal were higher student achievement in mathematics and the professional development programs were on reading instruction. Focus demonstrates to the staff that the goal is important and the leader is serious about accomplishing it.

It is important to implement an action plan that is *innovative*. Innovation does not have to be a new fad, which is often the perception. Instead, it needs to be an approach that captures the hearts and minds of those who will be part of the initiative. The staff must fully understand the action plan and be committed to its successful implementation.

Innovation involves changing the way things have been done. This change may result in the staff becoming upset. Innovation does not mean that a leader must make the staff happy, but they should sense their work is meaningful. The leader who has substantive innovative ideas makes work more challenging and causes people to grow professionally. Employees will have a greater sense of accomplishment when they believe the district goals lead to their personal growth as professionals. Looking for new ways to achieve improved performance will help prevent an organization from becoming complacent.

Creating a sense of purpose is the third DNA essential for establishing an organizational culture for world-class operation. Why is it important to achieve world-class performance in mathematics or literacy? What steps will be taken to get the organization on the path to world-class performance? How will the staff be rewarded for successfully achieving the goal? It should be understood the process evolves over time. The purpose is to continuously improve. For some schools the challenge is much greater but a sustained effort will support the purpose. It is important to create a shared sense of purpose so that everyone is working toward accomplishing the same goal. While we do not want to appear negative, it is not only important to offer rewards for success, but sanctions for failure. To achieve world-class performance in mathematics or literacy, the leader must establish a culture that understands failure is unacceptable. The sports metaphor is winning the championship. The great coaches and managers succeed because their teams understand the purpose for playing and strive to win. Players do not always love those coaches and managers; however, they are usually admired and respected because they win. Educational leadership does not need to be so harsh, but it must instill purpose in a serious manner, stand firm on its expectations, and take the time to achieve them.

Exhibiting *passion* for the goal is the fourth DNA that a leader must demonstrate. When a leader exhibits passion, it generates enthusiasm throughout the workforce and instills a positive climate in the organization. We learned how important passion for a world-class project can be when we served as leaders of the First in the World Consortium. The Consortium, a group of eighteen school districts was the first group of U.S. schools to ever participate in the TIMSS. The superintendents who initially led the Consortium worked diligently to make the project successful. When the project began, their passion encouraged their staffs to become actively involved in the activities. Eventually teachers assumed leadership roles for a variety of Consortium projects. Teachers took what they learned from their Consortium work back to their local districts and implemented that learning in their own related projects. The Consortium model is a positive example for all districts in our country.

The Consortium was a unique endeavor that would have failed without the initial passion and commitment of its leaders. The participants and their communities were rewarded with a visit and education speeches by President William Clinton, Secretary of Education Richard Riley, and Congressman John Porter, chairman of the U. S. House of Representatives subcommittee on Labor, Health and Human Services and Education. The leadership in the Consortium was unrelenting in its pursuit to accomplish the world-class goals. The school staffs and communities supported them by becoming actively involved in the project. Our experience with the Consortium only reinforces our belief that leaders must be passionate about their work.

The last DNA for changing organizational culture is earning the *trust* of the staff. The culture of an organization depends on a satisfactory level of trust between the leader and members of the group. It is important for leaders to clearly articulate their expectations for the group and elaborate in detail the process for achieving them. There can be no hidden agendas; they are detrimental to trust in an organization. Sustained cooperation from the staff requires open communication. Members of an organization may not agree with the leader, but if the goals and process for implementation are discussed with them, people will recognize that their leader is honest and trust will be established. Even when the message is difficult to deliver (for example, dealing with budget reductions), clearly communicating specific intended solutions will create an environment of trust between the leader and staff.

Edward M. Marshall discusses in one of the best resources on building trust in an organization, relationship-based corporations. He says, "Our challenge is to leave behind the politics of fear and to evolve toward what will be called a relationship-based corporation."[25] To build trust he suggests two tasks. The first is to commit to evolving from a culture of fear to a culture of trust. Leaders will have to move from theories of the past regarding relationships between managers and employees to more contemporary concepts of collaborative work. One example of a collaborative project could be a lesson study group. The group could work together on a chromosome to identify the genes for its school or district.

The second task, and one we consider very important for the leadership chromosome, is for leaders to adopt a philosophy recognizing that people make change happen, and the workforce must own that change to implement it successfully. Achieving world-class performance in schools will require all members of the staff, as well as students and communities, to support the goal. Absent trust, the process toward achieving the goal will inevitably fail.

Empower Teachers Through Participatory Decision-Making

The next gene on the leadership chromosome is to empower teachers through participatory decision-making. Warren Bennis summarizes the importance of involving the staff in decision-making when he says, "No matter how wise, shrewd, or visionary a leader is, a corporation is a collective endeavor and it needs the collective wisdom, canniness, and vision of all of its employees to function at the optimal level. Failing to appreciate the importance to the organization of the people who are already in it is a classical mistake, one that new managers and change-oriented administrators are especially prone to make."[26]

Empowering teachers through participatory decision-making is a significant cultural shift from a bureaucratic organization. If managers were solely responsible in the past for making decisions, then an approach to involve the staff requires new processes that are built on trust and evidence that their input is valued. In today's complex school environment, group decisions made by the staff most affected by those decisions will lead to better results. Each participant has a role in decision-making. Simply because it is participatory does not mean everyone must have the same viewpoint. The advantage of working in a group is that the organization gains from the collective wisdom of its staff.

There are several concepts to bear in mind when creating a new structure for participatory decision-making in an organization. The leader must recognize that empowerment means sharing ideas and responsibility. First, everyone must be given the opportunity to participate and the group must respect their viewpoints. If the group treats a participant rudely, the process will discourage others from becoming involved. The process will then come to an abrupt halt.

When making decisions, it should be an expectation to obtain a variety of viewpoints or perspectives from the staff. The more information the group collects and processes before a decision is made, the more likely it is that a good decision will result. Again, all members of the group need to believe their viewpoints are valued even if their ideas are not incorporated in the final decision. The fact that they participated enabled the group to explore what decision would be in the best interest of the organization. In the end the leader must thoroughly explain the rationale for the decision to capture group support.

It might be helpful to pose the problem and then divide the participants into small groups with a charge to bring several possible alternatives back to the large group. Using small group dynamics reduces the chance that individuals might feel their ideas were rejected based on personality issues.

Each group in participatory decision-making should have a facilitator to ensure that an effective process is used. The facilitator can stimulate discussion, ask clarifying questions, and make sure everyone participates in the deliberations. When the group finishes, the facilitator should summarize what was said.

The process of participatory decision-making leads to a more positive organizational culture. It provides employees a better understanding of the rationale for decisions and affords each one an opportunity to express differing viewpoints before the decision is made.

Involving employees in decision-making also enables them to better understand the responsibilities of a leader. One possible outcome is that new leaders will emerge and will accept responsibility for leadership of future organizational activities. The leaders that emerge from the group could have the respect of their peers and, therefore, help the organization achieve its goals.

Finally, participatory decision-making demonstrates employees are valued. When decisions are collectively developed, they will be more accepted and sustained.

An effective leader understands that the organization, like a human organism, is complex. Decisions that are made involving those individuals most affected will be better received and more effective. If world-class performance is the vision, the input from all of the participants is crucial. Using the genetic model will lead to implementing practices that enhance the quality of the organization, making successful achievement of goals more likely.

Organize a Guiding Coalition

The Motorola transformation demonstrates the importance of effective leadership to the organization. School leadership is no different. Leaders must articulate a clear vision for what they believe the organization should accomplish. Then, there needs to be a culture for continuous improvement. Leadership that achieves a goal should continue to direct the organization to improve even after the goal is met. Using processes that involve people in decision-making enhance the chances for successful outcomes.

Finally, the leader needs a guiding coalition. John Kotter inspired our decision to incorporate this gene on the leadership chromosome. The concept of the guiding coalition supports the adage that without followers there is no leader. A leader with a vision who works to organize a culture of continuous improvement and uses participatory decision-making will not complete the task without a committed group of followers. Thus, Kotter's concept of a guiding coalition is the final gene on our leadership chromosome. Kotter cites two tasks for creating a guiding coalition. They are putting together a group with enough power to lead the change and getting the group to work together like a team.[27]

The school team working on achieving world-class performance must include people who have the authority to make decisions. It stifles group work when the participants on an important project arrive at consensus only to find that a supervisor rejected the plan. A person with authority who can bridge communication between the working group and top management is an essential component for a guiding coalition. When Motorola's Chris Galvin reflected on his leadership style, he decided to be more hands-on to better understand the work and decisions of his executive team. His decision did not remove authority from his executives. Instead, it made the process more of a team approach. Leading schools to world-class performance will necessitate some difficult decisions on change and substantial commitment of both resources and personnel. The guiding coalition must include within it someone with the authority to approve decisions.

Kotter's second task is not a simple challenge, getting the group to work together like a team. Earlier in this section we discussed the responsibility of sports managers and coaches. The successful ones have the uncanny ability to blend the talents of their athletes with strategies that enable them to be winners. The guiding coalition in schools working on world-class performance must accomplish its goals in a similar manner. The coalition must be comprised of people who have the knowledge, talent, respect and authority to implement the genetic model. Working on six chromosomes with genes that reflect a district culture seeking world-class achievement is a significant undertaking. Without effective leadership and staff commitment, the task might be unrealistic. Using the other leadership genes with the guiding coalition will create a work environment in the organization that should be successful.

Conclusion

There has been so much written about leadership over the years. Numerous researchers and authors have studied leadership and arrived at their own conclusions regarding what behaviors are essential for success. Despite all the research, we know there is not a prescribed formula for successful leadership. Not all people want to lead. Leadership can be a very lonely responsibility, especially when the stakes are high. As Colin Powell said, people can become angry because of the leader's actions. On the other hand, successful leaders bring results and contribute to successful organizations. In schools, that leadership comes from a variety of sources. Superintendents lead by virtue of their position but not necessarily on all projects. The same premise holds true for principals. We hope our overview of leadership contributes to more teachers accepting responsibility for leading schools to world-class performance. Today's workplace is in continuous change, and there is not one *de facto* leader. It is for this reason we have designated leadership as one of our six chromosomes. When building organizational capacity, the change process, and professional development will require knowledgeable, committed, and effective leaders. We now turn to the second capacity-building chromosome, change.

Leadership

by Paul D. Houston
Executive Director of the American Association of School Administrators

Lately there has been an amazing discovery in education—leadership is important. Now it might seem silly that something so obvious should be a new discovery, but the fact is that education has been victimized by such oversights before. For a long time there was a search for "teacher-proof" approaches to education. The thinking was that teachers weren't very good and that you needed to get around them to produce better education for children. Since the classroom is the central point of the process and teachers are the focal point in the classroom, folks finally decided that improving rather than discounting teachers might make more sense.

Then came the era of "educator proof" reform. This was based on the idea that schools needed to be reformed and that educators were not up to the task so that those outside of education would conduct the reforms. Governors, legislators and policy "wonks" led the movement for better education. This didn't work either. Once again came the realization that the work was not done in state capitals or in think tanks. The work of education is done in schools, so educators were invited back into the process.

More recently there has been the thought that leaders, particularly system leaders were not important. Leadership should come from the "top down" via state bureaucracies or "bottom up" from local schools. Some states have passed laws that superintendents were not required for systems. Something was missing—the system connector in the middle. Like the previous faulty assumptions, the belief that anything in an organization can improve without strong system leadership has proven to be a bankrupt idea. So once again the spotlight is moving to leadership as a key to school improvement.

What is it about leadership that is required for schools to achieve world-class performance? Well, we must start this vision. Someone has to dream about that as a possibility and to translate that dream into a real vision for the rest of the organization. Leadership starts with a sense of the possible. Great leadership senses a possibility that others cannot even imagine. For an organization to move from mediocrity to excellence a great vision must be present. And then that vision must be translated into a mission. The goal must be set and the course charted.

But dreams must be grounded in reality. Great leaders provide the support system and scaffolding to allow the organization to build itself into the future. Leadership, particularly system leadership is about the creation of capacity. Resources must be gathered and organized. Since there has been much recent interest in drafting military leaders into the school leadership role, I'll put this in military terms. The provisions and weaponry must be gathered and organized so that the troops can move forward.

There must also be a battle plan developed. Specific allocation of resources and personnel must be made to assure that the tactical as well as the strategic goals are met. Part of leadership is creating the right plans to move things to successful completion.

And throughout the process, the leader must be at the head of the convoy moving the process forward. When I visited Cuba a few years ago I was discussing Castro and his hold on the people with some of the residents. Even those who admitted that they didn't like him much expressed great admiration for his courage. When the fight was being conducted, he was in the front vehicle leading his men into battle. He wasn't back at headquarters poring over maps and books on strategy.

Here lies the key to whether school leaders can take advantage of the moment they have been given in the public's awareness. People have come to see that leadership is as important in schools as it is in other areas. We know good armies need good officers. Good companies need good CEOs. Good churches need good ministers. And world-class schools need world-class superintendents.

The key ingredients can be found in the classic children's movie, "The Wizard of Oz." Good leaders need the brain to know what is needed and know how to organize it. They need the heart to understand those who follow and how to work with them so they will follow, and they need the courage of the lion to lead fearlessly toward a possible future that others might see as impossible.

And they need to understand the final lesson from Oz. The wizard didn't give anyone anything that they didn't already have. Leadership is first and foremost about eliciting from the organization what it is already capable of achieving. It just needs to understand it is already smart enough, and already good enough to do it, and leaders need to be smart enough and good enough to make it happen.

Change Chromosome

Introduction

While many leaders believe that they understand the nature and process of change in organizations, school districts continue to experience considerable frustration over the fact that change is not realized. It seems as if leaders can talk about change concepts but when it comes to actually implementing them, they cannot overcome the common obstacles. This disconnect between rhetoric and action suggests that organizational leaders do not fully understand the critical elements necessary to successfully engage in change.

The disconnect between rhetoric and action regarding change is problematic. A common scenario unfolds. Leaders embark on new initiatives with high motivation but encounter problems and resistance along the way and soon become discouraged. The initiative loses momentum and is ultimately abandoned. Yet, leaders claim some success in the program so as not to give the impression that the idea was bad or that the school district was experimenting with programs that did not necessarily help the students, or worse, impeded their learning.

It is for this reason that we advocate leaders gain a comprehensive understanding of the change process and make conscious decisions about the critical steps that they will follow to initiate the process.

As we develop this chromosome, we suggest asking the following question: What are the most important principles that need to be implemented as districts engage in the change process? We recommend five genes for making decisions to effectively implement change:

1. Plan and Act Believing that Change Is a Necessity and Reality of Organizational Life.
2. Understand the World of Change and What to Anticipate.
3. Develop a Preferred Future for Your District.
4. Build the Capacity for Change Initiatives.
5. Sustain Momentum for Change Initiatives.

Change Chromosome: Five Genes

Plan and Act Believing that Change Is a Necessity and Reality of Organizational Life

We often hear educators say, "Is this change simply for change's sake?" That phrase has become virtually meaningless in the 21st century. With the rapid growth and uses of technology, new research on curriculum and instruction, the standards-based and accountability movements, increased diversity, evolving social issues, the advent of the new global marketplace, and the impending teacher shortage, school districts are continuously confronted with the daunting task of adapting to change. These trends demonstrate that there is a sense of urgency for education to address the new priorities of the 21st century. Leaders cannot approach change with fear or skepticism.

The current challenge for teachers and administrators is to maintain a sense of stability within the context of continuous change. Teachers may develop skills to implement one new program and then be challenged with new expectations. They may feel a need to continue refining these skills at the same time that other demands are being placed on them. Simply stated, the "horizon keeps moving" on teachers. Just when they gain proficiency and a comfort level with one change initiative, there are others following that push the horizon further out of reach. Teachers feel that they cannot keep up with all the new demands being placed on them. While they do their best to embrace a new program, it is only one of many they are required to implement. Change can create stress and anxiety when teachers feel ill prepared to implement all of the new programs expected of them. Consequently, these teachers question whether they can help students become more successful.

In addition to the ever-changing expectations for staff members, there remains the proverbial question: Does this new program really enhance student learning compared with the former one? Evaluations of new programs rarely validate the improvements they purport to make. Teachers often become frustrated at the lack of evidence demonstrating that their work on a new program made a positive difference for the students. The absence of this evidence, coupled with increasing expectations for change, causes teachers to question what they should really focus on or how to implement it well.

Administrators and teachers need to understand that they work in an environment where change is continuous and stability is needed. It is important for the organization to bring a sense of stability to people's work life. This stability can come through focus and support—focus, in the sense of maintaining a reasonable number of priorities. By doing so, they know what will be expected of them and how they can go about successfully accomplishing change initiatives. Support—in the form of time to learn and master new areas of learning, teacher empowerment to make decisions, and professional development programs that enhance their learning in a meaningful way—will help to successfully implement new directions and embed them in the teachers' value system and the district's organizational culture.

In his book, *Change Forces: Probing the Depths of Educational Reform*, Michael Fullan, a prominent researcher on change, indicates that educators need generative concepts and capacities. By this he means that educators must be learners, engaging in inquiry about new areas of learning. The prime strategies must be to seek mastery of new areas of learning and be innovative in doing so. He encourages leaders to express what is valued. He stresses teamwork and shared purpose as people work together, the guided coalition mentioned earlier. He believes that in a time of change people must embrace both individualism and collectivism for organizational learning. He stresses that these concepts are necessary to avoid extinction, as environments are always changing.[28]

What then does all this say about how leaders and teachers approach change? First, it reinforces the notion that change, for change's sake, does not need to be the first course of action. It comes in many forms. Second, educators can attend to only a few, if not just one, substantive change initiative at one time and must work diligently to understand all facets of the new program. Third, knowledge acquisition is ongoing. Finally, the change process will have its obstacles, but they can be overcome if educators are persistent and innovative using alternative strategies to work on problems collaboratively.

Understand the World of Change and What to Anticipate

Understanding the world of change is not easy. It requires us to nurture the change process and address its various challenges. We delineate six important challenges that the nature of change creates. These challenges require proactive leadership, and although the list is not exhaustive, we believe it captures the nature of change. These challenges include building the intellectual capital of the leadership team, implementing change at a reasonable pace, conducting litmus tests of progress, recognizing the complex nature of change, embracing resistance and conflict, and building change agents.

Nurture the Change Process

Over the past few years we have spoken to many groups around the country and have been impressed with their desire to approach change in a comprehensive manner. Yet, when we begin working on the new initiative with them, there is surprisingly little interest in spending time talking and planning for the dynamics of change. Rather, there is considerable interest in developing the plans to implement the change district-wide. We draw a clear distinction between planning the initiative and planning for change.

Planning the initiative focuses on the action plan of the project. It addresses the goals, objectives, timelines, implementation strategies, professional development, and available resources. Planning for change is nurturing the change process and addressing the challenges of change. As we have mentioned, leaders speak in detail about the problems that organizations have bringing about lasting change. While they say they can attend to these problems, they find it very challenging to translate their theoretical understanding of problems related to change into practical ways to manage them. Leaders must take into consideration the dynamics of human interactions and feelings, stages of acceptance to the initiative, conflict and resistance, approaches to unknown factors, strategies to deal with unsuccessful implementation, and so forth. Planning for how the district will attend to these dynamics and resolve them will determine the level of success a district will experience. It acknowledges that if leaders do not build in strategies to address the dynamics and problems of change, the effort is destined to fail.

Leaders should expect problems to arise and need to plan how they will support people to overcome them. They must prepare people to be able to adjust when the unknown issues arise. Michael Fullan stresses that the change process is so complex and so fraught with unknowns that everyone must be on guard and apply themselves to investigate and solve problems.[29] Then, when the problems arise, teachers and administrators can feel confident that there are ways they can address the problems.

Jerry Patterson in his book *Coming Clean about Organizational Change* describes twelve harsh realities about people and organizations as they relate to change in the organization. These realities are explained and then illustrated through practical examples. Leadership implications are then discussed.[30] It is these issues that leaders must consider as they nurture the planning process. Patterson's book is helpful in thinking about and planning for change. It is important for leaders to understand the realities and view them within a context of asking two important questions: How will the individuals in the district interpret the change initiative? What organizational and leadership steps should be taken in order to address these twelve realities?

Michael Fullan eloquently describes the journey of change. He writes: *It is a world where change is a journey of unknown destination, where problems are our friends, where seeking assistance is a sign of strength, where simultaneous top-down-bottom-up initiatives merge, and where collegiality and individualism coexist in productive tension. It is a world that mirrors life itself in which you can never be perfectly happy or permanently in harmony, but where some people manage much better than others.*[31] It is to this environment that leaders must plan as they nurture the change process.

Six Challenges of Change

Challenge 1: Build Intellectual Capital of the Leadership Team. There is frequently a tendency to move quickly into the planning process for a new project. Leaders begin involving as many people as possible without devoting the necessary time to build the intellectual capital of the leadership team to guide the process. Intellectual capital, in this instance an in-depth understanding of organizational change, needs to be developed with a smaller team before the district involves others in the process. This intellectual capital includes building the capacity to nurture the change process and addressing the various challenges that will arise. It also includes building knowledge of the actual project to be undertaken: understanding its scope, defining goals and objectives, creating an organizational plan for participation of staff, timelines, professional development plans, and strategies to sustain the change initiative over time.

Once this leadership team has taken the necessary steps to build its intellectual capital, an action plan for the project can be developed and implemented with the larger district community.

Challenge 2: Implement Change at a Reasonable Pace. The leadership team is the support group for the change process. The group must be mindful of the obstacles and work to eliminate them. They create the action plan for the project and ensure that the project is implemented at a reasonable pace. Change cannot be forced or rushed.

Time is always a primary factor in the implementation of any new project. Teachers must have the time to learn new skills, practice them, and refine them. Most of all, teachers need support implementing new strategies. They need opportunities to reflect on their practice and discuss ways to adjust to the unexpected issues that occur. Unknown factors always play a role in new projects, and time must be available to address and resolve them.

Any project worth implementing should be given the time to succeed. Leaders are encouraged to incorporate "adjustment time." Time for teachers to try new strategies, reflect on them, adjust them, and try them again. Change is not only about implementation of an action plan but also about its impact on learning. Providing the support for these evaluation and feedback processes builds staff trust and confidence. This investment of time pays huge dividends.

Challenge 3: Conduct Litmus Tests of Progress. It is important to remember that change is about transforming the organizational culture. There are litmus tests that can signal whether a culture of managing change exists in the organization. We suggest three examples. First, engaging in change is not merely about accomplishing the goals of the leader. While that is certainly an important part of the process, the change effort must be grounded in **new values and beliefs** on the part of the people who are living the change. If these values are not well grounded, the new direction will soon dissipate once the leader is no longer with the organization. The staff will revert to former practices of the organization that were valued in the old culture.[32] Second, the **relationships among people** will offer insight into the organizational culture. If people feel positive about the change process, they will generally respond favorably about being empowered, exhibit trust in the process, sense support, and believe that the pacing of the change effort is appropriate. The grapevine will then generally support the change initiative. Finally, people will seek to **celebrate the benchmarks of success** but recognize that the initiative is not finished; celebrating benchmarks recognizes progress and achievement and signals moving to another stage of development. Celebrations sustain momentum for the change initiative. People will observe the beginning of a value-driven mindset verses an event-driven mindset that seeks short-term, unrelated outcomes. Event-driven outcomes only serve to bring momentary exposure and no systemic change. They do not serve to change people's beliefs and values. However, a value-driven mindset leads to systemic change where people value the initiative and the necessity to continue to meet students' needs.

Challenge 4: Recognize the Complex Nature of Change. The change process is very complex. Richard Pascale describes productive educational change as roaming somewhere between control and chaos.[33] Accepting this as an accurate description, one cannot try to control all aspects of change. One reason is that we cannot anticipate all of the unknown factors at the outset. They will need to be addressed at the point that they arise. Unplanned factors are inevitable. It is important to realize that every new variable entering the equation produces other ramifications that in turn produce other reactions and so on. Senge says no one could possibly come to figure out all these interactions.[34]

We will illustrate this challenge with an example. During the past six years as leaders in the First in the World Consortium, we encountered many factors that at the outset of the project were unknown. The first major activity of the Consortium was to participate in the TIMSS. We planned to take the TIMSS data set, have four Teacher Learner Networks study various aspects of it, and make recommendations for instructional improvement the participating districts could implement. We expected the data within six months, but they were not available for ten months. When we received the data almanacs, they were massive in size and were in a raw form requiring alternative formatting. Until the data could be structured into a usable form, they could not be interpreted. Moreover, the reports we received were limited, providing only broad, descriptive information.

The Consortium needed to look for a way to understand the data. We decided to form a partnership with the North Central Regional Educational Laboratory (NCREL). This partnership required us to resolve how to pay for NCREL's technical support, define a scope of work, restructure the "year-to-year" activities we originally planned for the Learning Networks, alter the summer institute agenda, and explore other data gathering activities to support the data analyses we were conducting. In essence, our original data analysis and reporting plan needed to be rewritten.

With NCREL's help we were able to provide the Learning Networks with meaningful data. Together, the teachers and NCREL researchers studied the data and learned from it. This partnership helped us understand more about our achievement and the factors that influenced it. NCREL's assistance was immeasurably more helpful than the general reports we originally received. In the end, we were able to co-develop Web-based tools and resource manuals for other school districts to use to compare their student performance with the Consortium and the highest achieving countries in the world.

One reason we experienced problems with the TIMSS data was that we were creating a new paradigm for using large-scale data in a local setting. Many of the processes used at the international level do not meet the needs of a local school group that is trying to learn from its data. The solutions that were created, however, made it possible for us to delve more deeply into the data and learn about our performance. It also made it easier for others to use this type of information in a fraction of the time it took the Consortium.

The TIMSS study has been fascinating. We learned how to merge our work with our partners. This international project taught us valuable lessons about unknown factors of change. We discovered that when we are breaking new ground we all have valuable information to contribute to the solutions of our problems. We also learned that there are other potential partners who can help. Finally, we learned important ways to bridge gaps between research and practice and have now created working tools to help districts understand how to use performance data from other countries. This problem actually became our friend by forcing us to move out of our comfort zone and create more effective tools for learning.

Challenge 5: Embrace Resistance and Conflict. Probably the most challenging aspect of change is resistance and conflict. From a leader's perspective it is easy to assume that everyone will embrace a new project with the same enthusiasm. Reality and experience have proven that this is not always the case. It is important to recognize that there will be some conflict along the way. The real issue is how leaders address this conflict to ensure the initiative moves forward.

Leaders should be encouraged to develop a positive approach to conflict. Patterson suggests three leadership implications and recommendations for addressing conflict. First he stresses that leaders should accept the reality that conflict is inevitable and acknowledge the fact that its existence is natural. Second, leaders should create a safe environment for confronting conflict in a constructive way. He encourages leaders to value the energy of dissent and recognize that conflict provides the fertile ground for rich solutions. Finally, he recommends that leaders provide the training in the organization for members to become skilled in conflict resolution and consensus building.[35]

Michael Fullan also offers a constructive approach to conflict and resistance. He advocates the only effective way to deal with resistance is to invite and work with (rather than against) those who resist. He believes that today's resistance carries the seeds of tomorrow's support.[36] The most productive response to resistance for a leader is to engage others, seek ways to learn from those who resist, and look for ways to find common ground to join forces with them. By doing so, leaders can build support for the change, develop relationships that build a foundation for future change, offer opportunities for creative solutions where everyone might benefit, and keep people from making decisions without enough information.[37] In the end, if leaders embrace the conflict and work with people to find sound solutions to the issues that have been raised, the new project will result in success.

Challenge 6: Build Change Agents. Fullan states that at the core of productive educational change is the ability to survive the vicissitudes of planned and unplanned change while growing and developing. To become expert in the dynamics of change, educators must become skilled change agents.[38] He states that the problems associated with advancing productive change simply cannot be addressed unless we treat continuous teacher education as the major vehicle for producing teachers as moral change agents. As school districts embark on curriculum development, instructional practice, professional development, and partnerships, it is important to lead everyone toward the mindset of being change agents in a larger learning organization.[39]

Understanding the world of change is important to the successful implementation of a change initiative. If leaders commit to nurture the change process and take to heart these key challenges of change, they will establish a foundation for success.

We encourage leaders to give attention to the various dimensions of change and plan to lead staff through the various stages. All participants in the change initiative should have a clear understanding of what constitutes the new initiative and how they will work through it.

There is a myriad of prominent researchers who have written practical ways to translate the change research into practice: Michael Fullan, Andy Hargreaves, Jerry Patterson, Peter Senge, Richard Pascale, and Robert Quinn. This literature base can serve as a foundation to better understand the change process. This reading list is included in the chapter endnotes.

Develop a Preferred Future for Your District

Educational leaders have the responsibility to develop the preferred future of the school district. A district's preferred future is its vision for action. As discussed in the leadership chromosome, a preferred future is what the district aspires to become, what it wants to accomplish, and what its expectations are. How will it serve its constituents? The articulation of this shared vision is the way a district takes a stand for a preferred future. Developing the vision causes the district to examine its purpose for existence, content, and practice and becomes the means by which the district leaders and the stakeholders articulate what is important to them.

Developing a preferred future should be done with the collaborative efforts of a board of education, the community, staff, and students. All of society is changing rapidly; no one is at a loss for topics or projects to undertake. School leaders must ask critical questions to determine what the future should be for their districts. Strategic planning processes and similar structures can help to establish criteria that will help formulate their decisions.

When a district clarifies a vision of what it wants to be, it is able to see current reality more clearly. Senge explains it this way: "The juxtaposition of vision (what we want) and a clear picture of current reality (where we are) generates "creative tension."[40] It is this tension that helps a district to move forward productively with change.

This gene stresses the importance of recognizing how a vision shapes the direction and potential implementation of new district initiatives. It purports that any new initiative must support the achievement of the district vision and be integrated holistically. While any number of initiatives could be started, educators must be very selective about deciding which ones will have the greatest impact on raising achievement toward world-class performance. This is particularly important since the district will invest considerable time and resources on the project. Consequently there are some important questions to consider when determining involvement in a new project:

- Does this project characterize a world-class concept or practice that the district currently does not demonstrate?
- Does the project help the district achieve its vision?

- How will the students and the educational process be improved because of the district's work in this area?
- In what areas does the district want to invest its time and energy?
- What resources will be needed to accomplish the project and for how long?
- What priority level should this endeavor hold in the totality of the district?

There are times when the district must implement changes because they are mandated from outside sources or because politically it would be difficult not to do so (for example, IDEA, Title programs, state and federal requirements). Despite what changes may occur, educators can still approach them as leaders and not victims. More often than not, leaders can integrate these mandated changes into programs, affect improvement, and still maintain cultural integrity. However, the change may involve considerable time and effort and will need to be carefully developed before implementation.

For a program to foster the vision, it must be carefully planned. When developing a new initiative, it is not only important to define its goals but also a long-range action plan with benchmarks. Appropriate time to accomplish these benchmarks and clear articulation of how the new initiative integrates with the district's existing programs must be built in. We cannot over emphasize this last point! If a district has other projects underway, what impact will a new project have on staff? How will planning and implementation expectations be received? Who will be most affected? Will this program adversely affect other programs that are currently being implemented? These are the types of issues that must be discussed before the district begins a new initiative.

As districts seek to achieve a better learning environment, they may use various means to select future programs. However, it is important to recognize what impact these decisions will have on teachers and the implementation of other programs. The overall reason to begin a new program is to advance the district's preferred future. If it does not do this, then the program should not be implemented.

Building the Capacity for Change Initiatives

Building the capacity to implement change is one of the most challenging endeavors a leader can undertake. It requires creating a working culture where staff accept and expect certain character-istics to be a natural part of their thinking and action. This culture generates energy throughout the system by virtue of the interact-ing dynamics among people. The leader must consciously build these characteristics in the culture and commit to them. Absent any one of them, there is no hope for sustained change. We present five interrelated characteristics of a capacity-building culture: staff in-volvement, shared vision of the initiative, continuous improvement emphasis, collaborative partnerships, and time to implement change.

Characteristic 1: Staff Involvement

Fundamental and long-lasting change requires the active in-volvement and support of the participants in the organization. Warren Bennis states, "Failing to appreciate the importance to the organization of the people who are already in it is a classical mis-take, one that change-oriented administrators are especially prone to make."[41]

Leaders must ensure that no staff member is left out of the pro-cess. This begins with an emphasis on communication. Staff should be informed about all aspects of the process and understand the time period over which the new program will be implemented. Knowing the scope of the project can help people grasp the overall picture of the task before them. It will also help them to gain a per-spective of what it might take to achieve this goal.

Staff members must also be involved in planning the project and making appropriate decisions about those aspects of the project that will have an impact on them. This will build ownership and trust among the staff. Finally, teachers will want to build their knowl-edge and skills to implement the project. Failure to take these im-portant steps could send the message to participants that their involvement is unimportant and could jeopardize any hope for long-term success. With staff supporting the project and being actively involved in its development, the first characteristic of capacity-build-ing culture is in place.

Characteristic 2: A Shared Vision of the Initiative

Leaders that seek to implement change must develop a shared vision of the initiative. This implies teachers must share and accept the vision for the project they are expected to implement. Their in-volvement in the initial discussions and planning of the project will help them to gain a commitment for what the district will seek to accomplish. Change for change's sake is no longer acceptable. There must be evidence to support the reason for making change. Teachers deserve the opportunity to discuss this evidence and gain an understanding of why a new direction would improve learning opportunities for the students.

Creating a study group is an excellent strategy to start the dialogue on a new project. We suggest that districts provide opportunities for staff to become familiar with the literature on the new initiative. Study group discussions and a written action plan for the project are ways to provide ongoing communication. Regardless of the approach that is used to engage teachers, the result should be that they share a common vision and understanding for the new program.

Characteristic 3: A Continuous Improvement Emphasis

Continuous improvement is grounded in the belief that it is necessary to regularly analyze programs and practices if the district is to become world class. A continuous improvement emphasis diminishes the perception that the improvements are sought because of people's weaknesses or incompetence; rather, the goal is to continually examine district practices and attempts to improve in light of what they are learning. Gaining more knowledge about programs and instruction can improve practice. It is important for people to embrace this mindset and embed it in their daily interactions and tasks.

UCLA professor and head researcher of the TIMSS video study, James Stigler puts it succinctly when he says that the process of improvement is about teaching, not teachers. Improvements should be made not because teachers are doing their jobs poorly, but because they are learning more about their practice and providing better learning opportunities for students.

Continuous improvement necessitates a fundamental shift in the way people approach their work. This shift is being proactive, seeking ways to improve. Without this shift, a district will face two incompatible forces, the *concept* of a continuous change theme in conflict within a *working* system characterized by a safe, nonrisk, and status quo environment. The system that incorporates continuous improvement seeks to be a learning organization. Michael Fullan calls for districts to make ongoing evaluation and examination of practices the norm, not the exception; where continual modification is expected.[26] Therefore, districts that approach change appropriately do not merely respond to the latest policy or initiative; nor do they rest on designing better reform strategies for the moment. Rather, they view change and improvement as a normal part of their operation.

How then does the district support continuous improvement? Several strategies serve to build teachers' capacity to improve. First, inquiry and study are critical to successfully implement change. Districts must provide opportunities for teachers to learn and grow in their profession. Learning communities serve as an effective way to engage teachers in valuable discussions. Teachers can study the research on new programs and gain knowledge. They can learn the theoretical underpinnings of the proposed change, strategies, and pedagogical skills that are crucial to the success of any change effort.

A second strategy is that teachers must teach new content and practice new skills so they can develop mastery. Competence and mastery of content and skills are necessary for effectiveness. They are also the means for achieving deeper understanding of the change being implemented. Michael Fullan states that people change their thinking as they gain greater mastery of the skills and concepts they are learning. He writes, "New mindsets arise from new mastery as much as the other way around."[43]

Third, teachers must reflect on their experiences with their colleagues. They must discuss those aspects of lessons that were effective and those that were not. They must then strategize how to modify their behavior to reach desired results. By doing so, they are determining the effectiveness of their new strategies on the learning environment. In the Instructional Practice Chromosome we offer several ways teachers can reflect on their teaching with their colleagues.

Finally, teachers should analyze student achievement data to determine if students are, in fact, achieving at higher levels. Ultimately, the changes we make in content and instructional delivery should have a positive impact on learning. An analysis of data will provide valuable information about student progress and program effectiveness.

When school districts emphasize continuous improvement, they embark on change for the betterment of their students and the profession. As education uses research-based evidence to improve, it is taking a major step toward becoming a mature profession. This step is needed in education and a continuous improvement approach will serve to move the profession toward maturity.

The continuous improvement notion is similar to one that has been practiced in the medical field for years. Through medical research, new discoveries result in medicines and procedures that better meet the needs of patients. In education it is equally necessary to build on current knowledge to improve practices that enhance the quality of education for children.

Characteristic 4: Collaborative Partnerships

Building capacity for change requires collaborative relationships. Research on effective professional development states that collaboration is a crucial activity for teachers to learn new skills. Small-scale collaboration involves mentoring new teachers, organizing study groups, and team building. Using these types of collaborative groups to engage in the continuous improvement strategies just discussed will enhance teachers' ability to gain understanding of new content and skills. In these groups the teachers must be free to take risks knowing that they will be supported and can reflect on how they can improve.

On a larger scale, collaboration consists of organizations forming cross-institutional partnerships such as school district, university and school-community and business agency alliances. The partnership that the First in the World Consortium formed with NCREL is a perfect example of how a collaborative builds the capacity to achieve its goals. Without this partnership, the Consortium would not have been able to analyze TIMSS data and learn from it.

Partnerships should be encouraged whenever the learning can be enhanced beyond working in isolation. Whether it is within the organization or across institutions, the incentive for the partnership should be to gain greater knowledge and skill because of the relationship.

Characteristic 5: Time to Implement Change

Earlier, in our discussion of the challenges facing leaders, we indicated that change should be implemented at a reasonable pace. From a capacity-building perspective, this challenge translates into providing sufficient time to implement the new project the way it was intended. Teachers consistently report that they do not have sufficient time to learn new strategies and skills. We agree! There is little time for teachers to collaborate with each other. The many demands on their time detract from their need for reflection and dialogue with colleagues.

Implementing change requires teachers to engage in trial and error at times because the answers are not always clear. Senge states that the real leverage for change involves the following: seeing interrelationships rather than linear cause-effect changes; and seeing processes of change rather than snapshots.[44] To grow, teachers must have the capacity to engage in meaningful interactions.

Districts need to provide professional development opportunities for teachers to participate in learning communities. This means that appropriate time parameters must be established for teachers to work through the continuous improvement process. We encourage leaders to be innovative in their efforts to provide time for this process.

Sustain Momentum in the Change Initiative

Sustaining the momentum of a change initiative is one of the most challenging tasks that leaders have in an organization. A typical scenario follows: A new project is launched with a great deal of emphasis and planning. Teachers begin the project with enthusiasm and high motivation. However, as the process unfolds, staff becomes discouraged. Sometimes it is due to insufficient progress. Other times, staff feel that they cannot achieve what is needed in the limited time that they have to complete it. Discouragement can also result when staff is not recognized appropriately. Sometimes it is because they believe their views are not being heard. Some staff have left and new staff have taken their places. These new staff may not share the same passion for the project that others shared. Whatever the reason, the initiative is struggling and is threatened to fail.

These problems are very real but correctable. In this gene we encourage school districts to plan for sustaining their school improvement initiatives. We say this with an emphasis on how important it is to be aware of potential problem areas and take the necessary steps to correct them. We have experienced failed endeavors and learned that taking some very simple but definitive steps can make a major difference in the success or failure of a project. Ignoring problems as they arise is at the heart of most failed efforts to change.

What critical areas should not be neglected when planning change? First, keep the end in mind. Recognize and celebrate incremental successes. Define those incremental successes in the plan by setting benchmarks. (This was mentioned earlier as one of the litmus tests of managing successful change.) The reason for celebrating successes is that reaching benchmarks is a success story. The celebration encourages participants to keep working and helps them gain confidence. It sends a message that the project is progressing and that the work is successful. It also provides the opportunity to thank people for their efforts.

Second, be prepared to make adjustments along the way and not view them as failures or setbacks. If what Michael Fullan says about the existence of unknown factors is accurate, then when they occur, it is simply necessary to make adjustments. Sometimes it will slow down the progress; other times it may be necessary to try something different. This should not be a source of discouragement but a "correction indicator" designed to strengthen the implementation process. Above all, do not view the need for adjustments as a sign of failure; rather, they are opportunities to learn.

Third, change initiatives take several years to develop, implement, and evaluate. It is likely that some of the individuals who were in the district at the start of the project will not be there to see it to fruition. Attrition is a reality in organizations; therefore, the organizational goals, values, processes, and culture must transcend the people that comprise them. To address this reality, there must be a process in place to mentor new staff. Mentoring can take two specific paths for very different reasons. The first path is staff that joins the planning team must be brought up to speed on the project. This means that they must be provided with the following:

- A complete historical review of the project
- A synopsis of the goals and processes being followed in the initiative and an explanation of how/why they were developed
- A summary of the research underpinning the work of the project
- A summary of what steps of the project have to be completed and why they look the way they do. This would include any barriers that have been encountered and how they have been addressed.

- A professional development program to scale up skills
- Opportunities to receive ongoing feedback when questions arise

The second mentoring path pertains primarily to staff that are trying to implement the program. These individuals may not have the same background or training on the project that other staff have. The district needs to provide a means for those staff to acquire background information and new knowledge and skills. They must be included in a group where they can discuss the project with their colleagues and have the support they need to implement it. In both mentoring scenarios, the key concept is that the individuals who are expected to implement a new program must feel that they understand the expectations and have the skills to accomplish them.

Fourth, we have already mentioned the need to develop a long-range action plan for a new project to ensure that it progresses in a reasonable manner for teachers, parents, and students. It must be integrated into the overall academic program so that a staff can give it the attention it needs. We iterate this point because the success of any new initiative is dependent on the attention that the staff can reasonably give it. If staff feel that they are expected to implement too many new programs, they will self-determine the program that they feel most committed to or passionate about and focus on that program. Think about the following very real scenario.

A high-performing school district is scaling up its practices and programs. Teachers across the district have worked hard making improvements to the programs. The board of education is also considering new directions. It is now a new school year and teachers are presented with the following new initiatives.

- A new science curriculum is introduced that requires teachers to learn new instructional strategies and different content. Several professional development sessions are scheduled to help the staff members learn the new program.
- The district assessment committee revised the current reading assessment measures and wants the teachers to implement them four times this year. The assessments are substantially different, and the teachers will need to score them, provide summary sheets on each student, conduct analysis on what the data tell them, and offer differentiated instruction in response to what is learned.

- The board of education set a goal to conduct a feasibility study on teaching elementary foreign language and is seeking feedback from the community and staff. Several informational meetings will be scheduled for staff members. Focus groups will be organized to discuss the value of the program. Teachers will be expected to give their input and spend professional development time studying the issue.
- Finally, the special education department has revised several of its reporting processes in conjunction with state and federal regulations. The changes require staff members to provide additional support data on student issues and to complete new forms. The process also requires teachers to attend additional staffing and case study meetings to support the placements and needs of students.

If you were a teacher in this district, think about the overwhelming responsibilities that have been placed on you. If you hold the same teaching assignment as before, the challenge is great. If you are a new teacher or one that has changed assignments within the district, the expectations may be unrealistic. As a teacher, how will you go about trying to prioritize your time for these new initiatives? Some aspect of your job will not get the attention that it really needs. This scenario is one that causes teachers stress and anxiety. They know that their best efforts will not be sufficient to meet the demands of the project. School districts need to pace the implementation of new initiatives appropriately and place reasonable expectations on teachers; otherwise, the change efforts will fail. The most important role of the teacher is to offer the best learning opportunities for children. Teachers must have the time, resources, and energy to translate new initiatives into learning opportunities. The development and implementation of a long-range action plan must be communicated to staff members so that they know what is coming and can plan for it.

Finally, it is important to evaluate whether the change process is working. This is an important step to sustain motivation and to correct those aspects of the project that may be faltering. To evaluate the process, the district should establish indicators to assess if the change process is functioning as planned. Some suggested indicators could be as follows: staff satisfaction with the development of the project; achievement of the benchmarks in the project; and staff perceptions of how well they were prepared to implement the project, and their involvement in the planning process. These indicators support the following types of activities. The leaders may want to reflect back on whether the vision of the project is still well focused. The district may want to gather teacher feedback as to whether they had sufficient opportunity to learn, practice, and reflect on the new program. Finally, the district may want to inquire whether there was sufficient collaboration in the process to ensure that most people could embrace the decisions that were made. Similar indicators could be developed that would give the leadership a sense that it is appropriately attending to the process of change.

Next, the leaders must determine if these indicators are being met. There can be various ways to accomplish this. One way to do so is to organize dialogue groups to reflect on the process. Teachers can talk about what is going well and what is not working. Their dialogue can be centered on accomplishment of the established benchmarks. These dialogue groups must provide people a safe and open environment. There needs to be an opportunity for a free exchange of ideas, and teachers need to feel their views are valued. When that occurs, there is empowerment and ownership.

A second way to determine if the indicators are being met is to make changes as a result of the dialogue. When this occurs, staff tends to view the change process as a total district effort and not one person or group's personal agenda. Providing people a sense that they are making a contribution to the project and that their voice is heard empowers them. This cannot be overstated.

Our primary message in this gene is that an initiative should never lose momentum as a result of a poorly developed process of change. Overwhelming staff members with multiple and diverse expectations will guarantee failure for a new project. If people become discouraged or uninterested in the initiative, it is a valid signal that their needs are not being met. Many laudable programs have been initiated with the expectation of creating lasting change but have fallen short because the district has ignored basic planning and implementing steps. A fundamental paradigm shift about educational change is required. It begins with a continuous improvement emphasis and is sustained by a well-developed process that adjusts to the unknown factors that will occur and supports teachers throughout the process.

The action plan should account for the appropriate pacing of the project and for ways to sustain it over time. The plan should also take into account the fact that the initial motivation for the project will wane if a process is not put in place to mentor and educate new people to assume key roles. Districts will constantly be faced with the challenge of revisiting the vision and goals of the project and with sustaining the momentum that launched the initiative. As leaders work together to develop goals and year-to-year activities, they will need to create strategies that will help critical players stay invested in the project until it is fully implemented.

Professional Development Chromosome

Introduction

It is impractical to draw any conclusions about professional development that are applicable to approximately 15,000 American public school districts. Our observations and conversations, as well as our experiences as educational administrators, have led us to conclude that high-quality professional development programs are just not very common. Very few boards of education commit the necessary personnel and funds to assure a well-trained education staff that is prepared to make knowledgeable decisions about teaching, learning, curriculum and assessment. We often hear from colleagues that they have good training programs for their teachers. Upon further investigation, however, the result is usually more of the same, an event-driven plan, not developed to be sustained over time and not aligned with the district goals and curriculum.

Other professions rely upon building knowledge to continuously improve. About 40 years ago, my father, Philip Kimmelman, had cataract surgery. He had to go to another state to find a specialist who could perform the operation. Then, blocks supported his head so he would not move for at least a week. Several years ago I had the same cataract surgery. I went into the operating room at 9:00 AM and left the hospital at noon. I was able to carry on a normal work schedule at home the remainder of the day.

We mention this example because medicine in many respects is no different as a science than teaching. A major difference, however, is that in medicine doctors build on previous knowledge to improve their techniques. Educators tend to try new methods and rarely use what they learned to improve their practices. This is an unfortunate commentary on the profession. Nothing should be considered more important than ensuring classroom teachers are well trained and involved in an organized professional development plan that is intended to inform their instructional practice.

Consider the raging debates that are occurring in reading (phonics vs. whole language) and mathematics (computation vs. understanding). Why is it that these debates seem to always be philosophical rather than rely on useful evidence regarding practices proven to work? Why is it that the participants in these debates tend to become so wedded to their philosophical positions and fail to use research to understand that different approaches and materials might result in different results for a variety of students? Educators often lack the necessary scientific knowledge to make informed decisions about teaching and learning. A very small percentage of teacher time is devoted to learning. Even more discouraging is that very little of that small percentage of time is used for teachers to collaborate on practice; therefore, they cannot learn from each other.

Special education is another example where science has not been the basis for improving instruction. In the 1960s, the goal was to place special education students in their own self-contained classrooms with a teacher who had specialized training to teach students with disabilities. In the 1990s, these students are being moved into regular classrooms with teachers ill equipped to meet their complex learning needs. There is more information about the brain and learning and the technology to support teaching these students, yet educators continue to struggle in classrooms unprepared to meet the challenges of teaching them.

To effectively improve teaching, it will be necessary to make a commitment to offer a new form of professional development unlike the plans currently in place. It will require aggressive leadership calling for an improved educational workforce with a plan that is ongoing and linked to the school/district learning goals and curriculum. This new professional development program must include benchmarks to determine if the goals are met and assessment plans to measure how well those goals are met. There will need to be more financial support, more time for the staff to engage in professional development activities, and a total staff commitment to the plan. Although a daunting responsibility, this approach is realistic and integral to implementing the genetic model.

There are many terms used for professional development, such as staff development, institute days, and in-service among others. However, for purposes of our work, we will refer to it as professional development. Incorporated in our use of professional development are professional learning strategies for teachers that include curriculum analysis and writing, textbook reviews, videotaping classes for analysis of teaching, workshops, lesson study groups, seminars, action research, mentoring, networking with peers to discuss teaching, graduate classes specifically in the subject taught, and membership in professional organizations.

There are six genes on the professional development chromosome. These genes, used together, form the framework of a high quality professional development plan. They include:

1.   Create a Philosophy Statement, Purpose, and Goals.
2.   Deepen Understanding of Content Knowledge.
3.   Design and Implement a Professional Development Framework.
4.   Change the Organizational Culture.
5.   Implement Professional Learning Strategies that Support Adult Learner Needs.
6.   Assess the Effectiveness of the Professional Development Program.

We consider these genes to be an integral part of professional development planning, and they need to be implemented in a manner that improves teaching and student achievement. We will offer some suggestions regarding the DNA of these genes, but professional development plans must be carefully written to meet each district's or school's specific goals. Most important, when working with the genes is how they will be communicated and implemented.

Professional Development Chromosome: Six Genes

Create a Philosophy Statement, Purpose, and Goals

So far we have discussed professional development in the context of what it should be conceptually. We have been critical of the education profession for failing to provide high-quality professional development to its workforce and for not making a serious commitment to what should be a top priority in every school district. Imagine any other profession approaching continuous learning using the education model that is based on the working assumption that teaching will improve through event-driven plans. There is an overemphasis on inviting a speaker to a single event to instill teachers with ideas and calling it professional development. The speaker finishes and the teachers are usually left to figure out how to implement the ideas. If other professions used the education model, doctors would still use scalpels, lawyers would research cases in large volumes of books, auto mechanics would guess on needed repairs, and accountants would complete tax returns with calculators. The point is that each of these professions has improved and evolved to a mature level by building on previous knowledge, using quantitative data to make decisions, collaborating on what works and even discussing what did not work, using technology to support their improvement, and being driven by competition to get better. It is time for a paradigm shift in education by implementing professional development as a regular component of the teacher workday.

Two of our guest authors have provided keen insight into what might be a world-class professional development plan. Dennis Sparks and Susan Loucks-Horsley are highly recognized for their thoughts on professional development. Sparks and Loucks-Horsley's works can be used to develop a philosophy, goals, and purpose for planning a professional development program. Sparks identifies the following critical components for effective professional development.

- Deepen teachers' knowledge of the content they teach.
- Expand teachers' repertoire of research-based instructional skills to teach that content.
- Provide ongoing classroom assistance in implementing new skills.
- Provide teachers with the classroom assessment skills that allow them to regularly monitor gains in student learning resulting from improved classroom practices.
- Surround teachers with a culture supported by structures that encourage innovation, experimentation, and a collegial sharing of new ideas and practices.

Susan Loucks-Horsley integrates research, theory, and experienced wisdom into her thoughts regarding world-class professional development. Loucks-Horsley lists the following principles in her plan.

- Teacher learning experiences have students and their learning at the core, and that means all students.
- Professional development focuses on a number of critical goals, all linked to improved student learning.
- Principles that guide the improvement of student learning also guide professional learning for teachers.
- Professional development is based in teaching practice.
- Professional development both aligns and supports system-based changes that promote student learning.
- Professional development is carefully designed for each context and circumstance.

A "World-class" Professional Development Program

by Susan Loucks-Horsley
Associate Executive Director, Biological Sciences Curriculum Study

"World class" professional development programs are designed with close attention to research, theory, and the "wisdom" of experienced professional developers. They have the following characteristics:

1. Teacher learning experiences have students and their learning at the core—and that means all students. Science and mathematics education reforms—and the national, state, and local standards on which they are based—share a common commitment to high standards of achievement for all students and not just for the few who are talented or privileged. This implies a different perspective on the content students should learn and the teaching strategies that should be used by their teachers. To meet this challenge, all professional development resources, including teacher time, must be focused on rigorous content and the best ways to reach all students.

2. Professional development focuses on a number of critical goals, all linked to improved student learning. These goals include (I) deepening the knowledge of teachers of the content they will teach and (2) strengthening and broadening their knowledge and skills of how to teach it. The latter, called "pedagogical content knowledge", involves teachers' abilities to select content, teaching examples, and strategies that are developmentally appropriate for their particular students, are keyed to student thinking and learning needs, and address common conceptions and misconceptions students are apt to have about the particular content. Excellent teachers are distinguished from even the most learned scientists and mathematicians by their well-developed pedagogical content knowledge. Other important goals of professional development include building a professional learning community to support ongoing learning for each and all teachers, and developing leadership skills to enable teachers to support others' learning and participate in important decisions beyond the classroom.

3. Principles that guide the improvement of student learning also guide professional learning for students. Excellent professional development experiences mirror how teachers should work with their students. Engaging in active learning, focusing on fewer ideas more deeply, and learning collaboratively are all principles that characterize learning for teachers if they in turn are expected to apply these to helping their students learn. Further, like approaches to student learning, effective professional development is ongoing and sustained, not one-shot and fragmented, for meaningful learning takes time, practice, and support.

4. Professional development is based in teaching practice. The most effective professional development helps teachers examine their own practice and that of others for its impact on learning and needs for change. Teachers who work with their own curriculum materials, view videos that demonstrate student thinking and classroom lessons, read cases of teaching dilemmas, and examine student work, deepen their understandings of student learning and effective teaching.

5. Professional development both aligns with and supports system-based changes that promote student learning. Professional development cannot be separated from other critical elements of the education system. In "world-class" programs, it works in concert

with changes in standards, curriculum, instruction, and assessments so that these changes are effectively implemented, sustained, and have maximum influence on student learning. School-based professional development engages teachers in simultaneously developing their own knowledge and skills, and making important decisions about the educational experiences of the students within their school community.

6. Professional development is carefully designed for each context and circumstance. Although the general principles previously mentioned all hold, each professional development program needs to be tailored to the particular situation in which teachers are learning new skills, content, and approaches. Like teaching, professional development identifies a set of goals, assesses where teachers are and what they need, selects the strategies that will best support teacher learning, and changes dynamically based on progress and problems facing the teachers. Different professional development strategies—I5 have been identified in studies of effective programs—can be combined in different ways over time to constitute the maximum set of learning experiences for individual and groups of teachers.

Well-designed, ongoing, content-driven, and challenging learning experiences for teachers can make a major contribution to building "world-class" opportunities for student learning.

Sparks and Loucks-Horsley's ideas mirror what others are saying is necessary to improve the quality of American education professional development. They offer a number of principles that can be used to write a philosophy statement, purposes, and goals for a professional development plan. It is critical to begin with these three activities in order to organize a professional development program that is focused on meeting specific learning goals. Those goals should always be to improve the quality of teaching and student achievement.

Deepen Understanding of Content Knowledge

The gene on teachers' content knowledge is very important. Teacher understanding of content formally begins in college. College signifies the preparation period for teachers and should include a requirement that these students take a comprehensive series of classes to build their content knowledge for the subjects they plan to teach. The process should be career-long, however. After graduating, the need for more knowledge about subject matter does not stop. To use a football metaphor, the college "hands off" to the teacher's new employer. It is incomprehensible to assume that in this information age a school district would not implement a professional development program that regularly provides opportunities for teachers to learn more about the subject matter they teach. Regardless of whether a teacher teaches music, science, mathematics, or physical education, a thorough understanding of subject matter is essential.

There are a number of studies on the importance of teacher content knowledge. These studies will be discussed in detail in the instructional practice chromosome section. They do, however, conclude that teacher content knowledge has a direct influence on student achievement. The essential gene of teacher content knowledge for the professional development chromosome is to plan activities with the specific intent of helping teachers gain more knowledge about the subjects they teach.

Design and Implement a Professional Development Framework

The research on the various components of professional development should be part of a plan that supports the following effective professional development practices: professional development should be sustained over a period of time, build teacher content knowledge, provide opportunities for collaboration, improve teaching practices, align to the district or school's goals, and result in higher student achievement.

There are two research papers on professional development that we offer as guidelines for this gene. The first study was completed for the U.S. Department of Education by Andrew Porter, et al in 2000.[45]

Porter's study is relevant because it tracked professional development activities over a three-year period. The purpose of the study was to determine those characteristics of professional development programs that improve teaching practice and their relative existence in professional development programs as they are currently offered. First, they found that professional development focused on specific, higher order teaching strategies increases teachers' use of those strategies in the classroom. An example of a higher order teaching strategy would be working on a problem with no obvious solution. More significantly, they found that the effect is even greater when the teachers work on the problem solving activity in a network or study group rather than in a traditional workshop.

They also found that the quality of professional development for teachers varies from year to year and that teachers in the same school have very different professional development experiences. These findings support their observation that in their longitudinal sample they saw little change in teaching practice over the three-year period.

Their findings support a suggestion we make in the instructional practice chromosome regarding consistency of instruction between classrooms. They observed that teachers in the same school had quite different teaching practices. This variance in teaching practices could have a profound influence on student achievement if any of those teachers are using ineffective teaching strategies.

Our second reference is to a paper prepared for the Council of Chief State School Officers in 1998 by Tom Corcoran.[46] Corcoran's paper offers an overview of the critical issues in K–12 professional development and ways states might improve the learning opportunities available to teachers and their impact on practice.

Corcoran found that the current state of professional development for teachers is primarily local and that many teachers do not value it as a source for improving practice. Most teachers have been subjected to local "in-service" programs that reflect fads in education and have had little impact on helping them with their work. Teachers were offered involvement in activities that were purported to be high-quality professional development. In reality, those activities tended to be weak and poorly focused. Corcoran found that the teachers receive salary increases for participation in just about any program regardless of whether it adds value to their work; and, teachers tend to select professional development activities that require the least amount of work.

Although more structures for defining good practice are emerging, Corcoran says they do not have much impact on professional development programs. There needs to be greater acceptance of new practices that are effective and they need to be implemented into professional development plans.

Lack of time and quality control are two current problems with professional development as cited by Corcoran. For high-quality professional development, time must be allotted as part of a teacher's regular work schedule—not merely added to an already busy schedule. Further, what is offered as professional development must be relevant to what teachers need to improve. School districts must insist that presenters show evidence that their programs and materials are effective.

Finally, effective professional development will be expensive. Reducing teacher workloads and offering high quality programs is going to cost more money. While it may be possible to redistribute some current funds, more money will be needed to lead school performance to achieve world-class goals. However, substantive programs should be the most important factor, not money.

Porter's and Corcoran's work are essential considerations for this gene. We include research because it has significant implications for planning high-quality professional development programs. Corcoran offered background on the current state of professional development, and Porter conducted a three-year study on the effect of professional development on teaching practice. We believe their research, as well as the high-quality work of many others on professional development, must be considered when writing a professional development plan. We provide a sample framework for professional development in appendix B. This framework includes the quality component discussed thus far. It demonstrates the connection between education goals and teachers' professional development goals; and it illustrates the need to define specific content to be learned, professional learning strategies to engage in, and specific measurable outcomes to seek.

Change the Organizational Culture

Connecting teachers within and beyond their schools is an important idea. It is somewhat basic; yet, we are surprised that it is not a common practice. Many American teachers are teaching in isolation. Unlike their Asian peers, little, if any, time is scheduled to bring them together to discuss and reflect on their instructional practice, curriculum, and students. The Asian practice of lesson study is gaining popularity in America and is a strategy that brings teachers together to work collaboratively on improving lessons and teaching strategies. We are highly critical of the protectionist practices of teachers who choose to do things their own way rather than collaborating with peers to bring consistency to teaching across grade levels and departments. Guarding one's own teaching materials and plans does little to improve schools. If it works, share it with your colleagues! A school's performance is dependent on the success of the entire staff, not one who considers teaching an individual responsibility rather than a team concept.

The team concept is embedded in Sparks' reference to culture. The culture of schools needs to be radically changed if professional development is going to be part of the school's culture. Richard Elmore has written a highly provocative article on school leadership that discusses transformation.[47] Elmore's work is bold and incorporates the essential ingredients of building a school culture that leads to accountability for student learning. Elmore states that the purpose of leadership is the improvement of instructional practice and performance regardless of role, and instructional improvement requires continuous learning. Our most significant concern for education is reflected in Elmore's statement, "One does not get to lead in education without being well socialized to the norms, values, predispositions, and routines of the organization one is leading." If Elmore is correct, the type of professional development transformation that is needed will not occur. Culture plays an integral role in organizations and effective leadership is needed to bring about this transformation.

The concepts of Edward M. Marshall are unique and applicable to changing the culture in organizations. In his book, *Building Trust at the Speed of Change*, Marshall discusses the importance of creating a relationship-based corporation and describes how to change the compliant management style, cultivate employee commitment, and reenergize the workplace.[48] While some educators may feel threatened by Marshall's emphasis on trusting employees, today's workplace in schools is so radically different from the traditional bureaucratic model of organizations of the past it is worth trying.

In summary, the culture of the organization must change in order for teachers to grow in their profession. They must develop working relationships with respect to sharing information. They must work in teams to improve their instruction, and professional development must focus on improving practices and student achievement.

Implement Professional Learning Strategies That Support Adult Learner Needs

The list of professional development activities for professional learning is endless and limited only to the imagination (vision) of the educator. Any activity designed to implement what we have described as high-quality professional development is a logical step toward a substantive effort to improve teaching and learning.

The next section presents some professional learning practices and strategies in more detail and provides references for further review. In most instances each of the activities we discuss is applicable to individuals or groups. Our descriptions are general in nature and intended to provide a basic understanding of the activity or strategy.

Reading Activities

The most convenient and least complicated professional development activity is individual reading of professional literature. Educational literature abounds on just about any topic. The challenge is to separate the "wheat from the chaff" and utilize materials that are relevant. Materials that are research-based, data-driven, and based on effective education practices are a good place to begin. Professional journals normally provide a periodic update on contemporary education issues.

A second professional development reading concept is book study groups. We have organized book study groups combining teachers from our respective districts. Our primary focus has been world-class schools using the books written by Haynes and Chalker (see chapter 2). Teachers and administrators were released from their duties up to five times each semester to participate in discussion groups on world class education concepts. Each study group concluded by participating in a dialogue with Dr. Haynes. These sessions led to district-wide initiatives in mentoring, assessment, and professional development among others. Each participant was granted the equivalent of credit hours for advancement on the salary schedule. The cross-district collaboration meshed two different organizational cultures and encouraged discussion of world-class education practices from different perspectives. We suggest the group be focused on a single concept that is aligned with district goals. New books are constantly published providing limitless topics for study group themes.

We have also selected the Internet as a source for readings. The caveat is that while there is excellent information available on the Internet, there is also material of questionable value. There is no guiding principle for searching the Web, but common sense should determine what sites you use. Universities, professional organizations, the federal research laboratories, and the U.S. Department of Education have useful sites with links to other sites on a host of topics (*http://www.ncrel.org*).

Professional Organization Membership

Membership in professional organizations should be considered an important responsibility for every educator. Professional organizations are available to superintendents, principals, and teachers of most every subject area. They provide opportunities for teachers to network through meetings and list serves and often publish professional journals that include articles on improving practice.

National Board Certification

An individual form of professional development can be undertaken to become nationally board certified. The National Board of Professional Teaching Standards offers a rigorous program that can improve content knowledge and instructional strategies. This program requires an intense commitment and can be completed in one year. Many states and local school districts are offering lucrative financial incentives to their teachers to become national board certified (*http://www.nbpts.org*).

The NBPTS has five core propositions.

1. Teachers are committed to students and their learning.
2. Teachers know the subjects they teach and how to teach those subjects to their students.
3. Teachers are responsible for managing and monitoring student learning.
4. Teachers think systematically about their practice and learn from experience.

5. Teachers are members of learning communities.

It should be noted that this program is not without debate. The primary criticism of the program is that while a teacher may go through a rigorous certification process, there is a lack of conclusive evidence that the instructional practices of a National Board certified teacher leads to higher student achievement. Nevertheless, we believe it is a substantive project for individual teachers and a meaningful form of professional development. It improves their reflective practice and can lead to improvement of teaching practices. For information regarding a new program that offers high-quality activities for teacher improvement, contact American Board Certification (*http://www.nctq.org*).

Videotaping

Videotaping lessons is rapidly gaining popularity among educators. Although not a new practice, the TIMSS project has ignited a renewed enthusiasm for reflecting on a lesson through the use of video. Digital technology is rapidly replacing the use of videotaping. Jim Stigler, a guest writer, oversees the TIMSS video study. Dr. Stigler's work has led to a scientific analysis of mathematics and science lessons taught in several countries through the use of a framework developed by international researchers. In general, the analysis examines the topics covered in the lesson, the lesson structure, including the amount of time devoted to the topic, the organization of the lesson, and the lesson coherence. The study also looks at what the students do during the class and provides comparisons of teaching in different countries. (A more detailed description of the video study is available at *http://www.lessonlab.com*).

We have found videotaping teachers, in conjunction with using the TIMSS videotapes, is an effective strategy to initiate discussion on instructional practice with teachers. We have worked with Dr. Stigler on developing an international video lesson study group using videotapes from eighth grade mathematics and science classes.

Action Research

Another effective form of professional development is action research. Its purpose is to conduct a study unique to the classroom or a limited population. It is intended to improve performance in that specific setting. Action research is a project undertaken by and for those who are involved in the study. It is used for practitioners and is not held to the same rigorous standards imposed on academic researchers. For that reason, it is normally not practical to apply the findings to other situations. Richard Sagor, a leading writer on action research lists seven steps in the process in his book, *Guiding School Improvement with Action Research.*[49]

1. Select a focus.
2. Clarify the theories.
3. Identify research questions.
4. Collect data.
5. Analyze data.
6. Report the results.
7. Taking informed action.

Action research provides data and can inform instructional practice based on relevant information. It separates the "If it feels good, it works" concept from decision-making by using evidence and analysis of effective practices.

Lesson Study

Japanese teachers participate in a professional development activity known as lesson study. This practice has gained popularity in the United States through a number of articles appearing in education journals and as a result of the TIMSS studies. Lesson study can be considered a form of professional development because it involves an actual classroom lesson written by teachers and observed by them. The result is a collaborative effort by the teachers with recorded documentation that is used for further analysis and refinement of the lesson.

When teachers participate in lesson study in Japan, they carefully prepare a single lesson, teach it in front of their peers, and refine it based on their observations. The lesson study groups are organized by grade level. The lesson writing can take up to one year and is part of a process that can last four years. The following is an example of the Japanese lesson study process.

YEAR ONE:
- Make preliminary plans for the lesson study.
- Investigate students' skills and abilities.

- Identify interests of teachers and create a lesson plan.
- Decide instructional goals.

YEAR TWO:
- Define goals of study.
- Establish a theme.
- Identify the students' abilities that teachers want to improve.
- Teach the lesson.

YEAR THREE:
- Reflect on fine-tuning previous year's lesson study activities.

YEAR FOUR:
- Reflect on Years Three and Four and continuation of cycle.

For American teachers, this process can be daunting. It is the antithesis to the American culture of teaching and lesson planning. American teachers are often left to their own judgment to write lessons while their Japanese counterparts work collaboratively to write the lessons and improve instructional techniques. Yet, this process can bring consistency to teaching across the grade level and department and help each teacher improve.

Some of the topics teachers discuss in lesson study are what is taught (topic), the materials to be used, anticipating solutions to problems, the kinds of questions students will ask, how to use board space, how time will be apportioned, how to handle individual differences, and how to end the lesson. In essence, the teachers are scripting the lesson.

Japanese lessons tend to be coherent, focused, and connect teaching and learning. They have been carefully developed over time and have resulted in high student achievement scores on international assessments. They are the product of planning, implementing, and reflecting.

Lesson study is a form of networking among teachers. It can lead to discussions beyond the school as recommended by Sparks earlier in this chapter. The emphasis on lesson design should be considered a high-quality professional development activity.

Assess the Effectiveness of the Professional Development Program

The primary goal of high-quality professional development programs is to improve teaching and student achievement. To determine if the professional development program is effective necessitates writing a plan. While it may be difficult to prove a cause and effect relationship between professional development and the intended outcomes, it is advisable to have benchmarks and data to support the activities. The assessment plan is very specific to each district or school's program. Some questions for assessing the program are:

- Is the program responsive to the needs of the teachers?
- Does it include all staff?
- Have priorities been identified using relevant data and information?
- Are there benchmarks to reach for a sustained effort?
- What student achievement data will be used to determine adequate progress?
- Are the professional development activities for teachers collaborative?
- Have consultants demonstrated that their materials and ideas are effective?
- Is there evidence of improved teaching practices?
- Are the activities aligned with the district or school goals?
- How will followup activities be planned?
- Is there a professional development planning committee representative of the participants?
- How will the program be funded?

These are some of the critical questions that need to be considered when writing an assessment plan for a professional development program. Without benchmarks and data, it is impossible to know if the program yields the intended results.

We have now completed our discussion of the three Capacity-Building Chromosomes. We sought to provide a research base of understanding and to give the reader a core set of genes to develop. It is now time to build the chromosomes that reflect your district. Section II provides this opportunity.

Section II

The Genetic Framework for Your District: Building Your Own Capacity-Building Chromosomes

Given the complexities and natural obstacles inherent in leading school districts, can districts really make progress toward world-class performance? Can meaningful school improvement be achieved? The answer to both of these questions is YES.

The place to begin is for school districts to build their own chromosomes using the genetic model. They must develop, integrate, and translate each core area of operation into results-oriented goals. This document becomes your genetic framework. An action plan should then be created to operationalize the district's values, beliefs, and commitments that are the essence of each chromosome. This plan becomes the working document to achieve the district's goals that will lead to world-class performance.

We remind the reader that any action plan should include reasonable timelines. Successful implementation does not, nor will it ever, occur quickly. As stated earlier, initiatives frequently are undertaken in piecemeal fashion without a coherent plan or timeframe. Time is needed to develop support for them. Building the capacity of staff to successfully implement new initiatives will be essential.

The goal in Section II is to build your district's genetic framework. In this chapter and the next, you will use the chromosome worksheets to:

1. Define the genes, the fundamental principles, to which your district will commit.
2. Articulate a value statement that represents your gene.
3. Delineate those DNA, research-based practices, that comprise the substance of your gene. These DNA provide the specific practices that clearly define what your district means when it says it is committed to a gene.

When you have successfully completed all of the worksheets, you will have the genetic framework for your district. You will have identified what you choose to accomplish in the future. You will have developed a set of ideas and recommendations that will take your district to a world-class level of achievement. The task of the district will then be to develop a working plan to operationalize the genetic framework. This will be your plan for school improvement. We recognize the reality that each district will want to utilize its own strategies to develop an action plan for the future. We encourage readers to take this step.

Where to Begin: The Process

As you begin the process of creating your genetic framework for world-class performance, three ideas should be kept prominently at the forefront of your thinking:

1. Fundamental principles and practices will be the genetic map for future success. They are the genetic blueprint for how the district will look and function.

2. All of the chromosomes, core areas, work systemically to achieve desired outcomes. It is the integration of the chromosomes that makes the whole greater than the sum of its parts.

3. World-class performance is achievable when the vision is set beyond the local environment to a global context. Districts must benchmark against international standards. After all, that is the world in which students will live and work.

We have provided three worksheets for each of the six chromosomes.

- Worksheet #1 is a diagram of the chromosome outlining the genes we have discussed. It also provides districts with the option to create their own genes. We encourage districts to select and develop only those genes they believe are relevant and can implement with integrity.

- Worksheet #2 is a prompt sheet of questions and guiding thoughts. This sheet is designed to help districts think through their beliefs and what they expect staff members to do in each core area. The readers should not necessarily try to answer all of the questions; rather, they can use them as a guide to define what they currently believe and might want to explore in the future.

- <u>Worksheet #3</u> is your working document to build the chromosomes. This document will include your genes and DNA. It will also provide you with opportunities to think about how the DNA of one chromosome may connect with those of another. This process is designed to help you begin to make the connections among the chromosomes. Finally, this worksheet encourages you to think about those genes and DNA that do not currently exist in your district and that you may want to develop in the future.

Steps to Complete Chromosome Worksheet #3

Step 1. There are two different worksheets: Capacity-Building Chromosomes Worksheets located in chapter 4 and Teaching-Learning Process Chromosomes Worksheets located in chapter 5.

Make sufficient copies of all the worksheets and place them in a notebook in six distinct sections. The six sections represent the chromosomes we recommend. You may choose to develop chromosomes beyond those we have identified. Simply make new sections in those chromosomes.

Label each section by chromosome title.

Step 2. Chromosome Worksheet #3 is labeled as the specific chromosome you are developing. If the chromosome is professional development, you need to duplicate the Professional Development Chromosome Working Document found in the Capacity-Building section. If you are developing a Capacity-Building chromosome other than the three we have suggested, a blank form has been provided for YOUR DISTRICT CHROMOSOME.

Step 3.   Identify the specific gene you want to develop. Again, we have provided genes that we believe must be developed for world-class performance, but we encourage the development of others the district might select. You may want to begin with the genes you currently have in place. This will help to define what currently exists. If you want to start by creating your ideal future, this is also acceptable. We encourage you, though, to have a clear understanding of your present values and beliefs; it is from this point that you will begin with your staff to contemplate change.

EXAMPLE OF A GENE

| Gene (Fundamental Principle) | Implement specific learning strategies that support adult learner needs |

Step 4.   Write the value statement that expresses the district's unwavering commitment to achieve that gene. This statement should be declarative and specific.

EXAMPLE OF A VALUE STATEMENT

| Gene Value Statement | The district will engage in a variety of professional learning strategies to support adult learner needs. These strategies will serve specific purposes in developing teacher knowledge and skill levels for effective instruction. |

Step 5. On the DNA lines state those research-based practices that the district will follow to fulfill its commitment and demonstrate the specific focus of the gene. In other words, these practices define exactly what the district means when it says it will commit to doing something. This is a critical step because the district needs to provide substantive content and understanding for the gene.

EXAMPLE OF RESEARCH-BASED PRACTICES

DNA (Research-Based Practices)	
Develop study groups on topics identified in the needs assessment	
Engage in curriculum analysis/revision	
Conduct and support college courses	
Conduct workshops Support conferences	
Analyze student data	

Step 6. Once you have defined your DNA, begin to think in terms of the connections that they have with respect to the other chromosomes. You need to ask: How does this DNA piece relate to or affect the other chromosomes? How will another chromosome be planned or operate to support or accommodate this DNA piece?

This is a critical step because you need to integrate all of these connections when you are finished building all of your chromosomes. This integration will need to be reflected in your district's action plan for the future.

EXAMPLE OF HOW PRACTICES CONNECT TO THE OTHER CHROMOSOMES

DNA (Research-Based Practices)	If applicable, indicate the chromosome these practices are connected to; if they are connected to a specific gene or DNA piece from another chromosome, indicate as such.
Develop study groups on topics identified in the needs assessment	*Change Chromosome:* Learning Communities *Leadership Chromosome:* Guiding Coalition
Engage in curriculum analysis/revision	*Curriculum Chromosome:* Curriculum Revision Process
Conduct and support college courses	
Conduct workshops Support conferences	
Analyze student data	*Assessment Chromosome:* Assessment Framework

Step 7. List the gene and/or DNA you would like to develop more fully in the future. This step is for those districts that developed their chromosomes based on their current values and beliefs. As you completed the worksheet, you may have observed areas that are not currently as well developed, as they need to be. There may simply be some incomplete pieces in your practices that should be examined more thoroughly.

The purpose of this step is to list those fundamental principles and practices that you want to improve. This step helps to develop recommendations for improvement.

EXAMPLE OF GENES/DNA TO DEVELOP MORE FULLY

Conduct video analysis	*Instructional Practice Chromosome:* Improving lesson design and pedagogy
Establish partnership with other organizations	*Assessment Chromosome:* Data analysis
	Change Chromosome Collaborative partnerships
	Instructional Practice Chromosome: Collaborative learning
Establish lesson study group	*Instructional Practice Chromosome:* Improving lessons and instruction

If you choose to build your chromosomes based on an ideal preferred future, you are already taking this step. However, you will still need to compare this future with your current status. We suggest that you also list those areas that will need to be addressed. In doing so, you will identify the points from where the district must start to build its preferred future.

Step 8. Repeat steps 1–7 for each gene that you want to develop on your chromosome. For example, if you want to use seven genes for professional development, you will need to complete seven sheets, one for each gene.

Complete these steps for each of the six, or more, chromosomes you are developing. We have provided a completed Sample Worksheet #3 for the reader's reference.

Sample Worksheet #3:
Professional Development Chromosome
Working Document

Gene (Fundamental Principle)   <u>Implement specific learning strategies that support adult learner needs</u>

Gene Value Statement   <u>The district will engage in a variety of professional professional learning strategies to support adult learner needs. These strategies will serve specific purposes in developing teacher knowledge and skill levels for effective instruction.</u>

If applicable, indicate the chromosome these practices are connected to; if they are connected to a specific gene or DNA piece from another chromosome, indicate as such.

DNA (Research-Based Practices)

Develop study groups on topics identified in the needs assessment	*Change Chromosome:* Learning Communities *Leadership Chromosome:* Guiding Coalition
Engage in curriculum analysis/revision	*Curriculum Chromosome:* Curriculum Revision Process
Conduct and support college courses	
Conduct workshops Support conferences	
Analyze student data	*Assessment Chromosome:* Assessment Framework

List those genes and/or DNA that you would like to develop more fully in the future and draw appropriate connections to other chromosomes as done above.

Conduct Video Analysis	*Instructional Practice Chromosome:* Improving lesson design and pedagogy
Establish partnership with other organizations	*Assessment Chromosome:* Data analysis *Change Chromosome:* Collaborative partnerships *Instructional Practice Chromosome:* Collaborative learning
Establish Lesson Study Group	*Instructional Practice Chromosome:* Improving lessons and instruction

Putting the Chromosomes Together

Once all of chromosomes are built, you will have the genetic framework for your future. You should then organize a leadership team to develop each of these areas into an action plan. As we suggested in the leadership chromosome, a leadership team can take responsibility for creating and integrating the various tasks of the overall action plan. Regardless of the planning process or organizational approach you use, it will be vital to have in place a process to understand the "big picture" and how all of the chromosomes interact to support the collective work of the district.

You are embarking on a project that will require commitment and persistence but can ultimately result in achieving your desired outcomes.

Capacity-Building Chromosomes Worksheets

LEADERSHIP CHROMOSOME

Worksheet #1: Leadership Chromosome Diagram

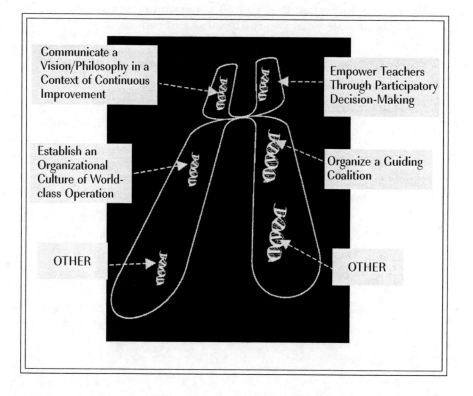

Worksheet #2: Leadership Chromosome Guiding Questions

Articulating the Values and Research-Based Practices Your District Has Regarding Leadership

We have delineated several leadership genes (fundamental principles) that contribute to effective leadership. In this activity we suggest that you use these leadership genes and others of your own choosing to identify the values and re-search-based practices that describe how the leadership should be developed and exhibited in your district. Guiding questions have been provided to assist in articulating these values and practices. Begin the activity by reading the questions and asking: *What do we value and what are our practices with respect to each of these genes?*

Note: It is not critical that you formally answer each of these questions. It is important that you take them into consideration as you contemplate what you really value and believe.

Gene 1: Communicate a Vision/Philosophy in a Context of Continuous Improvement

- What is the vision of your school district?
- Is this vision translated into district goals and initiatives that all staff seek to achieve?

Gene 2: Establish an Organizational Culture of World-Class Operation

- What leadership components exist in the district for the head of the organization as well as all other staff that work in leadership capacities?
- To what extent do the leaders work on components such as being focused on achieving goals; being innovative with the action plan; creating a sense of purpose; exhibiting passion; and earning trust.

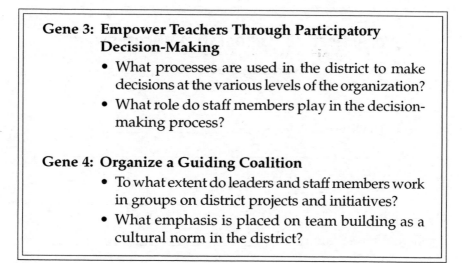

Gene 3: Empower Teachers Through Participatory Decision-Making

- What processes are used in the district to make decisions at the various levels of the organization?
- What role do staff members play in the decision-making process?

Gene 4: Organize a Guiding Coalition

- To what extent do leaders and staff members work in groups on district projects and initiatives?
- What emphasis is placed on team building as a cultural norm in the district?

Worksheet #3: Leadership Chromosome

Working Document

Gene (Fundamental Principle) _____

_____

_____

_____

Gene Value Statement_____

_____

_____

_____

	If applicable, indicate the chromosome these practices are connected to; if they are connected to a specific gene or DNA piece from another chromosome, indicate as such.
DNA (Research-Based Practices)	

List those genes and/or DNA that you would like to develop more fully in the future and draw appropriate connections to other chromosomes as done above.

Capacity-Building Chromosomes Worksheets

CHANGE CHROMOSOME

Worksheet #1: Change Chromosome Diagram

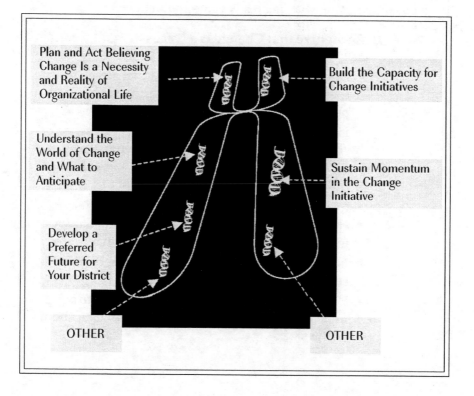

Plan and Act Believing Change Is a Necessity and Reality of Organizational Life

Build the Capacity for Change Initiatives

Understand the World of Change and What to Anticipate

Sustain Momentum in the Change Initiative

Develop a Preferred Future for Your District

OTHER

OTHER

Worksheet #2: Change Chromosome Guiding Questions

Articulating the Values and Research-Based Practices Your District Has Regarding Change

We have delineated several change genes (fundamental principles) that contribute to the successful implementation of change. In this activity we suggest that you use these change genes and others of your own choosing to identify the values and research-based practices that describe how the change process is nurtured and operationalized in your district. Guiding questions have been provided to assist in articulating these values and practices. Begin the activity by reading the questions and asking: *What do we value and what are our practices with respect to each of these genes?*

Note: It is not critical that you formally answer each of these questions. It is important that you take them into consideration as you contemplate what you really value and believe.

Gene 1: Recognize that Change Is a Necessity and Reality of Organizational Life

- Does the district provide a "big picture view" of the change initiatives in which teachers are expected to engage?
- In what ways does the district provide a sense of stability for teachers to cope with changes?
- What does the district believe it takes to change the culture to improve practice?
- In what ways does the district commit itself to changing the organizational culture and value system? What does it look like? How is it manifested?
- Is there a change model used in the district to serve this purpose?
- What, if any, process does the district use to adapt to changes and how does it communicate them to the staff?

Gene: 2 Understand the World of Change and What to Anticipate

- What does your district believe is important regarding the change process? What research underpinnings about change are embedded in your district's approach to change?
- Describe the district's basic beliefs and processes as it develops and implements change initiatives?
- What communication strategies are used with the staff during the change process?

Gene 3: Develop a Preferred Future for Your District

- What does the district believe its role is in developing its own future in light of the many outside forces that weigh on the district?
- What strategies are used in the district to develop and articulate the district's vision of the future?

Gene 4: Build the Capacity for Change Initiatives

- Describe the district's beliefs of sustaining a culture for continuous improvement? In what ways does the district develop or discourage this culture?
- How does the district build a shared vision for change initiatives?
- What structures are in place in the district to support teachers in their efforts to learn and master new skills and concepts (professional development)?
- What priority does the district place on providing time for teachers to reflect on their practice and to collaborate with each other in learning new skills and concepts?

Gene 5: Sustain Momentum in the Change Initiative

- Describe the ways that the district celebrates successes in a change effort?
- What mentoring processes are used to assimilate new people into the change initiative?

Worksheet #3: Change Chromosome
Working Document

Gene (Fundamental Principle) _____

_____

_____

_____

Gene Value Statement_____

_____

_____

_____

| | If applicable, indicate the chromosome these practices are connected to; if they are connected to a specific gene or DNA piece from another chromosome, indicate as such. |
DNA (Research-Based Practices)	
_____	_____
_____	_____
_____	_____
_____	_____

List those genes and/or DNA that you would like to develop more fully in the future and draw appropriate connections to other chromosomes as done above.

_____	_____
_____	_____
_____	_____
_____	_____

Capacity-Building Chromosomes Worksheets

PROFESSIONAL DEVELOPMENT CHROMOSOME

Worksheet #1: Professional Development Chromosome Diagram

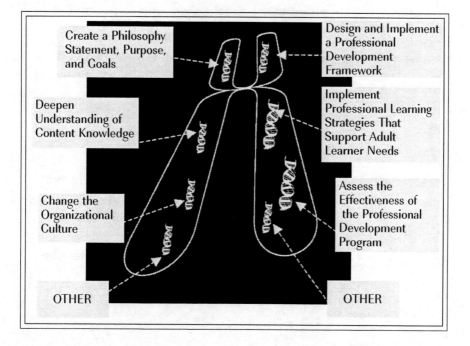

Worksheet #2: Professional Development Chromosome Guiding Questions

Articulating the Values and Research-Based Practices Your District Has Regarding Professional Development

We have delineated several professional development genes (fundamental principles) that contribute to the development of a high quality professional development program. In this activity we suggest that you use these professional development genes and others of your own choosing to identify the values and research-based practices that describe how professional development should be developed and implemented in your district. Guiding questions have been provided to assist in articulating these values and practices. Begin the activity by reading the questions and asking: *What do we value and what are our practices with respect to each of these genes?*

Note: It is not critical that you formally answer each of these questions. It is important that you take them into consideration as you contemplate what you really value and believe.

Gene 1: Create a Philosophy Statement, Purpose and Goals

- Describe the district's basic beliefs about professional development and its overall purpose.
- What are some of the fundamental goals that the professional development program is designed to accomplish in your district?

Gene 2: Deepen Understanding of Content Knowledge

- What value does the district place on deepening the content knowledge of teachers in the various subject areas?
- To what extent are teachers expected to have areas of content specialty?

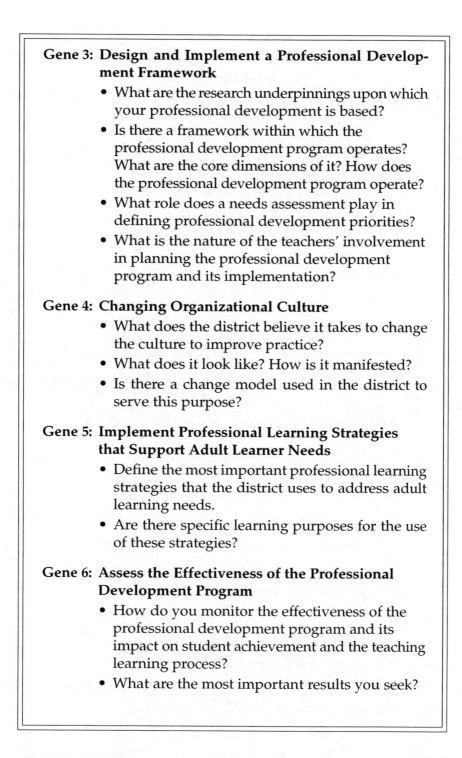

Gene 3: Design and Implement a Professional Development Framework

- What are the research underpinnings upon which your professional development is based?
- Is there a framework within which the professional development program operates? What are the core dimensions of it? How does the professional development program operate?
- What role does a needs assessment play in defining professional development priorities?
- What is the nature of the teachers' involvement in planning the professional development program and its implementation?

Gene 4: Changing Organizational Culture

- What does the district believe it takes to change the culture to improve practice?
- What does it look like? How is it manifested?
- Is there a change model used in the district to serve this purpose?

Gene 5: Implement Professional Learning Strategies that Support Adult Learner Needs

- Define the most important professional learning strategies that the district uses to address adult learning needs.
- Are there specific learning purposes for the use of these strategies?

Gene 6: Assess the Effectiveness of the Professional Development Program

- How do you monitor the effectiveness of the professional development program and its impact on student achievement and the teaching learning process?
- What are the most important results you seek?

Worksheet #3: Professional Development Chromosome

Working Document

Gene (Fundamental Principle) _____

_____

_____

_____

Gene Value Statement _____

_____

_____

_____

DNA (Research-Based Practices)   If applicable, indicate the chromosome these practices are connected to; if they are connected to a specific gene or DNA piece from another chromosome, indicate as such.

List those genes and/or DNA that you would like to develop more fully in the future and draw appropriate connections to other chromosomes as done above.

Capacity-Building
Chromosomes Worksheets

YOUR DISTRICT CHROMOSOME

Worksheet #1: Your District
Chromosome Diagram

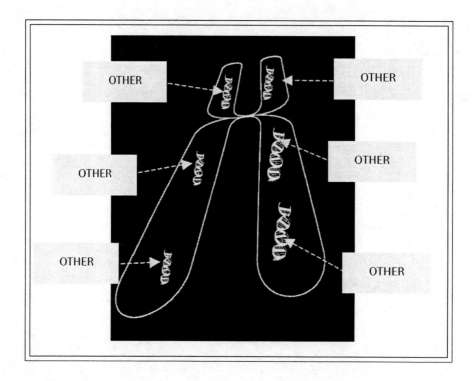

Worksheet #2: Your District Chromosome Guiding Questions

(To be completed by reader)

Gene 1:

-
-

Gene 2:

-
-

Gene 3:

-
-

Gene 4:

-
-

Gene 5:

-
-

Gene 6:

-
-

Worksheet #3: Your District Chromosome

Working Document

Your District Chromosome _____

Gene (Fundamental Principle) _____

_____

_____

_____

Gene Value Statement _____

_____

_____

_____

DNA (Research-Based Practices)

If applicable, indicate the chromosome these practices are connected to; if they are connected to a specific gene or DNA piece from another chromosome, indicate as such.

List those genes and/or DNA that you would like to develop more fully in the future and draw appropriate connections to other chromosomes as done above.

Summary

Leadership Chromosome

- A modern organization distributes leadership roles to members of the staff.
- Leadership is an important chromosome and essential for successful implementation of the genetic model.
- Leaders should change behavior when their strategies are not working effectively.

Change Chromosome

- Change is a reality of life for organizations in the 21st century and educators must engage in inquiry about new findings regarding how students learn.
- The district must maintain a sense of stability within the context of continuous change.
- In nurturing the change process, various dimensions of change must be addressed such as implementing change at a reasonable pace, monitoring its impact on the organizational culture, realizing unknown factors arise and have an impact on initiatives, dealing productively with the inevitability of resistance and conflict, and developing a mindset to be a change agent in the organization.
- Change must be implemented within the context of the district's preferred future. The district must be selective about the initiatives that will have the greatest impact on raising student achievement and moving closer to world-class performance.
- The district must build the capacity of its staff to implement the new initiative by creating a culture of continuous improvement, developing a shared vision of the initiative, valuing inquiry and study by teachers, mastering content and skills for effectiveness, creating collaborative groups and partnerships to enhance professional learning, and providing reasonable time allocations for the change process to be successful.
- Sustaining momentum for change initiatives requires proactive steps, which include selecting benchmarks of progress, celebrating incremental successes, being prepared

to make adjustments, implementing a mentoring process to train staff that are new to the project, developing a long-range action plan, and evaluating the change process to determine its effectiveness.

Professional Development Chromosome

- The six genes, philosophy statement/purpose/goals, content knowledge, research, changing organizational culture and assessing the professional development program provide the framework for having a world-class education staff.
- Professional development programs should involve participants in group activities.
- Professional development activities should build teacher content knowledge and improve instructional practice.
- It is essential to plan professional development programs as multi-year projects with specific goals for improved student achievement.

Endnotes

22. Colin Powell, *Lessons on leadership. http://blaisdell.com/powell*
23. "Motorola: can Chris Galvin save his family's legacy?" Roger O. Crockett, *Business Week* (July 16, 2001).
24. Warren Bennis, *Managing people is like herding cats* (Provo, Utah: Executive Excellence Publishing, 1997).
25. Edward M. Marshall, *Building trust at the speed of change* (New York: Amacom Books, 2000), p. 5.
26. Warren Bennis, *Managing people is like herding cats.*
27. John P. Kotter, *Leading change* (Harvard Business Press, 1996).
28. Michael Fullan, *Change forces: probing the depths of educational reform* (London: Falmer Press, 1993), pp. 12–41.
29. Fullan, *Change forces: probing the depths of educational reform,* p. 25.
30. Patterson, *Coming clean about organizational change,* pp. 7–14.
31. Fullan, *Change forces: probing the depths of educational reform, pp. vii–viii.*
32. Kotter, *Leading change.*
33. Richard T. Pascale, *Managing on the edge* (New York: Touchston, 1990).

34. Senge, *The fifth discipline*, p. 281.
35. Patterson, *Coming clean about organizational change*, p. 8.
36. Michael Fullan, Seminar on Educational Change (Urbana, IL, March 1999).
37. Fullan, Seminar on Educational Change.
38. Fullan, *Change forces: probing the depths of educational reform*, pp. 5–6.
39. Fullan, *Change forces: probing the depths of educational reform*, pp. 42–84.
40. Senge, *The fifth discipline*, p. 142.
41. Bennis, *Managing people is like herding cats*, p. 11.
42. Fullan, *Change forces: probing the depths of educational reform*, pp. 3–6.
43. Fullan, *Change forces: probing the depths of educational reform*, pp. 15–17.
44. Senge, *The fifth discipline*, p. 73.
45. Andrew Porter, et al, "Does professional development change teaching practice? Results from a three-year study," (Washington, DC: U.S. Department of Education, 2000).
46. "Effective professional development systems," paper prepared for the Council of Chief State School Officers Annual Meeting (1998), Consortium for Policy Research in Education.
47. Elmore, "Getting to scale with good educational practice."
48. Marshall, *Building trust at the speed of change*.
49. Richard Sagor, *Guiding school improvement with action research* (ASCD: Alexandria, VA, 2001), pp. 4–7.

Chapter 5

The Teaching-Learning Chromosomes

Overview of Key Concepts

- The Teaching-Learning Chromosomes (Core Areas) are the "Rigorous Academic Program" components that comprise the substance of what students learn and how they learn it.

- Three core areas comprise the Teaching-Learning Chromosomes: The Curriculum Chromosome, the Instructional Practice Chromosome, and the Assessment Chromosome.

- The interaction of the Teaching-Learning Chromosomes makes it possible to continually improve the academic program for students.

- Each district must determine its own set of organizational "genes" and "DNA" that will define how it will operate and what products it seeks to develop.

Curriculum Chromosome
- Local control of curriculum has been as much a hindrance to student learning as it has been a protection from unwanted subject matter.
- Standards provide the basis of rigorous curriculum for all students to learn but they must be implemented with a balanced view in mind.

- The written curriculum must be built with coherence and rigor.
- A curriculum revision process serves to guide the improvement of curriculum.
- The alignment of instructional materials to the curriculum ensures coherent instruction.
- Evaluating the curriculum determines whether it is achieving its intended expectations.

Instructional Practice Chromosome

- A shared language is essential for working collaboratively on instructional practice.
- Providing time for teachers to reflect on instructional practice and build content knowledge is an important priority.
- Knowledge of learning theory is essential for all teachers.
- Only high-quality instruction is acceptable.

Assessment Chromosome

- Assessment is the most underutilized of the three teaching-learning process chromosomes.
- Teachers and administrators need to become assessment literate in order to take advantage of the information that data have to offer.
- Districts must build a cultural context for using assessment data.
- An assessment program must identify clear purposes and goals.
- An assessment framework is needed to help teachers gather, use, and interpret data, and it must be an integral part of the district assessment program.
- Evaluating the assessment program will help to determine if it is having a positive impact on the teaching-learning process.

Introduction

In chapter 4, we addressed the Capacity-Building Chromosomes that enable the school district to create the contextual environment to implement a rigorous academic program. We now turn to the substance of schooling for students, the Teaching-Learning Process Chromosomes. These consist of Curriculum, Instructional Practice, and Assessment.

As a caveat for studying these chromosomes, we recommend that districts develop all three. It is important for a district to clarify how it will approach the development and implementation of these core areas. We contend that there must be a clear alignment among the curriculum, instructional practices, and the assessment practices of the school district. This alignment provides the means to ensure that each area interacts effectively with the other.

These chromosomes explore the content of what is expected to be learned, the instructional delivery system, and the measurement of growth components of the learning process. First, the Curriculum Chromosome makes clear what we expect students to learn and recognizes that over time the focus needs to be altered. Therefore, a well-developed curriculum is essential.

Second, we must explore and modify the way that students are taught. Regular examination, analysis, and evaluation of the impact of instructional practice are the keys to helping students learn at high levels. Research has isolated and verified many effective instructional practices that have a positive impact on learning. This research is not a critique of the teacher but the process for improving teaching. Study and reflecting on instruction provide the fundamentals for instructional improvement. Therefore, educators must move beyond a myopic view of focusing on teachers to analyzing teaching and the effects that various instructional practices have on student learning.

Third, student progress must be assessed, instruction informed by using data, programs evaluated, and reports provided to stakeholders. A well-developed assessment program makes valuable use of data to inform appropriate decisions that guide teachers to more focused instruction with students.

This relationship is depicted in Figure 5.1.

FIGURE 5.1—THE INTEGRATIVE NATURE OF THE TEACHING-LEARNING PROCESS

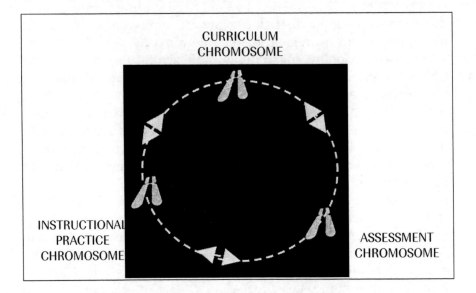

CURRICULUM
CHROMOSOME

INSTRUCTIONAL
PRACTICE
CHROMOSOME

ASSESSMENT
CHROMOSOME

As in chapter 4, we present a discussion of the research under-pinnings for the three chromosomes in Section I. Section II then provides readers with the opportunity to build the three chromo-somes for their own districts.

In this chapter we will present a clear alignment of the three areas and contend that they must always be viewed collectively in order to provide a rigorous academic program. If viewed and imple-mented in this manner, student achievement will improve.

Section I

Curriculum Chromosome

Introduction

School districts have sought to maintain local control of curriculum for over one hundred years. The notion of deciding what is the most important content knowledge and what are the most important skills for students to learn provides a sense of security for a district in that what students learn can be as political as it is cognitive. This control over what students learn will continue to be a cultural aspect of American schools.

Maintaining control over the content of learning has a benefit for a local community but can also provide a danger. Primarily, the danger is districts could take a myopic view of what students should learn. Students could be deprived of learning specific content and skills that are vital to their development. They would be woefully prepared to function in a global society. The TIMSS study and second administration of TIMSS in 1999 provide convincing evidence that American students are, in fact, not being challenged in the same way that international students are because American school districts tend to make local decisions that result in low expectations. Consequently, many U.S. students do not compete favorably on an international basis.

In an age when mobility is common there is reason to be concerned that students are not given reasonably consistent opportunities to learn and be well educated. The development of nationally accepted standards is an appealing thought but raises concern that a "national curriculum" might be instituted. We do have middle ground on this issue with the development of content standards in the various subject areas. International frameworks for assessment also provide a global context for viewing learning standards. These standards, coupled with state learning standards, provide a reasonable set of curricular guidelines that school districts can use to develop local curricula.

We believe that no matter where students are educated in the United States, their jobs will take them all over the world, even when performed from the comfort of their own homes. The information society has broken down the school walls as the sole environment for learning. Instructional practices that involve collaboration of students outside of the school use the world as a new learning environment (classroom).

We are highlighting this issue because the notion of local control has been as much a hindrance to student development as it has been a protection from exposure to unwanted subject matter. While communities may seek to control what students learn, they must bear in mind that they are preparing students for a global society. Sheltering students from specific content and ideas in today's society is like trying to capture running water in your hands. It is not possible. Providing a constructive environment to study controversial topics may be a more productive way for students to be introduced to them.

School districts have been writing and revising local curricula for years and will continue to do so, but it must be done with the understanding that there is much to be learned from a global perspective. To provide a world-class curriculum means offering students the opportunity to learn and problem-solve using content and skills that enable them to be part of a worldwide community of excellence. It is with this perspective that we address the development of the curriculum chromosome.

As we develop this chromosome, it will be important to make some distinctions between the terms curriculum framework and curriculum. They each represent different components of the larger curricular program. For the purposes of this discussion, a curriculum framework is defined as the set of core standards, topics, concepts, and skills that students will be expected to learn and when those learnings should be mastered. The curriculum is what we view as the units of study, lessons, activities, and tasks that teachers use to instruct students. These are typically developed in-district. These units of study include instructional materials that are purchased for classroom use. The focus of this chromosome is to build the curriculum framework. We recognize that once this component is determined, the units of study will naturally follow. It is not our intent to delve into the process of writing curriculum units; rather, it is in developing the curriculum concepts and skills to be learned.

What then become the most important principles that need to be included in the development of a world-class curriculum? We present five genes for districts to develop in the writing and revision of curricula:

1. Define the Role Standards Play in the Curriculum.
2. Write the Standards and Curriculum: Build Coherence and Rigor.
3. Follow a Curriculum Revision Process.
4. Align Standards, Curriculum, and Instructional Materials.
5. Evaluate the Curriculum.

Curriculum Chromosome: Five Genes

Define the Role Standards Play in the Curriculum

Prior to the mid-1980s there were few nationally accepted guidelines to help local educators define a set of core content standards and skills. As a result, there was a lack of consistency across school districts and states with respect to what students were expected to learn. While there were curriculum models available to assist in writing curriculum, the "what" and "when to teach it" were not well formulated. School districts primarily used textbooks to guide what they taught to students. They used the scope and sequence charts in the textbooks to help them. This resource actually provided some curricular structure for school districts, but it actually led them to be textbook-driven in their approach to curriculum. In essence, if a school district selected what it believed was a "good" textbook, it believed it had a good curriculum.

The beginning of the standards movement in the mid-1980s brought a focused emphasis on determining what students should learn to be well educated. School districts then could determine the best instructional materials to use. Almost every state in the country now has legislated learning standards for school districts. The districts must have local curricula to reflect these standards. State assessments are given at selected grade levels to determine if students are meeting the learning standards.

Textbook-driven vs. Standards-based Approach to Writing Curriculum

At this point it is worth making some distinctions between a textbook-driven and standards-based approach. A textbook-driven approach uses a dependence on the textbook as the curriculum rather than as one instructional resource; the goal is to teach the content of the book without regard for identifying the most important concepts and skills. Therefore, the rigor and coherence of the curriculum rests solely on the quality of the textbook. A standards-based approach stands in contrast to a textbook-driven approach in that it seeks to define a core set of benchmarks, concepts, and skills to be learned by students. This approach requires school districts to develop a philosophy and rationale that underpins the very nature of the district's curriculum. Moreover, it promotes the notion that districts can decide when student mastery of concepts and skills should occur, the sequence in which they will be taught, and the amount of instructional emphasis that will be devoted to learning these core concepts and skills.

The Standards Paradox

by Andrew Rotherham

Director of the 21st Century Schools Project at the Progressive Policy Institute

This is a book about standards, about measurement, and about using data to make educational decisions and improve the quality of education that youngsters receive in schools. One would assume that these things would be noncontroversial, however standards, assessments, and the meaning of the corresponding data are some of the most contentious issues in education today.

While there are some who attack standards and testing to protect adult interests and thwart the push for greater accountability for schools, most critics of the push for higher standards are well intentioned. They believe that standards and assessments stifle creativity in schools, turn schools into test-preparation centers rather than places of learning, and measure only superficial knowledge and memorization, not real learning.

Some critics raise valid points. When confronted with low test scores too many schools have simply piled on more of the same rather than re-evaluate their curriculum and instructional program. In some places schools have simply taught to the test rather than seek to refine their instructional methods to ensure that students are learning the more challenging material that states have incorporated into their curriculum during the past 10 years. However, these criticisms don't impugn the drive to higher standards and better assessments, only the implementation of this effort in some communities and schools. And, these issues can be addressed and corrected with strong leadership and sufficient support.

The larger criticism, however, that standards will result in the standardization of schools misses one of the most promising aspects of the standards movement. Standards, rather than restricting innovation and flexibility in schools are actually the instrument that could usher in a new era of greater innovation and choice in public education. For the first time clear expectations exist for the academic performance of schools. forty-nine states have developed a common set of standards, statewide, laying out the content that students are expected to master in at least math and reading. While not putting the issue to rest, common standards do allow us to move past the tired argument about what we should expect from our schools in terms of outcomes. For better or worse, states now have established expectations for what students should know and be able to do at some specific points during their education.

And these common expectations present a paradox, because in their commonality lay the potential for great diversity. The paradox of standards is that rather than restrict the diversity of schools, standards can unleash it. If we can arrive at a common set of expectations for what students should be able to do, then we can focus on those educational results and less on the particular educational delivery model. A range of schools, theme schools, focus schools, charter schools, even virtual schools can all compete for students so long as they are meeting these defined benchmarks or outcomes. What should be most attractive about this approach to the current crop of testing critics is that this diversity means instructional diversity—different methods suited for different children. This way, both adults and children can gravitate toward schools with educational philosophies that they are comfortable with, rather than being restricted to what are frequently now, standardized schools.

Such a system, where the publicness of a school is less defined by the particular governance arraignment than by its admissions and performance criteria, will move us past the stale debate over vouchers as

continued

well. In a standards-based system any school that agrees to admit all students (space permitting or in an equitable fashion) and be held accountable for meeting publicly defined performance standards is a public school. Whether this school is run by the school district, a local community group, or even a faith-based organization (in a secular manner) is largely irrelevant as long as the school is open to all and meeting standards defined by and for all. Likewise, schools that don't wish to abide by these public guidelines will not be eligible to receive taxpayer support. This is essentially the charter school concept writ large, entire school districts made up of schools of choice, open to all students and competing for their attendance, and free to pursue various missions and focuses so long as commonly defined performance benchmarks are met.

This book illustrates how better standards can lead to better instruction and more learning for students. This is the immediate promise of the reforms of the last decade. However, these same standards can also spark a fundamental rethinking of what a public school is and in the process create a greater diversity of high quality schools for students. That is the long-term promise, and paradox, of standards. (*http://www.ppionline.org*)

A standards-based approach encourages districts to think carefully about what core knowledge and skills students are expected to learn at each grade level. It helps school districts to be clear and conversant about what children should learn and by when.

When a district uses a standards based approach we offer some caution. It must be implemented with a balanced view in mind. On the one hand, a standards-based approach promotes greater clarity of purpose and sets the benchmarks for what students should know and be able to do. It clearly defines the core learning in each discipline. However, it should not define the totality of the curriculum. By this we mean that there must be freedom for teachers to explore their own inquiry in teaching. Teachers have gifts, talents, and interests that should manifest themselves throughout their instruction. Some of this may not fall within the identified core standards to be learned. These areas of teacher specialty and interest should be linked to professional development and the school or district goals and initiatives. In other words, these inquiry areas should be taught with the knowledge and approval of district leadership.

A concern with the standards-based approach is that it may be used to make unrealistic promises or inappropriate expectations. For example, there is the political reality for school districts to score well on large-scale assessments such as state assessments. State legislators proclaim this expectation. However, it is easy to talk the standards game, but sooner or later tests need to measure whether the standards are reached. School districts need to be supported in their improvement efforts. If they do not meet the standards immediately, they should not be viewed as failing schools; rather, their performance should be evaluated in light of their improvement over time.

Second, assessment results measuring standards are sometimes used to embarrass districts. This concept may be flawed. Districts need to be encouraged to improve and be given reasonable time and support to do so.

Third, the standards movement contains the seeds of its own heresy. Striving for high standards should not be confused with standardizing the teaching-learning process. Standardizing tends to prescribe how to teach and how to measure the accomplishment of standards. This approach does not take into consideration differences in people—both in the way students learn and teachers teach. Teachers must be open to explore new ways of teaching and learning. If we standardize processes and procedures, we run the risk of locking into the practices of the past, not looking at inquiry for the future. We must continue to seek ways to effectively help students learn and promote those instructional strategies that best suit their learning styles. Therefore, the standards movement should be about achieving high standards not about prescribing standardized approaches.

Interestingly, many school districts still depend on textbooks to serve as their curricular focus. The textbook companies now provide supplementary materials to align their lessons with the state standards. These materials can be helpful if a district uses a standards-based approach because they can align the textbook to their set of standards, not merely follow the textbook. There is a difference.

Textbooks often do not provide a coherent and focused curricular program. The textbook analysis from the TIMSS study clearly demonstrates that American textbooks are not coherent and lack focus and rigor in comparison to many textbooks from other countries where student performance on the TIMSS was at the highest levels. For example, in Japan the typical middle school textbooks are approximately 200 pages compared with the typical American textbook of approximately 700 pages. The Japanese textbooks are organized with a clear content focus and an appropriate progression of concepts and skills for students. We recommend that the reader examine *Splintered Vision*[50] for a complete study of American textbooks from the TIMSS.

Using Standards to Develop Core Curriculum
What role then should standards play in the development of curriculum in a school district? First, state standards should be one of the basic elements of the district curriculum because the district will be held accountable for meeting them.

Second, we would encourage a district to look at other reliable standards documents that have a more global view of curricular expectations. There are several credible content standards documents with which to compare, build, or revise a district curriculum. Take for example the mathematics and science disciplines. Several of the content standards documents listed in Table 5.1 and Table 5.2 have similarities and differences in content and design. One commonality among them is that they all typically contain more content than a district can reasonably address; therefore, the district is obliged to make careful choices of what will be taught.

Standards documents selected by districts will be influenced by any prior curriculum analysis that has been conducted. This analysis should identify strengths and weaknesses in the existing curriculum. What we encourage is that the district raise questions from the analysis of its current curriculum and then seek solutions to problems that were identified. As the district revises the curriculum, it is important to examine and align it with two or three content standards documents that are comprehensive and that will support the strengths and enhance those areas where weaknesses exist. As afore mentioned, we suggest districts make one of those comparative documents their state's published content standards. This document will no doubt be one to which the district will be held accountable. Suggested content standards documents the district can use for mathematics and science include the following:

TABLE 5.1—DOCUMENTS TO CONSULT FOR REVISING YOUR MATHEMATICS PROGRAM
Content Knowledge: A Compendium of Standards and Benchmarks for K-12 Education (Kendall, J.S. & Marzano, R.J. (2nd Ed., 1997).
Benchmarks for Science Literacy and Standards for Science Literacy. Project 2061.
Mathematics Framework for the 1996 National Assessment of Educational Progress. National Assessment of Educational Progress. (n.d.)
Principles and Standards for School Mathematics. NCTM. (2000.)
California Mathematics Content Standards Prepublication Edition, Feb. 2, 1998.
Terra Nova (Grades 4 & 8), CTB/McGraw Hill.
TIMSS Mathematics Items: Released Set for Population 1 (Third and Fourth Grades) - All publicly released items used to assess third- and fourth-grade students in the TIMSS study.
TIMSS Mathematics Items: Released Set for Population 2 (Seventh and Eighth Grades) - All publicly released items used to assess seventh- and eighth-grade students in the TIMSS study.
Mathematics Program in Japan (1990)
Primary Mathematics Guide (1A & 1B) (Singapore 1994).

TABLE 5.2—DOCUMENTS TO CONSULT FOR REVISING YOUR SCIENCE PROGRAM
Content Knowledge: A Compendium of Standards and Benchmarks for K-12 Education (Kendall, J.S. & Marzano, R.J. (2nd Ed., 1997).
Benchmarks for Science Literacy and Standards for Science Literacy. Project 2061.
Science Framework for the 1996 National Assessment of Educational Progress. National Assessment of Educational Progress. (n.d.)
Terra Nova (Grades 4 & 8), CTB/McGraw Hill.
TIMSS Science Items: Released Set for Population 1 (Third and Fourth Grades) - All publicly released items used to assess third- and fourth-grade students in the TIMSS study.
TIMSS Science Items: Released Set for Population 2 (Seventh and Eighth Grades) - All publicly released items used to assess seventh- and eighth-grade students in the TIMSS study.

We encourage school districts to define the specific grade levels in which they expect mastery of concepts and skills. Standards documents are typically presented in grade-level groupings called bands, for example, grades K–2, grades 3–5, grades 6–8, and grades 9–12. We believe banding leads to clustering concepts and including them in all of the representative grades rather than identifying the specific grade level where the concepts should be mastered. Consequently there is unnecessary repetition and a lack of coherence and rigor. We address this issue in depth in the following section of the chapter.

School districts should learn how to set, measure, and reach standards. Marc Tucker and Judy Codding, president and vice-president of the National Center on Education and the Economy, provide a compelling case for setting high academic standards using rich assessments to measure progress. Their book, *Standards for Our Schools: How to Set Them, Measure Them, and Reach Them,* provides an excellent analysis of how standards can be developed and attained.[51] We suggest our readers use this resource to support their development of a standards-based curriculum.

Write the Standards and Curriculum: Build Coherence and Rigor

School districts have been writing curriculum for many decades; therefore, we do not want to address the actual process of curriculum writing in this book. There are many rich resources available to school districts to assist with the actual writing of lessons, activities, and tasks for the classroom teachers.

We do want to focus on the notion of coherence and rigor of the curriculum. The TIMSS study found that the U.S. mathematics and science curricula were not coherent or rigorous in comparison to curricula from high-achieving countries.

When we speak of coherence in the curriculum we focus on three distinct but related ideas: (1) breadth of the curriculum, (2) flow of the curriculum, and (3) duration of time that topics, concepts, and skills remain in the curriculum.

Breadth of the curriculum refers to the number and range of topics, concepts, and skills that are taught at each grade level. Some topics may be taught with less emphasis while others may be taught in greater depth. The breadth of curriculum needs to be such that a teacher can devote sufficient attention to developing conceptual understanding of the topic.

If there are too many topics, concepts, and skills to teach, it stands to reason that some or all of them will not be given the emphasis needed for students to learn what is most important. In the TIMSS study of mathematics, there were substantially more topics in the U.S. curriculum than in curricula from high-performing nations. This led to the conclusion that only limited attention was being given to most topics and student mastery was difficult to attain.[52] Students should be taught a reasonable number of concepts in any given year and be expected to understand them.

Flow is the progression of topics, concepts, and skills entering and leaving the curriculum from early elementary through high school. The issue here is to identify the appropriate grade levels to introduce concepts and skills—appropriate, in the sense of being developmentally appropriate for the age of students. (Developmentally appropriate is determining when a typical student should reasonably be expected to master specific concepts and skills.) TIMSS found mathematics topics frequently entered the curriculum at an early grade level and remained in the curriculum for many years.

More challenging topics such as algebra and geometry concepts were not readily present in the U.S. curriculum, even in the middle school years. The concepts and skills of these topics were not being taught, and their absence was markedly apparent in comparison with the international counterparts that performed well. The U.S. curriculum emphasized arithmetic topics throughout the middle school years and did not focus on more rigorous topics.

As a school district addresses the issue of flow, it needs to determine very specifically when it wants to introduce and emphasize various concepts and skills. It also must determine when it expects a typical student to master them. Once mastered, that topic, concept, or skill should be removed from the curriculum and other, more challenging, concepts should be introduced.

Curricular duration refers to the number of years (or grades) that topics, concepts, and skills are retained in the curriculum. The U.S. curriculum maintains topics in the curriculum two years longer on average than the international mean. Many mathematics topics remain in the curriculum for seven to eight grade levels before they exit the curriculum. This extended duration is reinforced in most American textbooks. School districts that are textbook-driven will, by default, spend considerable time on topics that are more arithmetic rather than complex, such as algebra or geometry. When topics remain in the curriculum for extended amounts of time, less emphasis will be given to the more rigorous concepts that students need to learn.

Coherence begins with the standards that are defined by the district. It then carries through to the lessons that are taught and, ultimately, to the assessments that are used to measure progress. There must be a logical sequence of topics and concepts through the grade levels to build deeper understanding of the subject matter. It is important to consciously plan a coherent curriculum.

When we speak of the rigor of the curriculum we refer to how academically challenging it is and the depth of understanding that is expected of students on each topic. As we examine curriculum for its rigor, we would look at two specific areas: the degree of topic difficulty at specific grade levels and the diversity of topics at specific grade levels.

One analysis of rigor examines the degree of difficulty with respect to topics at specific grade levels. Is a district teaching topics and concepts that are developmentally appropriate and at a proper difficulty for the grade level? For example, are children in younger grades addressing number sense, fractions, decimals, and so forth, and are students in the higher grades learning algebra, geometry, data representation, and so forth? Is a district deciding to have more challenging topics taught at lower grade levels contingent on the students' learning abilities? When students are capable of learning challenging topics at an early age, they should be provided the opportunity to learn them.

Second, the number of topics and concepts at a grade level can have an impact on rigor depending on the amount of emphasis that is given to these topics. If a district has too many topics at a grade level, there is a possibility that some topics are not being thoroughly covered. Students may not be acquiring a comprehensive understanding of the concepts, hence, less rigor.

It is important to remember that breadth, duration, and flow are all critical components of how rigorous a curriculum may be. We suggest that a district conduct a review of all the topics, concepts and skills taught from grade level to grade level in a subject area and draw some inferences about the rigor of the curriculum. Any district interested in conducting this type of review in mathematics and science should contact the North Central Regional Educational Laboratory or log onto the NCREL Web site at *www.ncrel.org/currmap* for an interactive process to complete an analysis in these areas. We also would refer the reader to the *TIMSS-1999 Guidebook* (2002) for a structured curriculum analysis process that includes these concepts. A curriculum analysis to address coherence and rigor will help a district identify curricular patterns and make statements about the substance of the current curriculum.

Once a school district has an understanding of its curricular program, the next step is to compare that information with state and national content standards documents. This was discussed in the previous section on standards. The purpose of this next step is to identify, by grade level, content standards, concepts, and skills that comprise a coherent and rigorous curriculum. It is in this phase of analysis that a district must make decisions about when a typical student should learn specific concepts and skills and when mastery of those concepts and skills is expected.

The outcome of this task will provide the district with a grade level framework of content standards to which it can begin to write lessons, activities, and tasks and/or align these standards with relevant instructional materials. In appendix C we offer a suggested seven-step process for developing a coherent and rigorous curriculum framework upon which to write a curriculum.

Follow a Curriculum Revision Process

Articulating a curriculum revision process is an important task for all school districts. It indicates the cycle to revise the district programs and serves several purposes. First, it helps to guide school district efforts to maintain up-to-date curricular programs. Second, it provides a visual timeline of the various revision initiatives. Some programs can be revised in a brief amount of time while others will take considerably longer. It is important to know when projects will start and finish, how many revision initiatives are occurring at any given time, and what the expectations will be for the staff to implement them.

Third, a curriculum revision cycle provides a plan for all staff members to know when specific expectations will be a priority in the district. Ultimately, it will signal when teachers will need to assume the responsibility to learn a new program. This cycle must coincide with the professional development plan so that districts give proper emphasis to the current priorities. Finally, it articulates a detailed approach for updating the curriculum. Phases of the revision process guide staff through the steps leading to the new program. The curriculum revision process helps to assure staff members that the district is not vacillating from one fad to another. It conveys a well-thought out, systemic approach to updating curriculum, and prepares staff members to effectively implement new curricular programs.

If there is one critical feature to remember about curriculum revision, it is that professional development must be a required component. We have heard from many teachers that they were given a new curriculum to teach but not the support to learn and implement it effectively. They receive new instructional materials (such as textbooks) but are not given the training to use them as intended. As a result, they are not able to implement the program effectively. They also cannot inform parents about the value of the change. Parents become confused about why the new curriculum is being implemented and the district devotes considerable time to defending it rather than educating parents as to why the new approach is better. When teachers do not have the training, they cannot effectively communicate the rationale for the new program.

We have outlined a curriculum revision model, which presents a systemic approach for curricular review and development. This is one approach to curriculum revision. We encourage districts to use whatever approach best meets their needs. The most important factor is that a process should be in place. It should be implemented and adjusted as necessary, and it should be communicated to staff, the board of education, and parents.

Four Phase Curriculum Revision Model

The curriculum revision model we present includes four phases: Evaluation/Research, Revision/Writing, Implementation/Professional Development, and Refinement. This curriculum revision model is intended to help teachers, administrators, parents, community members, and the board of education understand the process of curricular development and revision. Ultimately, the curriculum revision model should be used to produce continued improvements in the educational program.

FIGURE 5.2—FOUR PHASES OF THE CURRICULUM REVISION PROCESS

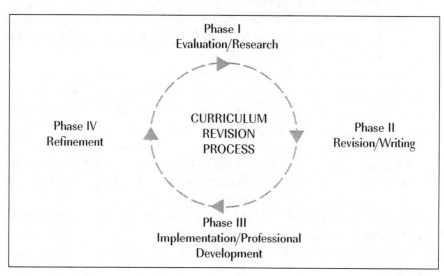

The relationship of the four phases is illustrated in Figure 5.2. The model outlines the nature of curriculum evaluation, revision, implementation, and refinement based on principles of continuous improvement. It also highlights the important relationship that exists between curriculum revision, instructional delivery, assessments, and professional development. Following is a description of the phases:

Phase I: Evaluation/Research. Phase I requires a careful examination of the existing district curriculum in light of current research and effective practices regarding content, skill development, instructional strategies, and assessment. Through an internal and/or external review, analysis of the curricular strengths and areas for improvement should be conducted. State and national professional standards can serve as a guide for the review and provide new directions, purposes, and objectives of the curricular program.

There are several key tasks in this phase of the process. They include:

- Conduct an internal and/or external review of your existing program to identify strengths and areas for improvement to the program.
- Determine the level of coherence and rigor (gap analysis, breadth, duration, flow) in the current program.
- Review current research in this discipline and identify new ideas and approaches.
- Identify/confirm the project scope and timeline to complete the revision process based on the extent of revision that is necessary.

Phase II: Revision/Writing. Phase II is the actual revision of the program. Standards, outcomes, concepts, skills, and ideas are developed in this phase of review. Identification sheets referred to in appendix C should be completed at this stage of the process. Specific units, activities, resources, and student assessments are also developed. These are related to specific curricular outcomes for each grade level, K–12. Articulation of curricular outcomes, instructional approaches, and materials is also an essential task in this phase. Products and activities developed in this phase culminate into the completion of a curriculum document.

There are several key tasks in this phase of the process. They include:

- Identify core standards, concepts, skills (standards documents).
- Make revisions to curriculum.
- Verify coherence and rigor of the revised curriculum.
- Develop lesson strategies.
- Identify instructional materials.
- Align instructional materials with curricular objectives.
- Plan and begin to deliver professional development to support staff members.
- Conduct pilot activities of the revisions as appropriate.
- Develop assessments that measure student learning of the new curriculum.

Phase III: Implementation/Professional Development. It is during Phase III that teachers and administrators deliver the new program and assess student progress. It is also the phase where extensive professional development is offered. This professional development should be ongoing for the staff as they deliver the curriculum. Teachers and administrators will need the necessary support to make lasting changes in instructional practice. Finally, teachers begin to identify areas to refine the curriculum. By this we mean that teachers will discover issues with the curriculum and materials and suggest modifications to met the intended goals of the programs. We introduce the concept of refinement because we believe that curriculum and materials should continuously be improved as teachers become knowledgeable about the details of it. Continuous evaluation of the program is expected during this phase.

There are several key tasks in Phase III. They include:

- Offer ongoing professional development for staff members.
- Implement the new program.
- Administer the new assessments.
- Identify areas of the curriculum or instructional materials that may need refinement.

Phase IV: Refinement. Phase IV includes the careful review of the curriculum and assessments as they have been implemented during the first two years. This phase allows for modification of the curriculum and the assessments as well as the augmentation of new materials. Many of these modifications will have been identified from Phase III implementation. It is also the time to review instructional approaches being used and the analysis of student achievement data to determine if students are making expected progress. Refinement of instructional approaches is necessary as a commitment to meeting the diverse needs of the students and maintaining the integrity of the written curriculum and intended outcomes. Assessment data will identify if students are achieving at the levels expected. If they are not, then the assessments should uncover when there is a curriculum issue or an assessment adjustment is warranted. Finally, professional development opportunities should be planned and provided to support the new refinements.

There are several key tasks in this phase of the process. They include:

- Review assessments and assessment data to discover areas of needed modification.
- Make refinements to program.
- Make refinements to instructional approaches.
- Make refinements to assessments as needed.
- Implement refinements to program.

The curriculum revision process provides an excellent opportunity for staff members, the board of education, and the community to learn how the district is attempting to improve. It also demonstrates that changes in the program and its delivery take time. In some cases, a revision process could take several years. This process will help the board of education members support the change effort and provide the necessary time to accomplish the task properly. There is often a tendency in schools to view change in small time increments (for example, 10-month increments beginning in August and ending in June). Change does not work that way, yet educators try to orchestrate it in neatly packaged time frames. Change initiatives must be developed in a thoughtful and substantive manner.

Align Standards, Curriculum, and Instructional Materials

Aligning the instructional materials and curriculum (lessons) to the curricular framework is a crucial, yet under-emphasized task. Without this very important task, teachers do not know exactly what lessons they should or should not teach to meet the core learning standards, concepts, and skills. A tight alignment of these components will result in greater coherence and academic rigor in that teachers will be able to determine precisely what to teach, the extent to which concepts and skills are emphasized, and how they align in adjacent grades.

The purpose of alignment is to identify the desired lessons and activities to be taught from the instructional materials, by grade level, and to determine what lessons, if any, need to be added, deleted, or moved to another grade level, or newly created to effectively focus on the concepts and skills that should be learned by students. There are no commercially produced programs available that will directly align to the district's locally developed curricular framework using a standards-based approach. The best way to secure a one-to-one alignment is to design the district's materials locally. Unfortunately, this is a cost prohibitive approach for most districts (both financially and through using staff resources). It is more prudent to select materials that most closely align with the district's framework and modify them to address the coherence and rigor issues.

The value of a tight alignment is that it focuses instruction on only those topics, concepts, and skills that the district wants students to learn. In most cases, the textbook that is used will contain lessons on substantially more concepts than the district wants included in the curriculum. There may also be lessons that should be included at another grade level. In some cases, the district may have identified concepts to be taught but the instructional materials do not address them. Therefore, teachers are left to devise their own lessons. In many cases, the concept may never be taught because there are no specific lessons and activities available to the teacher, and there are other lessons in the textbook making it more expedient to teach what is literally at the teacher's fingertips.

If a district were interested in exploring a process for aligning the district's instructional materials to the district curriculum standards and framework, we recommend that it refer to the *TIMSS-1999 Guidebook* for a detailed process. This process provides step-by-step instruction and worksheets that will enable a district to target all lessons that need modification. The outcome of this process is a tightly aligned curricular program.

Evaluate the Curriculum

The final gene on this chromosome is evaluating the curriculum. The essential goal of this gene is to make a commitment for ongoing evaluation of curriculum. Think for a moment about assumptions that we, as educators, make. First, we write a curricular program that we believe is coherent and rigorous. Second, we believe that the program reflects the current research and implements what we know to be the most effective practices in the field. We train the staff for effective implementation, and we believe that a typical student will learn the content, concepts, and skills that are taught. Assume that all of those critical factors are in place. How do you know that the students are learning the curriculum? The answer is to use valid data to assure that the curriculum is achieving its intended expectations.

Student assessment data is the best indicator of how well they are achieving; it provides useful information regarding how well all areas of the curriculum are being learned. Teachers' classroom assessments help to answer important questions such as: Are students learning the curriculum and are they demonstrating proficiency in all aspects of it?

In the earlier section on the curriculum revision cycle, we indicated that assessments must be developed to measure student growth. It is this data that can also answer questions about the appropriateness of the curricular program. This analysis requires that the district have a well-developed assessment program. In a later section of this chapter, we develop the assessment chromosome and address the fundamental questions that pertain to the evaluation of curriculum.

The value of using student achievement data is that a district can analyze the curriculum's effectiveness from the time it is implemented to the present. This analysis is different from the curriculum analysis process outlined earlier because these data are ongoing, longitudinal, and focus on student learning. The data that are used here examine student learning by objective and skill. They also observe student learning over time to determine if there are patterns and trends of student achievement. For example, are there particular concepts or skills on which a majority of students do not perform well? Are these skills consistently low each year at that grade level? Is the program meeting all of the needs of the students?

To answer these questions the leader can determine patterns identified in the data. They can then develop some hypotheses about why the trends are occurring. Some logical hypotheses might include:

- There may be a weakness in the lesson structure on certain concepts.
- Teachers may not be devoting the necessary instructional time for students to learn the concepts and skills.
- These particular concepts may be too difficult for the students to learn at this grade level. Is mastery being expected too soon?
- The test items may not be a reliable and valid measure of what students are being taught. Should the test items be altered to align more closely to the curriculum being taught?
- Students may be performing so well that mastery should be expected earlier than currently identified.

Other hypotheses can be posed to address the impact of the curriculum on student learning. The value of ongoing assessment is that the district can monitor the program and make informed revisions in a timely manner. Districts are encouraged to build curriculum evaluation studies into the revision process and monitor them closely so that appropriate revisions can be made.

In summary, we have introduced five genes that help build the curriculum chromosome. We have presented ideas for the role standards should play in the development of curriculum. We offered a process to study coherence and rigor as well as a model for curriculum revision. We stress the need to align the curricular framework to the actual instructional materials used, and we advocate ongoing evaluation of the curricular program to determine if it meets the intended outcomes. We now turn to the key component of the teaching-learning process: Instructional Practice.

Instructional Practice Chromosome

Introduction

If there were a dominant chromosome in our model, it would unquestionably be instructional practice. You can have effective leadership, consensus about your change process, high-quality professional development, a research-based curriculum, and valid assessment, but if there is not effective instruction for students, world-class student achievement is not possible. Instructional practice refers to the actual process of teaching for world-class achievement. The importance of high-quality instruction is supported in the recommendations of two important national commissions, the National Commission on Teaching and America's Future, (*www.tc. edu/nctaf*) and the National Commission on Mathematics and Science Teaching for the 21st Century (*www.ed.gov/americacounts/glenn*). In the report from the National Commission on Teaching and America's Future, five basic recommendations highlighted the future direction of teaching in America.

1. Get serious about standards, for both students and teachers.
2. Reinvent teacher preparation and professional development.
3. Overhaul teacher recruitment and put qualified teachers in every classroom.
4. Encourage and reward teaching knowledge and skill.
5. Create schools that are organized for student learning.

After an extensive review of research on the American school system, the National Commission on Mathematics and Science Teaching for the 21st Century was assertive in its conclusion that America is not doing the job that it should, or can do, in teaching its children to understand and use ideas from mathematics and science. The Commission believes that the most powerful instrument for change is teaching itself and, therefore, that is the place to begin. It offered the following recommendations regarding teaching:

1. Establish an ongoing system to improve the quality of mathematics and science teaching in grades K–12.
2. Increase significantly the number of mathematics and science teachers and improve the quality of their preparation.
3. Improve the working environment and make the teaching profession more attractive for K–12 mathematics and science teachers.

It is imperative that all teachers use effective teaching methods with consistency of instruction in every classroom. To accomplish this, it is necessary to create an environment for teachers to work collaboratively on teaching the curriculum and writing lessons. Teachers must think systemically about their work and participate in the process as members of learning communities. Simply stated, learning communities are groups of educators working collaboratively on a specific project over a period of time with the intention of improving practice. It is only through the practice of learning communities that teachers will have the opportunity to develop and improve their teaching techniques to meet the diverse needs of today's students.

Seymour Sarason, a prominent education theorist titled one of his recent books, *Teaching As a Performing Art*. In that book Sarason says, "In the theatre an actor is given a script and left to his or her own devices to interpret a role. Although in the process of becoming a role the actor is obviously crucial, it is axiomatic that the actor is an imperfect interpretive instrument. That is why there are many rehearsals before the play opens, and that is why there is a director whose main task is to assist the actor to understand, deepen, and enlarge the myriad of nuances of the role." [53]

This notion applies to our concept of what instruction in the classroom should be. We concur with Sarason's metaphor of teaching being a performing art. Practicing the teaching of lessons before actually facing the class is very important. The process of practicing should engage teachers with similar teaching assignments in an in-depth review of the particular instructional techniques that might be most effective. While this may not be practical for all lessons, it would be realistic for a grade level or department of teachers to select some lessons on which to work. Ideal lessons to select would be those that are considered the most difficult for students to learn. Together the teachers could study lesson development and instructional methods. They should be encouraged to observe their colleagues actually teaching a lesson and then meeting to review what worked well and what needs to be refined. Over a period of time numerous lessons could be revised and improved through this collaborative process.

The entire process should be archived by retaining video samples of the teaching and anecdotal comments of the teachers regarding the lesson. Archiving what they learned from the process can be used to inform future teachers and contribute to the continuous improvement of instructional techniques and lessons. The overarching issue for the instructional practice chromosome is to define the essential fundamental principles (genes) that comprise high-quality instruction.

We have delineated some of the fundamental principles that we believe are essential for high-quality instructional practice. These principles, when properly implemented, will lead to world-class teaching. The principles range from implementation strategies to the recognition that teachers must be empowered to teach. We do not mean using a laissez-faire approach to management; rather we advocate what might be called "guided professionalism". In guided professionalism teachers and their principal work collaboratively using proven effective practices to analyze and improve teaching. The process is grounded on the premise that the group has a positive and trusting relationship. The underlying assumption for the instructional practice chromosome is that when teachers are well trained and have sufficient time for collaboration to effectively implement the other genes (fundamental principles) on this chromosome, high-quality instruction will result. For example, most doctors perform routine procedures on a daily basis, but it is the unanticipated emergency and how they handle it that separates the best from the average. The best doctors are well trained, keep up with developments in their profession, understand their work, and have the latitude to make critical decisions on what to do in situations that call for a different approach. Such is the case for quality teaching.

We have identified eight genes, fundamental principles, for the instructional practice chromosome. As we have noted throughout this book, we are not writing a "how to" manual with prescriptive instructions. Rather, we want our readers to decide which genes best address their specific cultures. We are offering suggestions to consider when attempting to achieve world-class education performance. The eight genes on the instructional practice chromosome are:

1. Develop a Shared Language.
2. Reflect on Improving Instruction and Arrive at Consensus on Effective Instructional Strategies.
3. Understand the Curriculum, Possess Content Knowledge, and Develop Coherent Lessons.
4. Work with High-quality Instructional Materials.
5. Be Knowledgeable of Learning Theory Research, Learning Styles, and Human Development.
6. Use Technology to Enhance Teaching and Learning.

7. Empower Teachers Through Guided Professionalism.
8. Implement a Board Policy that Requires High-quality Instruction.

Instructional Practice Chromosome: Eight Genes

Develop a Shared Language

We are often struck by how educators have a different understanding of common terms used in various areas of education. We have learned that curriculum has different meanings for teachers. Class size interpretation (small or large) can vary depending on regional demographics and the perspective of the teacher or administrator. Assessment and cooperative learning can have different meanings to many teachers. The important point is to be certain that there is a shared and common language used by the participants. Take the time to identify the terms, discuss the definitions with the staff, and maintain a written log to use with new staff for future activities.

It is essential for participants working collaboratively on instructional practice to have a common understanding of the terms being discussed. That understanding can only be achieved through shared discussions about them. An interesting example of how teachers can have a different understanding of what a term might mean occurred during the TIMSS video interviews. The teacher was teaching a mathematics lesson and using what she thought was problem solving. In reality, her class was merely doing the mechanics of solving a mathematics problem. The class was not demonstrating an understanding of mathematical concepts by using what they knew about mathematics to solve the problem. In that instance, what the teacher thought was problem solving and what the researchers expected were very different. There needs to be a clear understanding of what the terms mean when working on education projects. That example from the TIMSS research highlights the importance of clearly defining the terms that are used for group work.

When teachers engage in dialogue about teaching strategies and practices, they should have a clear understanding of what these practices mean. One way to do this is to have teachers discuss their practices in very specific, descriptive ways, and to ask questions of each other. Paraphrasing what teachers hear from each other is an excellent way to bring clarification (for example, "So what I heard you say was . . ."). Giving examples of their strategies also enhances meaning and provides evidence of consistency or the lack thereof.

We would also suggest that a consensus process be put in place to reach agreement on terms. In this way teachers can support the definitions by having a voice in what they mean by the terms. This process will also build a very important cultural norm (shard language) in the organization that will enhance instructional practice.

Reflect on Improving Instruction and Arrive at Consensus on Effective Strategies

There are two DNA components contained in this gene. They are time and collaboration. These two components are interactive in the sense that without time there is little or no chance teachers will arrive at consensus on effective instructional practices. In other words, collaboration requires time. The culture of American education has been to assign teachers to their classrooms and let them teach on their own. Critics of American education cite the accepted practice of isolation as a root cause for teachers not working together to improve their practices. How can a teacher improve without feedback and analysis of performance? We are not referring to one or two short-term administrative observation visits to a classroom for evaluation purposes. Instead, we are suggesting ongoing collaborative work with the teachers' administrator and peers, a process we identified as guided professionalism in chapter 4.

The challenge of finding the necessary time for teachers to engage in collaborative learning activities and professional development necessitates creative thinking that departs from the traditional school schedule. Whenever the question of more time for teachers is raised, the usual answers involve a longer workday or year and finding more money to pay for it. That tactic may work in some situations, but surely there may be other solutions available by reviewing the use of time in the current school schedule. We suggest that school leaders carefully analyze how much time is devoted each day to noneducational activities that could be used in more productive ways. For example, a fourth grade student attends elementary school for 6 1/2 hours per day or 390 minutes. During that time assume the student receives 90 minutes of language arts, 60 minutes of mathematics, 45 minutes of science, 45 minutes of social studies, and on a revolving schedule an average of 60 minutes of physical education, music, or art. Of the total 390 minutes, 300 were devoted to classroom assignments and not all of those minutes are traditionally the responsibility of the self-contained classroom teacher. We would note that the hypothetical 300-minute daily academic schedule we use as an example would be considered rigorous and not as common as many people would like to believe. The point is that there are at least 90 minutes of nonstudent contact time in our hypothetical schedule that could possibly be used for teacher professional development activities. The nonstudent contact time for the teacher is probably for lunch, passing between classes, and recess. In addition to the student time, there is likely more time included in the teacher workday that could be factored into this example. The responsibility for school staffs is to find a balance between the time teachers need to complete their daily tasks and the time needed for professional development, capacity-building activities.

If teachers are expected to improve and understand the most effective instructional practices, they will need time to meet and discuss their work. Finding that time may require "out of the box" solutions, but without it there is little chance that effective practices will be used on a regular basis and with consistency throughout the school.

When we speak of the term instructional practice, we are referring to strategies being used in the delivery of lessons. There has been considerable research on effective instructional practice. We have suggested throughout this book that the decision of what genes (fundamental principles) to place on your chromosome be left to you. Effective instruction is comparable to effective leadership in the sense that not all effective instructional techniques work all of the time, and different techniques may be needed depending on the situation. That is why it is so important to organize teachers into learning communities to help them become familiar with what the research says about teaching. Teachers must engage in discussions regarding the various strategies they use in their classrooms, and they must reflect on how well those strategies work. Then teachers must be challenged to agree on what instructional practices are effective and support them with evidence that their students are successful. Expectations and opportunities for teachers to participate in collaborative discussions and consensus-building activities regarding their practices will facilitate the accomplishment of this goal. All of these actions will lead teachers to a better understanding of their work. It will be necessary to provide technical assistance for this work if the school district does not employ someone who is knowledgeable about the research on effective instructional practices. We emphasize here that we are not referring to annual education fads, buzzwords, or consultants offering an elixir that has no research-based support for their claims. Instead, we are referring to research and practices that have been proven to be effective and transferable to another setting.

Examples of Instructional Practice

While it would be impractical to list pages of instructional practices in this section, we discuss some of them in order to provide practical examples. It should be emphasized that while these instructional practices have been demonstrated to be effective, not all teachers may be effective using them. Different strategies can be used to teach students, but there must be evidence demonstrating that the students are learning what is expected of them in every classroom. The critical point is that teachers must be knowledgeable about an eclectic array of practices and capable of using them effectively to ensure that all of their students are learning.

Our first example centers around the belief that students should be required to think and build on previous knowledge. Engaging them in this process can involve a variety of teaching strategies. For example, a class begins with the teacher posing a difficult problem. She decides to divide the class into *small groups,* each group having the responsibility to solve the problem and present the solution to the class. The group may be required to select a spokesperson or each member could be required to present the solution to the class. In this instance the teacher selected a passive facilitator instructional strategy.

The teacher acting as an active facilitator using *whole-class instruction* could teach the same lesson. She poses the same problem but guides the entire class in a discussion in pursuit of the solution. Either the whole class or small group strategy can be used effectively, but they require different preparation and teaching skills.

Cooperative learning can be used as an effective instructional practice. Engaging students to work together on a project that is designed to fulfill the goal of a lesson can be highly motivational for the students. It is critical to outline a process for determining each group member's responsibility so that the work is evenly distributed. In cooperative learning, as well as small group activities, students also learn other important skills such as compromising, consensus building, decision-making, trusting, leadership, and sharing. Business leaders have said those skills are necessary so students can be successful in today's modern workplace.

In contrast to cooperative learning, *independent learning* is an instructional practice that should be used regularly. While the other practices should be part of the overall teaching plan, students must be expected to demonstrate the ability to accept responsibility for their own work. Independent learning activities require students to make personal decisions about their approach to classroom assignments.

Many lessons can begin by using a *lecture* teaching strategy. When using lecture, students should be required to take notes in order to record the flow of the lesson topics and create a summary of the lesson for studying. Teachers should help the students by providing a study sheet that guides them through the lecture specifying the key terms. The study sheet should also list the goal of the lesson and supporting resources the student can use to better understand the topic.

Homework, or followup practice and learning activities, should be considered an essential part of any instructional plan. It is an effective strategy for students to practice what was learned and should help the student build a deeper conceptual understanding of the lesson. There has been considerable debate among educators regarding the assignment of homework, but there is no debate that when used properly it can enhance a student's understanding of the subject. To avoid some of the criticisms regarding homework, we offer the following suggestions:

- Have a specific policy on homework including purpose and time guidelines.
- Make the assignment a meaningful extension of the learning from class and not just busywork.
- Be sure students are able to complete the assignment based on the class work and available resources.
- Clearly articulate how the assignment will be assessed.

The last instructional practice, *technology use to enhance teaching and learning,* is one of our genes for this chromosome and will be discussed later in this section. Suffice it to say, effective use of technology for teaching and learning is a critical part of teaching in a modern classroom.

All of these practices (small group, whole class, cooperative learning, independent learning, lecture, homework, and using technology) enhance teaching and learning. They are proven to be effective when used by high-quality teachers. While they serve as examples of effective practices, there are other practices that are also valid. Discussing these practices is not the entire solution to improving teaching. They need to be implemented after teachers have reflected on practice and have analyzed their work and the work of their peers.

Understand Curriculum, Possess Content Knowledge, and Develop Coherent Lessons

It is truly ironic that most of the attention given to American school reform by business leaders and policymakers has been on writing rigorous curriculum standards and using high-stakes assessment to ensure they are met. The consequences for failure to meet the standards include teachers losing their jobs, not promoting or graduating students, and closing schools. While we agree with rigorous standards and assessments based on those standards, we also think that more time and funding should be devoted to the people who are responsible for ensuring those standards are achieved. We would expect business leaders and policymakers to recognize that the best way to attain higher student achievement is to improve the quality of teaching. We have listed some effective instructional practices and devoted an entire chromosome to curriculum, yet there is an emerging body of evidence that supports the notion that teacher content knowledge is also important. How well teachers know their subject matter is related to their teaching effectiveness and ability to write lessons that contribute to improved student learning. It is our unwavering belief that understanding the curriculum, possessing content knowledge, and developing coherent lessons play critical roles in the process of attaining world-class achievement.

Teachers who do not understand what they are expected to teach stand little or no chance of communicating important learning standards to their students. Numerous studies and reports have emphasized that students receive an inferior education when taught by uninformed and unqualified teachers. Teachers must have a clear understanding of what concepts and skills they are required to teach. Being qualified is the second important factor in quality instruction. A significant criterion used to define a qualified teacher is one who has a content area major, or at the very least a minor, in the field being taught. Note we are only saying the teacher is qualified, not necessarily effective. But, without adequate content knowledge and preparation, the teacher should not be assigned to teach as a content area specialist.

The National Commission on Mathematics and Science Teaching for the 21st Century, mentioned earlier, reported alarming data regarding the number of teachers assigned to teach mathematics and science classes who were unprepared in their subject. The Commission's findings are further supported in a study conducted by Dan D. Goldhaber and Dominick J. Brewer in 1996. They found a significant positive relationship between teachers' degrees and students' achievement in technical subjects. While they concluded that the degrees were important for mathematics and science teaching, they noted that there was no evidence to suggest that their findings would not be applicable to other subjects.[54]

With ample evidence supporting the notion that teachers need sufficient content knowledge of their subject matter and a clear understanding of the curriculum, school districts would be well advised to implement activities that help teachers improve their content knowledge of the subjects they teach. It is unreasonable to expect students to sit through classes with teachers who do not understand what they teach; much the same way teachers deplore this in their professional development sessions and university coursework. People do not want to be served by unqualified doctors, lawyers, or practitioners in other professions, and their children should not get an inadequate education from an unqualified teacher. For the integrity of the teaching profession, all teachers should have a major or minor in their teaching field and ongoing professional development to build on their subject knowledge.

Understanding the curriculum and possessing content knowledge are the first two pieces of this gene. Now we move to developing coherent lessons. Understanding the curriculum is the prelude to developing content-rich, coherent lessons. Jim Stigler has often said that a lesson is a good story that is easy to understand and remember because each event has meaning in relation to other events. In essence, a good lesson incorporates the classroom environment, planning, effective instructional practice, use of technology when appropriate, and assessment. In a Japanese lesson study group as described by Stigler, a lesson is carefully planned with colleagues, focused with a specific learning goal that is aligned to the curriculum, and carefully analyzed by peers using data on student achievement and observation of teaching.

Lesson Planning

The *classroom environment* is very important to delivering a high-quality lesson. From the arrangement of the furniture to the complete elimination of distraction; all are part of the planning process. Is the furniture arranged in a manner that supports the instructional practice being used? It is critical to have furniture that can be moved if different grouping patterns are used. It is also difficult to teach a high-quality lesson when a teacher and class are interrupted. Planning the lesson should include strategies to avoid distractions.

The Japanese model of planning lessons is one that we offer for further consideration. The process, known as lesson study, incorporates the lesson analysis features we believe are essential for the improvement of teaching in the United States. We do not suggest merely importing another country's cultural practice, but instead encourage adopting some of the procedures and incorporating them into the American school culture. Using some form of lesson study would be a major stride toward achieving world-class teaching in this country. Teachers using lesson study in Japan meet as a group and use the following procedures for planning lessons.

- Define a problem.
- Plan the lesson.
- Teach the lesson.
- Evaluate the lesson.
- Reflect on what worked well and did not work.
- Revise the lesson by working collaboratively.
- Teach it again.
- Repeat the process listed above.

The process of lesson study enables teachers to build on the knowledge they gain from working together. It is at this point where we emphasize the importance of archiving this information. If schools want to improve teaching over time, they must build on knowledge gained from practices like lesson study. The information can be archived through video clips of teaching, audio, or written anecdotal comments from the teachers about the lessons. As new teachers teach these lessons, the archived materials will be helpful by informing them about what worked and did not work in the past. Far too often new teachers are left to their own judgment on how to prepare lessons. There is no substitute for the interaction of colleagues' shared ideas and reflection that is at the heart of the lesson study process used in Japan. It is simply too intuitive and logical to dismiss as an unimportant practice for American teachers.

A coherent lesson communicates the curricular expectations and should be understood by all of the students. A variety of instructional techniques should be utilized to account for differences in learning styles. Questioning techniques should require students to build on previous knowledge, engage in problem solving, demonstrate comprehension of the subject, apply what they learned to practical situations, and analyze the results.

The coherent lesson is a detailed, well-planned script that tells the story as Stigler suggests and has assessment measures that ensure students learned the important concepts. Writing coherent lessons requires a consistent lesson framework. It also serves as the basis for teacher collaboration to improve those lessons. The following lesson components can serve as one framework for writing a coherent lesson plan:

- Subject
- Grade level
- State or national learning standard used
- Objective of the lesson
- Lesson strategies to be used
- Grouping
- Activities
- Questions
- Resources and supplemental materials

- Vocabulary
- Technology to be used
- Homework
- Assessment measures to determine student understanding of objectives

There are volumes of research on teaching. This gene offers some suggestions and supportive information on the importance of understanding the curriculum, possessing a deep understanding of content knowledge, and developing coherent lessons. The reader is advised to remember that world-class practices are achieved by using research-based, data-driven, and qualitative reviews of proven effective teaching practices. This gene implies that teachers are qualified for the teaching assignment, by having a major or minor in their teaching field, and are actively involved in collaborative activities organized to write, teach, and analyze lessons aligned to the district curriculum and standards.

Work with High-Quality Instructional Materials

What materials should be used to support high-quality lessons? Using instructional materials that are aligned with the curricular expectations is an important consideration for teachers. Educators have relied too long on textbooks for the basic content and framework of their curriculums as described earlier in this chapter. The textbook publishers have had a significant influence on what is actually taught in many American school districts. Project 2061 of the American Association for the Advancement of Science conducted an analysis of middle grades mathematics and science textbooks and high school biology textbooks. The analysis process was a rigorous procedure that was based on considerable field-testing. It has been found to be exemplary in describing the strengths and weaknesses of curriculum materials. The objective was to see how well the materials aligned with national standards and how well they helped students achieve them. The results were not encouraging. Of the 45 textbooks that were analyzed, only five middle grades mathematics books and one stand-alone physical science unit were found to have potential for helping students learn concepts that are essential for mathematical and science literacy (*www.project2061.org*). Without high-quality instructional materials, teachers must have the knowledge and ability to develop curriculum and lessons that lead to students' understanding of complex ideas that align with rigorous standards.

The National Research Council of the National Academy of Sciences was asked by the U.S. Department of Education and the U.S. Department of Health and Human Services to establish a committee to examine the prevention of reading difficulties in children. The results of this study support the findings from the Project 2061 analysis of textbooks. The NRC committee found that textbook adoption procedures in school districts and the lack of incentives for publishers to customize their materials to meet specific needs in a school district resulted in teachers using less than adequate materials.

These two projects, which encompass mathematics, science, and reading, paint a bleak picture of the availability of high-quality textbooks for instruction in American classrooms. We emphasize that textbooks should not be the only source of instructional materials. There is no all-inclusive textbook that will meet the total needs of a curriculum built on a standards-based approach. Often they include lessons and activities that are not part of the district's curricular focus. The textbooks need to be supplemented with other resources to more effectively support the district's learning standards. As the standards movement gains momentum, it will become increasingly important for teachers to select instructional materials that align with their district's curricular expectations. Selecting these materials, developing an understanding of their content, and working collaboratively with colleagues on implementation strategies will require substantial time. Only knowledgeable teachers working with high-quality technical assistance will be able to effectively incorporate this gene using high-quality materials on their instructional practice chromosome.

We are often reminded of the time when a reporter contacted us regarding a textbook controversy over what series would be the best choice in her school district. Rather than offer her our advice regarding whether the textbook was good or not, we asked her if she would rather have her daughter in a classroom with the best textbook and an average teacher, or in a classroom with an excellent teacher using a poor textbook. Our premise is that bad genes lead to unsatisfactory results; however, when you combine good materials with good teaching the outcomes should be rewarding.

Be Knowledgeable of Learning Theory Research, Learning Styles, and Human Development

It is likely that this gene is the most difficult one to incorporate in instructional practice. Finding the time to read, review, and apply research is one of the most difficult activities for teachers to do. How to incorporate one more task into the teacher workday is not easy. Even if the time is available, much of the research is complex and not written in a manner that is easily understood and applied by classroom teachers. Nonetheless, being knowledgeable of learning theory research that is scientific and practical for classroom use (conducted by reputable researchers), and teaching by using strategies that appropriately align with learning styles can lead to high-quality instruction. Both of these bodies of research also attend to the developmental needs of students. All instruction must be developmentally appropriate with respect to a child's mental capabilities, age, prior knowledge gained through experience, and readiness for learning. We also suggest that new developments in cognitive neuroscience be explored. We emphasize the need to present lessons in a way for students to understand information and create mental images of that learning.

While there are volumes of research on learning, we have chosen to select five resources that we believe are significant research examples for this gene. Distinguished scholars have completed the work which is intended to improve teaching and learning. It synthesizes a large body of research on education thus providing an expedited path for building this gene. The resources are:

1. *Preventing Reading Difficulties in Young Children.* Catherine Snow, M. Susan Burns, and Peg Griffin, Editors, National Academy Press, Washington, D.C. 1998

2. *Teaching Children to Read: An Evidence-Based Assessment of the Scientific Research Literature on Reading and Its Implications for Reading Instruction,* National Reading Panel. National Institute of Child Health and Human Development, National Institute of Health, 2000

3. *How People Learn-Brain, Mind, Experience and School.* National Research Council, National Academy Press, Washington, D.C., 2000

4. *How People Learn-Bridging Research and Practice,* National Re-

search Council, National Academy Press, Washington, D.C., 1999

5. The Dunn and Dunn Model (*http://www.geocities.com/ ~educationplace/Model.html*)

Learning Styles

Rita and Ken Dunn originally developed their learning model in 1967, and it has been refined through the years. It utilizes cognitive style and brain lateralization theories. Cognitive style theory is based on the concept that individuals process information differently based on learned or inherited traits. Brain lateralization theory addresses the idea of two brain hemispheres, left for verbal-sequential abilities and right for emotions-spatial holistic processing. Thus, learning style is the way each learner begins to concentrate on, process, and retain new and difficult information.[55]

The Dunn model identifies four primary learning styles; visual, auditory, tactual, and kinesthetic. These learning styles are the preferred method for students to learn new or difficult information. Teachers who incorporate instructional strategies in their lessons that address the four learning styles are more likely to be successful with all of their students. Developing lessons using the learning styles strategies would be a time-consuming project and should involve teacher collaboration.

Students with a visual preference require the use of visual media or demonstrations. Auditory learners prefer listening to lectures, group discussions, or taped books. If a learner is tactual, learning activities should be hands-on, that is, note-taking, writing assignments, or building projects. Finally, kinesthetic learners perform best when they are actively involved in the lesson. We caution teachers that kinesthetic learners are mobile and their learning preference should not be confused with a student who is a disciplinary problem. Teachers should identify this learning modality in their students and accommodate the student's need to be active and mobile.

Incorporated in the Dunn Model are 21 elements organized into five strands. The strands are environmental, emotional, sociological, physical, and psychological. Each of the strands contains elements that can have an influence on student learning. The Dunn model utilizes a Learning Styles Inventory, an assessment instrument that can be administered by a classroom teacher that identifies the preferred learning styles of students.

The elements are:

- Environmental – sound, light, temperature, design
- Emotional – motivation, persistence, responsibility, structure
- Sociological – self, pair, peers, team, adult, varied
- Physical – perceptual, intake, time, mobility
- Psychological – global/analytic, hemisphericity, impulsive/reflective

Our presentation of learning styles is a brief overview of the model. One of our guest writers, Marie Carbo, has incorporated learning styles theory into reading instruction. Referring to Dr. Carbo's work will provide more depth for understanding this concept (see appendix A).

Learning Theory

Much of what has been discovered about the science of learning has taken place in the last decade. Two substantive projects on learning have been conducted by the National Research Council of the National Academy of Sciences and the National Institute of Child Health and Human Development. We reference these projects for our chromosome because each of the agencies is highly respected and their studies were completed using a distinguished panel of scholars, researchers, and educators. Their findings offer valuable suggestions for educators that could lead to improved teaching and learning.

The National Research Council report on how people learn provides these key findings on learning with three implications for teaching. This report presents a fundamental underpinning that can serve as the basis for the research gene on learning theory. To get you started, we list these three findings and three implications for teaching. There is considerably more information in the report that should be used for teacher/administrator collaborative discussions on the science of learning. (*How People Learn: Brain, Mind, Experience, and School* [expanded edition]).

1. Students come to the classroom with preconceptions about how the world works. If their initial understanding is not engaged, they may fail to grasp the new concepts and information that are taught, or they may learn them for pur-

poses of a test but revert to their preconceptions outside the classroom.

2. To develop competence in an area of inquiry, students must (a) have a deep foundation of factual knowledge, (b) understand facts and ideas in the context of a conceptual framework, and (c) organize knowledge in ways that facilitate retrieval and application.

3. A "metacognitive" approach to instruction can help students learn to take control of their own learning by defining learning goals and monitoring their progress in achieving them.[56]

Those findings have implications for teaching and should be used to inform practice. The implications for teaching are:

- Teachers must draw out and work with the preexisting understandings that their students bring with them.
- Teachers must teach some subject matter in depth, providing many examples in which the same concept is at work and providing a firm foundation of factual knowledge.
- The teaching of metacognitive skills should be integrated into the curriculum in a variety of subject areas.[57]

Our last reference is to a research-based study conducted by the National Reading Panel that was convened by Congress in 1997. The National Reading Panel based much of its work on the reading study conducted by the National Research Council in 1998 (*Preventing Reading Difficulties in Young Children*). Throughout this book we have cited a number of studies on mathematics and science teaching. Our intent was not to overemphasize these two subjects, but unfortunately most of the pertinent research has been centered on those two disciplines. While there is no evidence to indicate the findings from the mathematics and science studies could not be applied to the teaching of other subjects, we believe well-developed reading skills and strategies are the cornerstone to achieving world-class performance.

We cite the work of this panel because it meets three fundamental criteria this book stresses; it is research-based, data-driven, and discusses successful teaching practices. These three criteria align with the framework we have stipulated for using the genetic model.

The reading panel concluded that effective reading instruction incorporated:

- Alphabetics (the smallest units comprising spoken language; phonemics awareness and phonics instruction)
- Fluency (reading orally with speed, accuracy and proper expression)
- Comprehension (a complex cognitive process that involves thoughtful interaction between the reader and text)
- Vocabulary instruction (oral and print)
- Text comprehension and instruction (engaging readers in intentional, problem solving thinking processes)
- Teacher preparation and comprehension strategies instruction (teachers who possess a firm grasp of the content presented in the text and substantial knowledge of the strategies to teach reading)
- Teacher education and reading instruction (higher quality teacher preparation and continuing education in reading)
- Computer technology and reading instruction (newer technology that can deliver instruction)[58]

It should be apparent there is considerable research on teaching. Rather than use too many research studies in your work, it is advisable to find a few good scientific research studies that support your goals. Bear in mind that what comprises your research gene should reflect the cultural beliefs of your school. Then, it is important to be aware of new research and developments.

Use Technology to Enhance Teaching and Learning

Technology, when used properly, can be an effective resource to support high-quality teaching and learning. There have been education technology "fads" in the past, however, and we offer the caution that technology is viewed as a means to support teaching and learning, not as a substitute. A number of years ago, television was placed in many classrooms with the thought that they would lead the way to improved student achievement. Although the use of television has arguably been helpful for teaching, it was how teachers used high-quality programs to support lessons and not the television that made the difference. Today this is much like computers that require high-quality software to be useful. For improved learning to take place with technology, the manner in which the teacher integrates it into the lesson is what will determine whether students successfully learn the concepts. As we noted on a number of occasions, a shared language is important for this gene. Technology is a general term and overly used. When it is used in education, it must be in the context of how it can enhance teaching and learning and it must go beyond the hardware-software concept. Like a laser to a surgeon, hardware and software are only tools for a teacher to use to enhance student performance. They should not be expected to do the work. Examples of technology include calculators, video and DVD recorders, overhead projectors, computers, software, cameras, and personal digital assistants. But, be certain to define what is meant by technology for instructional practice.

Computer technology can enhance instruction. The fundamental issue with technology use is whether it creates a rich interactive learning environment or a passive one. The teacher must clearly define the products that will result from using technology. These results can be intellectual capital or tangible results. In either case, the teacher must determine if technology is the best means to derive those products.

Technology can be used for problem-solving questions, to provide sophisticated simulations, and to facilitate teacher/student communication around the world as well as a number of other basic tasks. When used for simple tasks that are primarily drill activities, it is reduced to nothing more than an electronic version of flashcards. While drill and practice activities can be effective if properly integrated into a lesson, the use of technology should be used for much more than simple practice exercises. It is important to understand, however, that it is the teacher who makes technology a more challenging interactive, instructional strategy and not technology that makes the teacher effective.

As districts develop the technology gene there are a few concepts to consider. First, technology can enhance teaching and learning, but only if it is used effectively. It is not a substitute for teaching or a time-filler for students. Effective use of technology requires substantial professional development. The continuous innovations in equipment and software require ongoing training for teachers to understand their effective application in the classroom. Teachers need to align technology applications with their lessons, curriculum, standards, assessment, and the district technology plan. There should be specific goals defining how technology can be used to meet the diverse learning needs of the students.

Selecting appropriate technology is also an important consideration. Computers, calculators, and videos can all be part of an instructional plan but each technology has its own unique features. They should be used to accomplish tasks that otherwise would be frustrating to do or extremely time consuming. These features should not replace foundational intellectual development. For example, a calculator should not replace learning computational skills. It can be used to efficiently check the accuracy of student responses. More sophisticated calculators can be used to support complex problem-solving questions, graphing, and other tasks for which a calculator is appropriate. Word processing provides students with editing capabilities that allow them to easily revise and improve their work. Teachers can make anecdotal notes on their writing, and students can correct their work quickly without a high level of frustration. Spreadsheets and databases provide a means for students to gather, organize and report data in a variety of formats. While these examples are simple, they illustrate how technology can be incorporated into instructional delivery.

Another concept for this gene is that the technology must be easy to use and accessible for teachers and students to incorporate it seamlessly in the instructional process. The quantity and quality of equipment and software are prerequisites for effective use of technology. Technical support must be available to assure that the technology is working or can be repaired quickly. When technology is not working, teachers' lessons are disrupted.

The critical requirements for working with the technology gene on instructional practice are to have a plan for its implementation and continuous professional development for the teachers. The plan should address how technology aligns with the district's learning standards and it should describe the performance expectations of both staff and students. Measures of accountability should be implemented to ensure that the district's learning standards for technology are met.

Empower Teachers Through Guided Professionalism

In the past the traditional organizational structure of a school was bureaucratic and hierarchical. The principal was viewed as the "expert" and was responsible for evaluating teachers and administering the school. Leadership theory has evolved over the years, and the role of the principalship has become more complex and sophisticated. Our leadership chromosome provides background regarding more contemporary approaches to working with people in a professional setting. It is unlikely that today's principal has the time to work with teachers on a daily basis or the expertise to meet all aspects of the teaching-learning process. The work demands of the principal necessitate a different approach to leadership and instructional practice. We believe that academic performance of students and quality of teaching are two important priorities for a principal; to be successful it will be necessary to facilitate an effective process of working with teachers by using guided professionalism.

Guided professionalism, as noted earlier in this chapter, is facilitating ongoing collaborative work with the staff on substantive professional activities. As principal, it would be important to develop a work schedule that provides regular time for teachers to reflect on practice to improve their pedagogical skills and content knowledge. We suggest that cooperative planning with staff members should lead to successfully implementing this concept. A work schedule must include time to build professional capacity.

Teacher evaluation is another example of how guided professionalism can be used. The evaluation process of observation and feedback sessions is not enough. The principal must work collaboratively with a teacher to engage regularly in discussions of successful teaching practices and use of assessment data to improve student achievement. Documenting the process and demonstrating growth using data based benchmarks will ultimately improve the overall quality of the school.

Leadership is important and guided professionalism is not a concept that diminishes a leader's responsibility for making critical organizational decisions and accepting responsibility for them. Instead, it suggests that there are a number of professional activities in a school that must focus on teaching and learning. These activities should be implemented through a knowledgeable leader using effective practices (for example, book study groups and data analysis teams). Collaborative use of these practices will yield positive results.

Implement a Board Policy that Requires High-Quality Instruction

Finally, the board of education must have a policy that stipulates that only high-quality instruction is acceptable. A board of education policy on instructional practice validates the work expected of the education staff. It establishes a context for planning, budgeting, and implementing a program that will ensure professionalism, high-quality teaching and opportunities for students to achieve at world-class levels. In this context, district expectations, practices, and resources can be focused on those priority areas that influence student achievement.

Recipe for World-class Teaching

by Laura Singer

Reading and Language Arts Staff Development Teacher, Northbrook School District 27

It was late Friday afternoon and a mom was baking a cake with her three young children. They were going to surprise their grandma for her 60th birthday. As they began the baking process, questions flowed smoothly from the young children's mouths . . . "How do we know what to add first?" "How many minutes do we stir it?" "How long does it stay in the oven?" As she answered these questions, she realized they had obvious answers because the recipe told them exactly what to do.

Unlike baking, teaching does not come with a recipe. Although this makes it more challenging, it also allows each teacher to provide the quality instruction that meets the needs of each and every unique learner. To be a world-class teacher, you must be like a baker who is able to mix all the necessary ingredients to allow your students to perform up to their potential. These ingredients are numerous and quite varied, and they change and grow with each unique group of learners that present themselves at the beginning of each school year.

The first ingredient is the ability to assess each student continually throughout the school year. These assessments may include observational records, paper and pencil tests, performance assessments, standardized assessments, and other appropriate measures. From these assessments, as well as the student's performance in class, the teacher must determine the students' strengths, weaknesses, learning style, past performance history, mastery of content, as well as any other needed data. All of these pieces of information then lead the teacher to instruct in an appropriate manner for each student.

Next, the teacher must provide instruction to challenge each learner at his/her own learning level. This will involve differentiating lessons, activities, and/or content of what is being taught. The teacher will need to obtain appropriate materials, apply diverse teaching strategies, and work with small, flexible groups of students to meet the needs of each one. Although this is often a very challenging, and sometimes overwhelming task, these are some of the very most important instructional decisions that an educator will make.

Once children are being instructed at the appropriate level, it is crucial that they feel engaged in the lesson or activity. Students need to understand what they are doing, and more importantly, why they are doing it. Hands-on, real world experiences are much more valuable to all students, no matter at what level they are performing. Assignments and projects should be meaningful, with a clear purpose in mind.

Good instruction must involve the use of varied discussion and questioning techniques, as well as a wide range of instructional strategies. As we know, students come to us with different learning styles and strengths. A teacher's instructional practices must reflect this diversity and encompass the learning styles of each and every student. Teachers must be able to choose wisely how they will present their lesson and assign any follow-up activities or projects.

To insure quality instruction, the teacher must have mastery of the content that she is going to teach. She must be able to present the basic information, but more importantly, she must be able to encourage students to question and probe above and beyond the basics to a level that challenges them. The teacher's goal is to teach the information from the content areas, but ultimately, to guide her students so that they can continue on as independent learners and seekers of information.

Finally, just as a baker must continually check on his cake to make sure it is done just right, a teacher must do the same with her instruction. Instruction is complicated and has many facets. The baker's task is complete when the cake comes out just right and is a masterpiece. The teacher, however, does not work with just one cake, but the numerous students she teaches. Each one comes with its own unique ingredients, but no recipe. Just as the baker may need to add more sugar or adjust the cooking temperature, the teacher must model this same behavior and constantly study and evaluate her instruction each and every day. Modifications and adjustments to her teaching on a regular basis make her a better teacher tomorrow than she was today.

It is an incredibly challenging job being a teacher in the 21st century. Thank you to all of the masterful teachers for their instructional practices and their ability to teach the whole child. Thank you for molding the future.

Assessment Chromosome

Introduction

The world is at an unprecedented time in history when communication among people is paramount. People in general want information and to fully understand why things are the way they are. With respect to their schools, parents want detailed information about their children's performance. They are seeking reliable information that will help them understand the nature of their students' learning. It is becoming an expectation to have quality assessment data about student achievement and to make instructional and placement decisions that enhance the students' opportunities to learn. These decisions need to be discussed with parents on a regular basis.

Despite the growing recognition that data can be used to improve children's learning, the assessment chromosome is the most underutilized and misunderstood of the three teaching-learning process chromosomes. *Testing* students has become commonplace in districts, but educators are struggling with the challenges of *assessing* student learning. By this we mean that districts are collecting student achievement data, but it is primarily being used to describe characteristics of student performance. Understanding why students achieve the way they do is a more challenging task. Teachers need to know how to use the data to inform their practice and understand student progress. In essence, they have an abundance of data but lack the proper understanding of how to make use of this information.

Michael Fullan in his book, *What's Worth Fighting For Out There?* encourages teachers and administrators to become more "assessment literate". He emphasizes that they can become assessment literate in several ways: (1) expand their assessment repertoires; (2) show parents and students how they have arrived at their assessment decisions; (3) collect assessment data as an ongoing part of classroom learning; (4) monitor how well their students are achieving over time; and (5) communicate the results clearly to parents and the public.[59]

When this "assessment literacy" is absent, teachers and administrators are unable to use the information that data offer. An assessment program enables teachers and administrators to understand various forms of data, helps teachers to focus on specific content, and informs their instructional practice.

The assessment chromosome interacts with the curriculum and instructional practice chromosomes to validate and improve them by providing substantive information. Data provide the evidence to support or change current programs and practices. Accurate assessment data and their interpretation also provide parents and other community members with detailed information about student achievement and how the school is meeting the students' needs.

As we develop this last chromosome, we want to ask the following question, "What are the most important principles upon which to base the district's assessment program that would lead to world-class performance?"

We offer four genes that are essential to build a quality assessment program. As with the other chromosomes, a sound research base will shape the values a district will need to provide a quality assessment program.

1. Build a Context to Support the Effective Use of Assessment Data.
2. Identify the Purposes and Goals for the District Assessment Program.
3. Design and Implement Systems to Gather, Use, and Interpret Assessment Data.
4. Evaluate the Assessment Program to Determine Its Impact on the Teaching-Learning Process.

Assessment Chromosome: Four Genes

Build a Context to Support the Effective Use of Assessment Data

Using assessment data effectively must be a culturally accepted norm in a school district. Building a context to support its use requires the district to develop an overall "big picture" of the significance of data and how it will be used. We offer nine research-based practices that will help to build an assessment culture.

Establish Continuous Improvement as a District Expectation

In order to use data effectively the district must believe in *continuous improvement*. As we mentioned in the change chromosome, the underpinning of continuous improvement is the notion that as good as a district may be, there is always room for improvement. Improvement does not mean present practice is poor or ineffective. Nor does it suggest that teachers are not competent; however, it does mean that the organization can be even better with refinement in light of new educational developments, information, and conditions.

In a continuous improvement environment, districts rely on new information that is research-based and data-driven. Data are the key to any improvement initiative because they provide evidence that supports or contradicts beliefs or perceptions that may be held. They are based on statistically sound psychometric principles to ensure that teachers are looking at valid and reliable information that can shape their views of student learning and program effectiveness. When interpreted properly, data unfold comprehensive stories that provide new understandings. The key to successful continuous improvement is that teachers believe that data can reveal what needs to be improved. Structures must be put in place to help teachers organize and understand the data and to guide them toward informed decisions that can be readily implemented.

Nurture a Culture of Assessment Literacy

Leaders must build an understanding and appreciation for assessment literacy. They must seek to nurture a culture that will use data to improve. In many respects the use of assessment data for school improvement parallels diagnostic testing used in the medical profession. A physician seeks various types of information before making a diagnosis. This information comes from the patient's description of the symptoms and tests designed to rule out some causes and/or confirm others. Once this information is collected, the physician is in a position to make an informed diagnosis and prescribe medical treatment. The physician will then monitor the patient to ensure the problem is corrected.

In the same way, schools gather data to determine how well students are learning and what areas need attention. Teachers are then in a better position to make informed decisions about how to teach the students. They collect ongoing information to measure formative and summative learning. When teachers use the information properly, they can provide optimal learning opportunities for students in the same way a physician can provide the best treatment for a patient. Physicians should not treat a medical condition without a diagnosis of the problem. In the same manner, teachers should not instruct students without understanding what they know and how they learn.

Becoming assessment literate is a commitment that must begin at the district level. This means that the district leaders must make it an expectation and provide the support for staff members to become proficient in the concepts and uses of data management. Furthermore, it must be an integral part of the teaching-learning process. Teachers and administrators must view assessment data as important information for their understanding of student learning. They must devote time to reviewing data and trying to make sense of it. This approach illustrates the fundamental distinction between testing (the process) and assessing (the analysis). Teachers must assess student learning.

Provide Professional Development Opportunities
Supporting the effective use of assessment data means providing professional development opportunities for staff members. Teachers need to understand how to use assessment data in a meaningful way, by incorporating it naturally into the teaching-learning process. Teachers must be given the time and guidance to understand the data. The time comes from the professional development program. The guidance comes from using a district assessment framework (to be discussed later).

Develop the Structural Pieces

Fortunately teachers have a myriad of data at their fingertips. What they typically lack is the framework to guide effective use and interpretation of those data sources. It is incumbent on the district to develop the structural pieces by which the staff will consistently use data to learn and improve. Developing a district-wide assessment framework is the most effective way to structure the use of data and direct staff members' energies toward understanding what the data say to them. By using a framework, practitioners can gain a clear understanding of how data relate to the complexities of the teaching-learning process; and they can more fully grasp the integral relationships that exist among curriculum, instruction, and assessment. Teachers are then better able to use assessment data for what is called "data-driven decision-making." There is a growing body of knowledge about aligning the components of the teaching-learning process (curriculum, instructional practice, and assessment). In particular, data can inform practice and lead to desired outcomes. This concept demands a clear understanding by everyone who uses assessment data.

The school's improvement planning process is another occasion to develop study questions at the district, school, and classroom levels to determine what data will be used and how it will be interpreted.

Integrate the National and State Emphases

The national political agenda for using assessments can take many different forms over the course of time. These directions are typically reflected in state mandates. The district must administer the externally required assessments. State assessments are a reality for most school districts and they come with their own expectations.

At this juncture it would be helpful to take a brief look at how national and state uses of assessment data have altered over time. There is considerable literature on the importance of assessing students' learning through state and national testing. This literature also increases our understanding of the effectiveness of curriculum.[60] Historically, however, this literature interprets the use of these assessments in light of the context of various national reform efforts at that moment in time. Robert Linn, Professor at the Center for Research on Evaluation, Standards, and Student Testing, University of Colorado, writes that over the past 50 years various national agendas defined the role that tests played in schools. In the 1950s the emphasis was on tracking and selection. The use of tests for program accountability was the call of the 1960s. In the 1970s minimum competency testing programs were in the spotlight, and the 1980s stressed school and district accountability. Currently standards-based accountability systems dominate the assessment landscape.[61] Regardless of the national emphasis on the use of assessment information, student learning should always be the basis for local district efforts.

Presently, the emphasis is for American schools to be results-driven. Assessment data is the means to demonstrate the achievement of those desired results. The current movement of reform from state and national policymakers calls for standards-based education. In this environment there will need to be changes in the nature of assessments. They must be aligned with the emerging content standards from the states. States will continue to play a key role in standards-based reform and school districts will need to demonstrate that their students are meeting the standards.

We mention this governmental emphasis because it holds significance for local practitioners when they develop local assessment plans. It affects the content standards to be measured both in the choice of concepts and skills, and the methods by which they are measured. Governmental requirement will have an impact at the district and classroom level. Linn writes, "It is critical to recognize first that the choice of constructs matters and so does the way in which measures are developed and linked to the constructs."[62] Therefore, districts must be mindful of state directed standards, but must not lose sight of what content area research emphasizes as the most important concepts and ideas for students to master.

Set High Performance Standards

Another important aspect of continuous improvement calls for the development of high performance standards in assessments. State assessments will be one important form of assessment, yet, the structure of those assessments may not provide all of the necessary information to determine if students have a meaningful understanding of the learning standards. Districts must develop high performance standards and emphasize the need for all students to meet them. Performance standards in essence specify "how good is good enough."[63] Linn notes that there are at least four critical characteristics of performance standards. He writes:

> First, they are intended to be absolute rather than normative. Second, they are expected to be set at high, "world-class" levels. Third, a relatively small number of levels (e.g. advanced, proficient) are typically identified. Finally, they are expected to apply to all, or essentially all, students rather than a selected subset such as college-bound students seeking advanced placement.[64]

These factors should be kept clearly at the forefront as districts develop their local assessment measures. Large-scale assessments (for example, state testing and norm-referenced testing) will play a small role in the overall assessment of student performance. The district will not determine the rigor of the performance standards by these assessments. Therefore, districts should identify their local baseline for acceptable performance and not merely rely on large-scale measures.

Align Assessments to Curriculum and Instruction

If the district assessment program is to be effective, it must be aligned with the intended curriculum. Teachers must teach the intended curriculum with integrity. Then, the assessment program must measure what is taught. Figure 5.3 illustrates this integrative relationship. When there is alignment, each aspect of the teaching-learning process informs and supports the other two parts of the process. The center represents the desired outcome of high student achievement.

The National Forum on Assessment describes the integrative nature of assessment with curriculum and instruction. It indicates that assessment systems must have coherence with respect to the practices and methods of assessment and they must be consistent with learning goals, curriculum, instruction, and current knowledge of how students learn.[65]

FIGURE 5.3—THE INTEGRATIVE NATURE OF THE TEACHING-LEARNING PROCESS

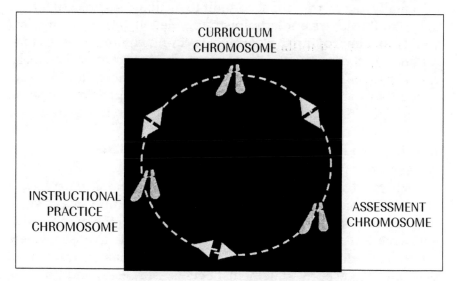

Work with High-Quality Information and Accept Responsibility for Using It

Another aspect of a continuous improvement culture is that leaders must commit to work only with high-quality, accurate information and be responsible for using it appropriately. These are crucial underpinnings of an effective assessment program. In the National Research Council's document, *Testing, Teaching and Learning*, the authors state that any education improvement system relies on information and responsibility:

> Everyone in the system—students, parents, teachers, administrators, and policy makers at every level—needs high-quality information about the quality of instruction and student performance. At the same time, everyone needs to be responsible for fulfilling his or her role in improving results. The key is transparency: everyone should know what is expected, what they will be measured on, and what the results imply for what they should do next.

> Such a system is never "complete"; educators and policy makers continue to modify and adapt it as they learn from their own experience and the experience of others . . .[66]

Evaluate the Assessment Program

Finally, the district must commit to evaluate its process for using data. If teachers and administrators devote time to using data and it is not improving the learning environment for students, then continuous improvement will not occur. The district must then make changes to its assessment program. This evaluation should reveal strengths and weaknesses in the program and provide direction for change. This concept will be discussed later in this section.

Identify the Purposes and Goals of the District Assessment Program

When a district creates its assessment program, it must have a clear understanding of the program's purposes and goals. What does an assessment program really contribute to the organization and what is it designed to accomplish? To be able to answer these questions, a district needs to articulate why it has an assessment program. Philosophy statements, beliefs, purposes, and goals all contribute to the rationale for assessment.

The literature indicates that an assessment program serves many purposes including the following:

- Improve student learning.
- Provide ongoing and cumulative data to measure student development and academic achievement.
- Provide purposeful and meaningful information to guide students' instructional programs.
- Provide a means to evaluate and improve the district's academic programs.
- Provide meaningful information to parents about the growth and development of their children.
- Hold schools accountable for meeting performance goals.[67]

With a clear understanding of the purposes of assessment, school districts can begin to articulate the overall goals of the program. Examples of goals include, but are not limited to the following:
The District Assessment Program will:

- Measure and evaluate student achievement and academic progress on a regular basis for the purpose of improving student learning.

- Diagnose students' needs in order to make informed decisions, choices, and judgments in guiding classroom instruction.
- Provide information to place students in appropriate programs that best support their instructional and developmental needs. (for example, Gifted Program, Foreign Language, English as a Second Language, Mathematics, Resource, and so forth)
- Provide the means for reporting student academic progress to parents.
- Explain and interpret student achievement to staff, parents, students, board of education, and other community groups.
- Comply with mandates.
- Gather longitudinal information to evaluate students' academic progress over time.
- Determine the effectiveness of the district's instructional and curricular programs.

In summary, as a school district develops its assessment program, it will be important to set the context for its implementation. Identifying the purpose and goals of the program provide that context. When a district articulates what it believes assessment should accomplish for the district, people will understand its value.

Design and Implement Systems to Gather, Use, and Interpret Assessment Data

School districts often have structured some of the components of the assessment program but lack a framework to organize them to improve the teaching-learning process. What is lacking is a methodology for gathering and studying the data. This is very significant to a district because it helps to understand the data that are important indicators of district-wide success. The North Central Regional Educational Laboratory's (NCREL) *Data Retreats* is one program that provides a large-scale methodology for studying data. It is this type of program that provides a "big picture" view of school district indicators of success and guides the improvement process. Districts interested in a large-scale methodology will find this program useful.

Dennis Fox, consultant with the Southern California Comprehensive Assistance Center, offers another conceptual model to help organize and view data on a broad basis in the district. This model provides a method to study various data sources and to identify trends and patterns. Figure 5.4 illustrates the contribution of these data sources to the decision-making process.

FIGURE 5.4—SCHOOL DATA SOURCES FOR DATA DECISION MAKING

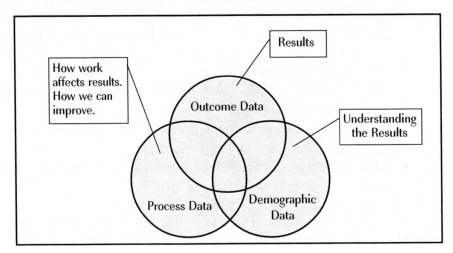

He categorizes data into three distinct groups as follows:

Outcome Data: These data measure the degree to which students demonstrate particular knowledge and/or skills, and achieve specified goals. Outcome data measure the impact of instruction on achievement. Examples of these data include: state assessments, norm-referenced tests, curriculum-based measures, portfolios, quizzes, homework, and teacher observations.

Demographic Data: These data measure the student and his/her family and community. These data characterize the group memberships and experiences, attitudes, and perceptions that are believed to affect the manner and rate in which students learn. Examples of these data include: gender, socio-economic status, ethnicity, limited English speaking, mobility, attendance rate, personal attitudes and perceptions, and discipline records.

Process Data: These components and practices comprise the instructional program in the classroom and at the school and district level. The process data are the only data that teachers and administrators can control in terms of making decisions that improve learning opportunities. Examples of these data sources are the curriculum, instructional time, classroom management, teacher attendance, instructional materials, equipment.[68]

Each of these three data sources contributes to the decision-making process. Practitioners can use these data sources to identify important connections among them and determine those factors that have an impact on the students' learning. These connections can be made at the district, school, or classroom level. It is then within the Process Data component of the model that teachers and administrators make decisions that will have an impact on the teaching-learning process. These decisions are called data-driven decisions.

It is at this point that we want to focus attention on the Outcome Data sources that teachers will work with on a daily basis. To do this we have provided a framework specifically to organize and understand these data. It is here where multiple decisions are made every day to improve learning opportunities for students. Teachers must have a working knowledge of these data. We are choosing to devote considerable time on this framework because it is manageable for teachers and should be a part of their everyday work with students. This framework depicts the day-in-and day-out use of Outcome Data (achievement and performance data) to make decisions with respect to the process component of the larger model. The framework serves to identify student assessment work within a working system of interrelated parts. It helps the teacher to use assessment data effectively.

This assessment framework provides a process to make data-driven decisions. It is designed to help teachers select data sources and use the data to measure student performance, improve instruction, and determine program effectiveness. It also provides reporting mechanisms for various audiences. Figure 5.5 illustrates the relationship between the fundamental questions the district seeks to answer, the relevant data sources to use, and the formative and summative learning that can be derived from thoughtful study of data. It also emphasizes the important role that reporting mechanisms play in the communication of what is learned from the data.

FIGURE 5.5—DISTRICT ASSESSMENT FRAMEWORK

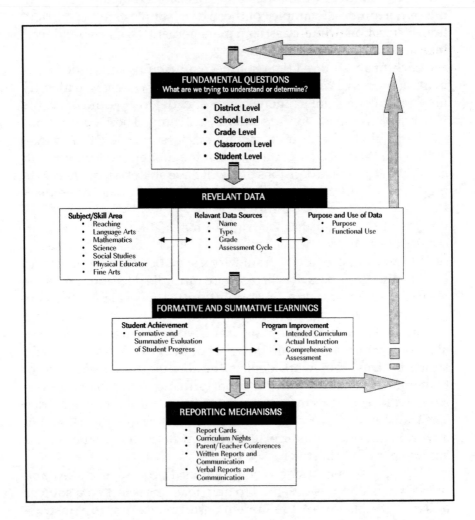

Fundamental Questions the Assessment Program Is Designed to Answer

Frequently school districts gather useful data, but they are merely descriptive of student performance. This information is not used in a consistent manner to guide teachers to more informed decisions about their instruction. Nor are the data used to meet other needs that the district may have such as placement of students in programs, monitoring student growth over time, and evaluating curricula. Moreover, parents could benefit from some of this valuable information to understand their child's progress. Data can provide many indicators of the district performance if used properly. When school districts agree on a set of fundamental questions to answer, they can focus their attention on specific areas.

Questions should be developed at all levels of the organization: the district, the school, and the classroom. For example, there may be questions that district level administrators want answered. The district-level questions are categorized by the following five areas:

1. Student Progress: How well are students progressing in each of their academic areas and within their respective grade levels?

2. Benchmarks: How well do students compare with local, state, national, and international counterparts?

3. Program Placement: How are students identified for placement in appropriate programs that best support their needs?

4. Reporting Mechanisms: To what extent is the district effective in reporting students' progress to various audiences (parents, teachers, community)?

5. Program Evaluations and Improvement: Are the district programs rigorous enough to enable the students to be competitive on a world-class level? Are the district programs diverse enough to meet the various needs of all students?

Each school team or individual teachers can use data to address the questions listed above. They can also develop their own set of questions. The value of developing questions is that they help to determine the specific type of data needed. When data are collected and used to answer questions, teachers gain new knowledge of how much assessment can support their instruction. It is important to make the distinction between testing and assessing. Testing is the process of giving tests and gathering data. Assessing is analyzing the data to improve the educational program for students. We often hear that testing takes away from instruction and is very time consuming. However, with guiding questions of study, the district can focus its assessment efforts more effectively and thus better meet the needs of students.

Relevant Data: Types of Assessment Data and Their Purposes

As a district determines what assessment measures to use, it is important to recognize that no single test or assessment can provide all the information needed to answer all of the questions of study in a comprehensive assessment program. The second level of Figure 5.5 illustrates that there are various types of achievement data that can be collected. These data are each designed for specific and unique purposes. With this in mind, it is important to have a shared language and understanding about assessment instruments, their purposes, and their ultimate uses, in order to support making data-driven decisions.

Overall there are two distinct categories of assessment: Classroom and Large-scale. Classroom assessments (also know as Informal Assessments) are those used by teachers on a day-to-day basis to provide a formative understanding of their students' achievement. Large-scale assessments (also known as Formal Assessments) are those mandated, designed, conducted, and reported from outside the classroom, usually for district or state evaluation, or accountability requirements.

Classroom Assessments. Classroom assessments comprise the majority of assessments used by teachers. They are the primary means through which assessment can inform their instruction and measure formative learning. Various classroom assessments can be used to obtain information about individual and group achievement. These include but are not limited to the following:

- Teacher-made tests
- Daily observation of student work in the classroom
- Checklists
- Brief skill tests included in workbooks
- Written quizzes
- Systematized behavior observations and anecdotal records
- Student projects and other performance-based measures
- Curriculum-based tests developed by the teacher, school, or the district
- Criterion-referenced tests

The National Forum on Assessment defines the role of classroom assessment and its interactive nature with curriculum and instruction as follows:

Classroom assessment is the primary means through which assessment affects learning. It is integrated with curriculum and instruction so that teaching, learning and assessing flow in a continuous process. By documenting and evaluating student work over time, teachers obtain information for understanding student progress in ways that can guide future instruction. Assessment also provides opportunities for self-reflection and evaluation by the student.[69]

Classroom assessment must always inform instruction. It can do this in several ways. One important way is in the daily continuous feedback that teachers give to students to help them improve their work. It also enables students to show their understanding through products they develop for authentic purposes.

Assessment and instruction need to be interwoven to meet student needs. Assessment plays a primary role in informing teachers' next steps in the classroom. Using data from various sources helps them to arrange students for small group instruction. It can help teachers create skill development groups as well as enrichment groups. It enhances their ability to determine student needs and then differentiate instruction geared toward those needs.

Large-Scale (High Stakes) Assessment. Large-scale assessment measures play a broader role in the assessment program than classroom assessment. They are primarily used in districts to improve program quality. They are also used to make policy decisions at district, state, and national levels. For example the Second International Mathematics and Science Study served as a catalyst in the writing of the well-known document, *A Nation at Risk.* It was this document that launched the reform movement in education. Large-scale assessments can have an important impact on classroom practices; but, they are more challenging to work with in this capacity. The TIMSS example we provided in the change chromosome illustrates this point.

Large-scale assessment has been implemented for decades but is now only starting to be used to inform practice at the state and local levels. One clear example is the work being done with the Third International Mathematics and Science Study (TIMSS). This is the first large-scale international assessment study offered to public school districts in the United States. In the re-administration of

TIMSS in 1999, 27 state, local consortia, and districts participated in it. Their data became available in the spring of 2001. The North Central Regional Education Laboratory (NCREL) has conducted analyses on the TIMSS data and developed protocols for using the curriculum and achievement data at the local level. These products are major breakthroughs for the use of large-scale assessment. For an in-depth view of the potential use of TIMSS for your district, we recommend the NCREL Web site at *http://www.ncrel.org*.

The value of a TIMSS study to local districts is multi-faceted. First, it allows a district to have benchmark comparisons with the highest achieving countries in the world. Second, the findings of this study challenge assumptions about the way U.S. students are taught. Third, it provides a frame of reference for developing what many so casually refer to as "world-class standards." Fourth, it helps teachers improve instructional practice. Finally, it provides a framework to align our curriculum, instruction, and assessment practices within a more global environment.

Table 5.3 provides examples of large-scale assessments:

TABLE 5.3—EXAMPLES OF LARGE-SCALE ASSESSMENTS	
TYPES	**EXAMPLES**
International Studies	• Third International Math and Science Study • Progress in International Reading Literacy Study and • Performance on International Student Assessment
General Achievement Tests	Terra Nova Achievement Test
Diagnostic Standardized Tests	Stanford Diagnostic Reading Test
State Standards Tests	Illinois Standards Achievement Test

As teachers seek to answer various questions that have been posed, they must determine the data sources for answering them. Then, they must be clear about how the data will be used and what purpose it will serve. Will it provide the necessary information to answer the questions? These data sources can be either formal or informal. As districts build their assessment program, we recommend that they determine the various types of district-wide assessments they will use and then specifically define the purposes for their use. This assessment standard will create a shared language and understanding for how assessments will be used across the district and will provide guidelines for teachers to follow in their study of questions. It will then focus their time and effort to improve student learning.

Formative and Summative Learnings

Once the data are analyzed and the answers to the questions are developed, teachers are able to describe what has been learned. It is this third level of the framework (Figure 5.5) that summarizes the findings of the data. The findings are in two areas: Student Achievement or Program Improvement. The focus of the learning will depend on the questions that were asked and the type of data that were used to study them. If the student achievement area was the focus of the question, then the interest is on measuring the progress of students. If program improvement is the focus, then the data were designed to determine if the program is adequately meeting the needs of students. In either case, the findings serve to guide the next steps to improving learning opportunities for the students. The findings from the data can also raise new questions for study. These questions would move to level one of this data framework, as noted by the return arrow.

Determine Reporting Mechanisms To Various Audiences

The data collected in the assessment program should take into consideration the various groups that need to be informed about the progress and development of students as well as the quality of the curricular programs. These groups can include parents, teachers, students, administrators, school boards, state departments of education, and policymakers at all levels of government. There is no one assessment measure that can adequately serve to provide the information desired by all of these groups. To determine the kind of assessments to use, we suggest that districts ask some critical questions that may help to identify the information they need to communicate to the various publics. What kind(s) of information do the assessments provide and what is the purpose of each assessment measure? Once you have determined the data source, you can then begin to structure the types of reporting that you want to use. Examples of reporting mechanisms include report cards, annual reports, parent-teacher conferences, and cable television broadcasts.

Evaluate the Assessment Program to Determine Its Impact on the Teaching-Learning Process

A district should always evaluate the plans and models it uses. The assessment program of a district is no different. It is important to improve all district-wide processes so that they can accomplish the district's desired results in the most effective way possible.

With respect to the assessment framework presented, teachers and administrators should ask several questions as they work with the program. For example, are we focusing on the right fundamental questions? Are our assessment measures informing us properly about student achievement? Are our students progressing adequately? Is our community well informed about our programs and achievement? Does our assessment information help improve curricular programs? Many other questions can be asked to determine the impact of the assessment program on the teaching-learning process and student performance.

We encourage all districts to ensure their assessment programs are coherent. They must employ practices and methods that are consistent with learning goals, curriculum, instruction, and current knowledge of how students learn. The National Forum on Assessment states that coherence can be achieved by ensuring that all assessments support important learning and are compatible with how students learn.[70] The extent of the assessment program's coherence can only be determined by evaluating the program and its systems.

The National Forum on Assessment writes that assessment of student learning is undergoing profound change. This is occurring at the same time reforms are taking place in learning goals, content standards, curriculum, instruction, the education of teachers, and the relationships among the various constituent groups. The Forum also states that assessment systems and practices must focus on improving classroom assessment while ensuring that large-scale assessment also supports learning. Learning assessment must be integrated with curriculum and instruction to best serve learning.[71] The changes that the National Forum on Assessment call for are daunting, but they can be achieved. The two models that we have presented in this section are designed to accomplish these very changes and are offered as a starting point for district discussions of how to approach data-driven decision-making.

More than ever, people desire to have detailed information about their child's progress. In this chromosome we emphasized the need for teachers and administrators to be assessment literate. Assessment literacy begins by building a context to support the effective use of assessment data. As districts develop their assessment program, we stress the importance of identifying the purposes and goals it seeks to accomplish. Then the district must design and implement systems to gather, use, and interpret assessment data. Finally, districts must determine if their assessment program is accomplishing its desired outcomes. We encourage districts to evaluate the assessment program to gain this valuable information.

Assessment

by David Clarke

Associate Professor, Education Faculty, University of Melbourne, Australia

Assessment should be recognized, not as a neutral element in the curriculum, but as a powerful mechanism for the social construction of competence. In the creation of a world-class school system, the imperative for educators is to realize and exploit the significant role that assessment plays in this process (see Barnes, Clarke, and Stephens, 2000). Assessment embodies the reflective function of the educational process, and improvement at the level of the individual student, the class, the teacher, the school or the school system should be informed and facilitated by assessment. However, the manner in which assessment has been undertaken in the past has alienated those whom it might most benefit: students and teachers.

To many teachers, assessment has been an unpleasant obligation imposed by the system, resented by students, and interrupting the teacher's principal activity: instruction. To many students, assessment has been stressful and arbitrary; an impersonal judgment on weeks or months of effort, much better at identifying failures than at documenting successes. Some of the faults are technical in nature. The persistently summative nature of most systemic assessment practices has consolidated the impression that assessment occurs after the event: documenting failure rather than promoting success. Inappropriate aggregation has misrepresented the understandings of individuals (Clarke, 1996) and the performances of nations (Bracey, 1996). Economic and political considerations have been allowed to override the messages of theory, the lessons of research, and the achievements of good educational practice.

In our assessment practices, we are in a position to benefit from an extensive body of theory, research and quality practice (Clarke, 1996). The messages are many. Wherever schools are able to draw upon the same activities for both instructional and assessment purposes, economies of time, effort and resources will occur. State-mandated and school-based assessment should model the full range of performances valued by the community. Student performance must be monitored in a manner that allows all students the opportunity to demonstrate what they have learned. For example, in the case of mathematics, the restriction of assessment tasks to only those requiring written responses or competency in calculation misrepresents mathematical activity and allows many important mathematical competencies of many students to go unrecognized.

Assessment can serve as a powerful agent for communicating standards. But both the standards and the assessment must be carefully and comprehensively conceived. Consistent with the increasing complexity of our society, student performances are expected to be more complex, frequently in response to real world tasks with several viable solutions. Teachers need to be even more active in the establishment of the tenets of excellent performance. Students cannot be expected to meet criteria that they themselves do not understand. In a world-class learning environment, the characteristics of good performance must be as much a part of classroom discussion as conventional academic content. A simple strategy to promote this is to have students evaluate samples of other students' attempts to solve a complex problem already attempted by the class. The ensuing discussion will identify those characteristics of quality performance that students are capable of recognizing and those that are only evident to the teacher. Class discussion can then relate these characteristics to their occurrence and development in the students' own work (see Clarke, 1995).

Government authorities must recognize that the political expediency of appearing to monitor key learning outcomes by measuring a narrow band of skills with out-of-date, discriminatory techniques will ultimately be self-defeating. State-mandated assessment should also be state-of-the-art assessment, consistent with local conditions. Quality assessment activities become quality instructional activities through a natural process of teacher adaptation (Barnes, Clarke and Stephens, 2000). Investment in quality assessment offers governments and school authorities a powerful, cost-efficient means to model exemplary practice, while meeting the evaluative obligations of public accountability.

References:

Barnes, M., Clarke, D.J., & Stephens, W.M. (2000) Assessment as the Engine of Systemic Reform. Journal of Curriculum Studies 32(5), 623–650.

Bracey, G.W. (1996). International Comparisons and the Condition of American Education. Educational Researcher 25(1), 5–11.

Clarke, D.J. (1995). Quality mathematics: How can we tell? The Mathematics Teacher 88(4), 326–328.

Clarke, D.J. (1996). Assessment. Chapter 9 in A. Bishop (Ed.). International Handbook of Mathematics Education. Dordrecht, The Netherlands: Kluwer.

Section II

The Genetic Framework for Your District: Building Your Own Teaching-Learning Process Chromosomes

Using the process outlined in chapter 4, Section II; you can build your Teaching-Learning Process Chromosomes. As with the Capacity-Building Chromosomes, we provide a blank worksheet for you to develop chromosomes other than the ones that we have presented.

Teaching-Learning Process Chromosomes Worksheets

CURRICULUM CHROMOSOME

Worksheet #1: Curriculum Chromosome Diagram

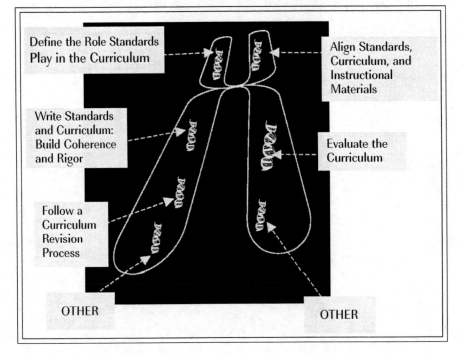

Worksheet #2: Curriculum Chromosome Guiding Questions

Articulating the Values and Research-Based Practices Your District Has Regarding Curriculum

We have delineated several curriculum genes (fundamental principles) that contribute to the development of a rigorous curriculum. In this activity we suggest that you use these curriculum genes and others of your own choosing to identify the values and research-based practices that describe how the curriculum should be developed and implemented in your district. Guiding questions have been provided to assist in articulating these values and practices. Begin the activity by reading the questions and asking: *What do we value and what are our practices with respect to each of these genes?*

Note: It is not critical that you formally answer each of these questions. It is important that you take them into consideration as you contemplate what you really value and believe.

Gene 1: Define the Role Standards Play in the Curriculum

- What approach (textbook-driven or standards-based) does the district use to delineate the curriculum by grade level?
- How does the district go about determining the content standards for student learning at each grade level?
- To what extent are standards documents used in the development of the curriculum?
- To what extent does the district expect teachers to be familiar with the standards documents that are the basis of the curriculum?
- To what extent is the board of education committed to the use of standards in the development of the curriculum?

continued

Gene 2: Write Standards and Curriculum: Build Coherence and Rigor

- When curriculum is written, what process is used to determine the concepts and skills that should be taught at each grade level?
- How are concepts and skills articulated through the grade levels?
- Does the district expect mastery of skills at specific grade levels and then drop the concept out of the curriculum to focus on more challenging concepts?
- What indicators does the district have to tell that the curriculum is rigorous?
- Does the district compare its curriculum against the curriculum of other high performing districts and/or countries?

Gene 3: Follow a Curriculum Revision Process

- What is the importance of each phase of the curriculum revision cycle and what purpose does it serve?
- Is there a district curriculum revision process? If so, what goals does the process attempt to accomplish?
- To what extent are the teachers familiar with the curriculum revision process and understand its value to them as professionals?
- To what extent is professional development a part of the revision process?

Gene 4: Align Standards, Curriculum, and Instructional Materials

- To what extent can teachers articulate how they use the instructional materials to teach the curriculum?

continued

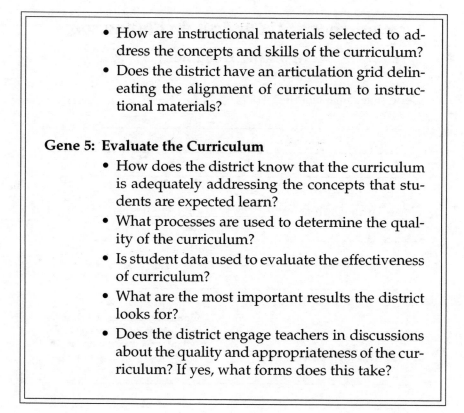

- How are instructional materials selected to address the concepts and skills of the curriculum?
- Does the district have an articulation grid delineating the alignment of curriculum to instructional materials?

Gene 5: Evaluate the Curriculum

- How does the district know that the curriculum is adequately addressing the concepts that students are expected learn?
- What processes are used to determine the quality of the curriculum?
- Is student data used to evaluate the effectiveness of curriculum?
- What are the most important results the district looks for?
- Does the district engage teachers in discussions about the quality and appropriateness of the curriculum? If yes, what forms does this take?

Worksheet #3: Curriculum Chromosome

Working Document

Gene (Fundamental Principle) _____

_____

_____

_____

Gene Value Statement _____

_____

_____

_____

DNA (Research-Based Practices)	If applicable, indicate the chromosome these practices are connected to; if they are connected to a specific gene or DNA piece from another chromosome, indicate as such.
_____	_____
_____	_____
_____	_____

List those genes and/or DNA that you would like to develop more fully in the future and draw appropriate connections to other chromosomes as done above.

_____	_____
_____	_____
_____	_____

Teaching-Learning Process Chromosomes Worksheets

INSTRUCTIONAL PRACTICE CHROMOSOME

Worksheet #1: Instructional Practice Chromosome Diagram

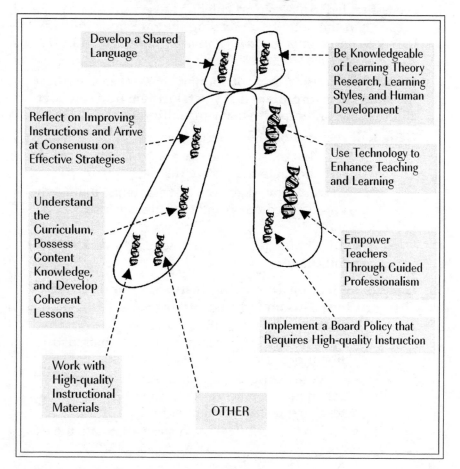

Worksheet #2: Instructional Practice Chromosome Guiding Questions

Articulating the Values and Research-Based Practices Your District Has Regarding Instructional Practice

We have delineated several instructional practice genes (fundamental principles) that contribute to the development of high-quality instruction. In this activity we suggest that you use these instructional practice genes and others of your own choosing to identify the values and research-based practices that describe how the instructional practice should be developed and used in your district. Guiding questions have been provided to assist in articulating these values and practices. Begin the activity by reading the questions and asking: *What do we value and what are our practices with respect to each of these genes?*

Note: It is not critical that you formally answer each of these questions. It is important that you take them into consideration as you contemplate what you really value and believe.

Gene 1: Develop a Shared Language
- To what extent is there a shared language of instructional terms in your district?
- In what ways does your district ensure that teachers have a common understanding of instructional terms?
- To what extent should teachers have a shared language?

Gene 2: Reflect on Improving Instruction and Arrive at Consensus on Effective Strategies
- In what ways does the district provide time and opportunities for teachers to discuss their instructional practices?
- Has the district come to a consensus of important instructional practices that must be a part of all teachers' instructional repertoire?
- To what extent does the district articulate the ex-

continued

pectations for consistent implementation of specific instructional practices throughout the school(s)?

- In what ways are teachers consistently exposed to research on effective instructional practices?

Gene 3: Understand the Curriculum, Possess Content Knowledge, and Develop Coherent Lessons

- To what extent are teachers informed about the specific curricular expectations and expected to adhere to them with integrity?
- What practices are in place in the district to ensure that teachers possess a deep understanding of their content knowledge?
- What qualifications does the district expect content specialists to have?
- What, if any, protocols or processes exist in the district for developing high-quality coherent lessons among staff members?
- How does the school protect classroom instructional time from interruptions?

Gene 4: Work with High-quality Instructional Materials

- What processes are used in the district to evaluate and identify high-quality instructional materials that are aligned with the district's curriculum standards and expectations?
- To what extent does the district support teachers in discriminating the most valuable parts of instructional materials and ignore those portions that do not focus on the curricular expectations for that grade level?

Gene 5: Be Knowledgeable of Learning Theory Research, Learning Styles, and Human Development

- What role does research on learning theory and learning styles play in the development of both the curricular program and instructional practice?
- Are there specific theories of instructional practice that all teachers are expected to implement? Identify them.

continued

Gene 6: Use Technology to Enhance Teaching and Learning

- In what ways does the district expect teachers to use technology?
- Does the use of technology create a rich interactive learning environment or a passive one? In what ways?
- Are the products (intellectual capital and tangible results) resulting from technology use indicators of rigorous learning and are they only because of the use of technology?
- Is technology in reasonable supply for all teachers and students to use when needed?
- To what extent is professional development provided for teachers to maintain their skills and learn new ones? This is critical if the district expects the technology to be used in a manner the district expects.
- Are incentives for technology use aligned with the district's learning standards and is there a well-developed plan for how to integrate technology into instruction to achieve lesson objectives and tasks?
- To what extent are students trained to use technology as a powerful learning tool?

Gene 7: Empower Teachers Through Guided Professionalism

- To what extent does the district expect schools to be structures to facilitate guided professionalism? What specific ways have been implemented?
- In what ways does the teacher supervision/evaluation process guide teacher collaboration and discussion around practices and use of assessment data designed to improve student achievement?

Gene 8: Implement a Board Policy that Requires High-quality Instruction

- What board policy exists that address the expectation, if any, for high-quality instruction?

Worksheet #3: Instructional Practice Chromosome

Working Document

Gene (Fundamental Principle) _____

_____

_____

_____

Gene Value Statement_____

_____

_____

_____

DNA (Research-Based practices)	If applicable, indicate the chromosome these practices are connected to; if they are connected to a specific gene or DNA piece from another chromosome, indicate as such.
_____	_____
_____	_____
_____	_____
_____	_____

List those genes and/or DNA that you would like to develop more fully in the future and draw appropriate connections to other chromosomes as done above.

_____	_____
_____	_____
_____	_____

Teaching-Learning Process
Chromosomes Worksheets

ASSESSMENT CHROMOSOME

Worksheet #1: Assessment Chromosome Diagram

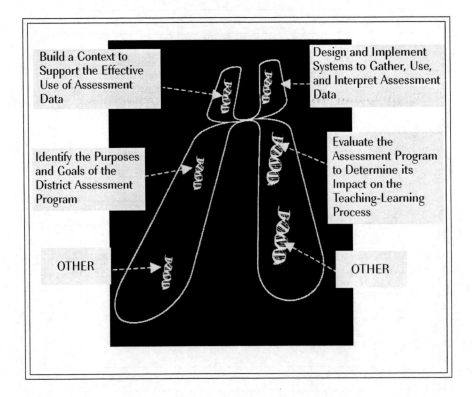

Worksheet #2: ASSESSMENT CHROMOSOME GUIDING QUESTIONS

Articulating the Values and Research-Based Practices Your District Has Regarding Assessment

We have delineated several assessment genes (fundamental principles) that contribute to the development of an effective assessment program. In this activity we suggest that you use these assessment genes and others of your own choosing to identify the values and research-based practices that describe how the assessment should be developed and implemented in your district. Guiding questions have been provided to assist in articulating these values and practices. Begin the activity by reading the questions and asking: *What do we value and what are our practices with respect to each of these genes?*

Note: It is not critical that you formally answer each of these questions. It is important that you take them into consideration as you contemplate what you really value and believe.

Gene 1: Build a Context to Support the Effective Use of Assessment Data

- Does the district have a local assessment program?
- What are the research underpinnings that guide the development and implementation of the program?
- What does *assessment literate* mean to teachers and administrators in the district?
- What views does the district hold regarding aligning assessment with the intended curriculum and the taught curriculum? Is this alignment important to the district?

Gene 2: Identify the Purposes and Goals of the District Assessment Program

- To what extent has the school district articulated the purposes and goals of the district assessment program? What are the theoretical underpinnings of those purposes and goals?

- How does the district expect the teachers and administrators to describe what the assessment program serves to accomplish?

Gene 3: Design and Implement Systems to Gather, Use, and Interpret Assessment Data

- Describe the framework for how the assessment program should operate in the district.

Fundamental Questions of the Assessment Program

- Does the district develop guiding questions regarding student progress, program effectiveness and rigor, student program placement, etc., at all organizational levels (district, school, classroom)?
- To what extent do the data collected focus on answering these questions?

Types of Assessment Data and Their Purpose

- To what extent are data organized and distinguished by their use and purpose?
- Do staff members understand what the data can tell them and whether the data they are using will provide the answers they seek?
- Is there a clear understanding of how various data sources can and should be used to meet teachers and the district needs?
- What role, if any, do large-scale assessments play in measuring student growth, placement issues, and program improvement?

Learning from the Data

- What are staff expected to learn about student growth from the findings of the data?
- What are the expectations that staff members will

use the findings of the data to improve current practice?

- What are the expectations that the district will use the findings of the data to improve curriculum?

Reporting Mechanisms

- Describe the various ways in which the findings from data analysis are reported to various audiences.
- What information does the district consciously believe is important to report to various groups in the district and the wider community?

Gene 4: Evaluate the Assessment Program to Determine Its Impact on the Teaching-Learning Process

- Describe the structure or system that is in place to determine if the assessment program is effectively measuring student learning, evaluating the curriculum, and appropriately informing teachers about their instructional practice.

Worksheet #3: Assessment Chromosome

Working Document

Gene (Fundamental Principle) _____

_____

_____

_____

Gene Value Statement _____

_____

_____

_____

	If applicable, indicate the chromosome these practices are connected to; if they are connected to a specific gene or DNA piece from another chromosome, indicate as such.
DNA (Research-Based practices)	

List those genes and/or DNA that you would like to develop more fully in the future and draw appropriate connections to other chromosomes as done above.

Teaching-Learning Process Chromosomes Worksheets

YOUR DISTRICT CHROMOSOME

Worksheet #1: Your District Chromosome Diagram

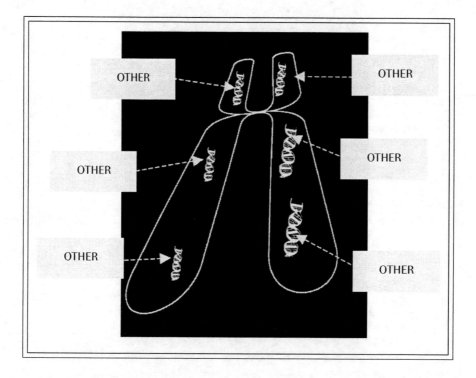

Worksheet #2: Your District Chromosome Guiding Questions

(To be completed by reader)

Gene 1:

•

•

Gene 2:

•

•

Gene 3:

•

•

Gene 4:

•

•

Gene 5:

•

•

Gene 6:

•

•

Worksheet #3: Your District Chromosome

Working Document

Gene (Fundamental Principle) _____

_____

_____

_____

Gene Value Statement _____

_____

_____

_____

DNA (Research-Based practices)   If applicable, indicate the chromosome these practices are connected to; if they are connected to a specific gene or DNA piece from another chromosome, indicate as such.

List those genes and/or DNA that you would like to develop more fully in the future and draw appropriate connections to other chromosomes as done above.

Summary

Curriculum Chromosome

- Local control of curriculum has been as much a hindrance to student learning as it has been a protection from exposure to unwanted subject matter.
- Standards provide the core of rigorous curriculum for all students to learn but they must be implemented with a balanced view.
- The curriculum must be coherent and rigorous. It must be coherent in the sense that there are a reasonable number of topics, concepts, and skills, to be learned at each grade level. The flow of the curriculum should be developmentally challenging to the students at all grade levels. Topics, concepts, and skills should remain in the curriculum only until students would be expected to master them. The curriculum must be rigorous in that it should delve into topics, develop depth of understanding, and expect students to learn content that is challenging for the age level.
- A curriculum revision process serves several purposes. It guides school district efforts to maintain up-to-date curriculum programs. It provides a timeline for various revision initiatives and a plan for all staff members to know when they need to assume responsibility for learning a new program.
- Aligning the instructional materials to the curriculum framework will result in greater coherence and academic rigor. Teachers will be able to know exactly what lessons to teach in order to meet the core learning standards, concepts, and skills.
- Valid data should be used to evaluate whether the curriculum is achieving its intended expectations.

Instructional Practice Chromosome

- Teaching is the most critical component if students are going to achieve world- class performance.
- High-quality teaching requires planning activities that involve teachers in learning communities that focus on specific themes.
- Teachers need to understand learning theory and human development to effectively meet the learning needs of all students.

- A lesson should be scripted and rehearsed in much the same manner that an actor rehearses for a part in a play.

Assessment Chromosome

- Assessment is the most underutilized of the three teaching-learning process chromosomes.
- Teachers and administrators need to become more assessment literate to take advantage of the information that data have to offer.
- The assessment chromosome provides substantive information to engage in continuous improvement. It provides information about academic progress, curricular programs, and instructional practices. It provides parents and other community members with high-quality information about how the district is meeting student needs.
- Districts must build a cultural context for using assessment data. Nine research-based practices can be developed to build an assessment culture: establish continuous improvement, nurture a culture for assessment literacy, provide professional development opportunities, develop the structural pieces to support the consistent use of data to learn and improve, integrate the national and state emphases for using assessment, set high performance standards and expectations at a world-class level, align assessment with curriculum and instruction, work with high-quality, accurate information, and evaluate process for using data to determine if it is improving the learning environment for students.
- An assessment program must identify clear purposes and goals. This will help the district determine how the program will contribute to the organization and what it will accomplish.
- Districts must articulate a well-developed framework to gather, use, and interpret assessment data. This can take different forms. Districts should conceptualize how they will view data in the broad sense of understanding patterns and trends. At the same time they must help teachers to understand and use data on a day-to-day basis to make instruction decisions to improve learning opportunities for

students. Two conceptual models are illustrated to address these district goals.

- Evaluating the assessment program will determine if it is having a positive impact on the teaching-learning process.

Endnotes

50. W. H., Schmidt, C. C. McKnight, & S. A. Raizen, *A splintered vision: an investigation of U. S. science and mathematics education* (Kluwer Academic: Dordrecht, the Netherlands, 1997).

51. Marc S. Tucker and Judy B. Codding, *Standards for our schools: how to set them, measure them, and reach them* (San Francisco: Jossey-Bass Publishers: 1998).

52. Schmidt, McKnight, Raizen, *A splintered vision: an investigation of U. S. science and mathematics education.*

53. Seymour B. Sarason, *Teaching as a performing art* (New York: Teachers College Press, 1999), p. 4.

54. Dan D. Goldhaber and Dominick J. Brewer, "Evaluating the effect of teacher degree level on educational performance," *Development in School Finance* (1996), p. 199.

55. Rita Dunn and Ken Dunn, *Teaching students through their individual learning styles* (Reston: VA, 1978).

56. How people learn: mind, brain, experience, and school. National Research Council. (Washington, DC: National Academy Press, 2000), pp. 14–18.

57. How people learn, pp. 19–21

58. Report of the National Reading Panel. National Institute of Child Health and Human Development (April 2000).

59. Michael Fullan and Andy Hargreaves, *What's worth fighting for out there* (NY, 1998: Teachers College Press), pp. 98–99.

60. Robert Stake, The goals on American education," *Phi Delta Kappan* (May 1999), pp. 668–672. Rebecca Simmons, "The horse before the cart: assessing for understanding," *Educational Leadership* (February 1994) Vol. 51, No. 5. Kathy Checkley, "Assessment that serves instruction," *Education Update* (June 1997) Vol. 39, No. 4. Robert L. Linn, "Assessments and accountability," *Educational Researcher* (March 2000) Vol. 29, No. 2, pp. 4–16

61. Stake, The goals on American education," Simmons, "The horse before the cart: assessing for understanding," Kathy Checkley,

"Assessment that serves instruction," Robert L. Linn, "Assessments and accountability".

62. Linn, "Assessments and accountability," p. 8.
63. Linn, "Assessments and accountability," p. 9.
64. Linn, "Assessments and accountability," p. 9.
65. "Principles and indicators for student assessment systems" (policy paper), National Forum on Assessment (Washington, DC, August 1995) pp. 1–29.
66. *Testing, teaching and learning: a guide for states and school districts* National Research Council (Washington Academy Press: Washington, DC, 1999), p. 3.
67. Stake, The goals on American education," Simmons, "The horse before the cart: assessing for understanding," Checkley, "Assessment that serves instruction," Linn, "Assessments and accountability," pp. 4–16.
68. Dennis Fox, "Three kinds of data for decisions about reading," *Using data for educational decision making*, Vol. 6, No. 1, Spring 2001, Comprehensive Assistance Center, Region VI.
69. "Principles and indicators for student assessment systems," National Forum on Assessment, p. 6.
70. "Principles and indicators for student assessment systems," National Forum on Assessment, p. 1.
71. "Principles and indicators for student assessment systems," National Forum on Assessment, p. 26.

Chapter 6

Final Thoughts

As we wrote this book we were aware that the education profession is immature compared with other professions such as medicine, law, and business. When we say that education is immature, we use the description put forth by University of California at Los Angeles history professor, Theodore M. Porter. In his book, *Trust the Numbers: The Pursuit of Objectivity in Science and Public Life*, he characterizes an immature profession as one where expertise is based on the subjective judgments of the individual professional, trust based on personal contact rather than quantification, and autonomy allowed by expertise and trust, which staves off standardized procedures based on research findings that use control groups. He goes on to say that a mature profession is characterized by a shift from judgments of individual experts to judgments constrained by quantified data that can be inspected by a broad audience, less emphasis on personal trust and more on objectivity, and a greater role for standardized measures and procedures informed by scientific investigations that use control groups.[72]

Education is at the point of needing to mature. It must begin to use quantifiable data that can be inspected by a broad audience and use sound research findings (qualitative and quantitative) that can inform our practice. This information can support the kind of decisions that will help our schools become internationally competitive and world-class. It is for this reason that we wrote this book, to help education take a significant step toward maturity.

It is our contention that we must prepare students to be functioning members of a WORLDWIDE COMMUNITY OF EXCELLENCE. School districts have no other alternative than to seek to be world-class. It is not about being number one in the world, but about being competitive. By this we mean that a district is capable of articulating and demonstrating the ability to compete and perform with the highest-achieving countries in the world. We also mean that this achievement must be accomplished within the context of the American culture. Practices that work in other countries may not work in American schools. Therefore, we must be judicious in taking potentially useful information and findings, and applying them with efficacy. Finally, we mean that school districts must embrace the concept of benchmarking, whereby comparing oneself against broader standards becomes the norm. We believe that world-class performance can be achieved when districts write a well developed course of action to do so.

The fundamental message of this book is that world-class achievement can be accomplished, by using a genetic model. The major premise of the genetic model is to use research-based, data-driven, and quantifiable work to guide the development of a theory of action for our profession. The model is the means to develop the necessary systemic connections among core areas that would lead to world-class performance and purports that no one approach or method is superior to another. To the contrary, it supports the notion that a district must make decisions based on its unique culture and circumstances, but it does so with this one important caveat; that all decisions should be guided by a comprehensive understanding and application of research, and quantifiable measures of achievement. By doing so, educators have the necessary information to make informed decisions regarding how their schools could become internationally competitive and world-class.

The genetic model builds a working theory of action by developing six chromosomes we call core areas. Figure 6.1 illustrates the integrative nature of these six chromosomes. These chromosomes are categorized into two groups. The first group requires a school district to build the intellectual and contextual capacity to lead people and empower them to grapple with the complexities of implementing world-class practices. Three chromosomes are developed in this group: Leadership, Change, and Professional Development. With visionary leadership, knowledge of the change process and an environment to nurture that process, and the ability to develop the capacity of people in the organization, schools can successfully implement world-class practices.

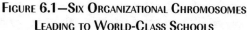

FIGURE 6.1—SIX ORGANIZATIONAL CHROMOSOMES
LEADING TO WORLD-CLASS SCHOOLS

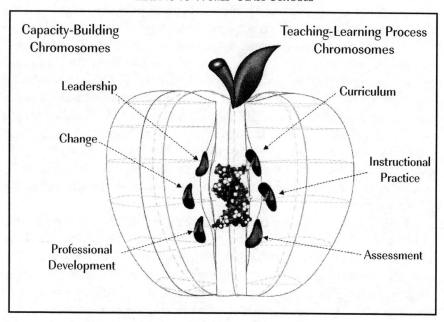

The second group of chromosomes is designed to address the fundamental aspects of the teaching-learning process. Three chromosomes are developed in this group: Curriculum, Instructional Practice, and Assessment. While all three of these areas are given attention in most school districts, we contend that districts need to use quality research to make better decisions about their development and that stronger connections need to be made between them. Their natural interactive aspects must be developed into a usable and practical theory of action for teachers. Collectively, all six chromosomes can be managed and integrated for the purpose of bringing organization to the disconnects that frequently exist in schools. The concept of the genetic model can help bring organization from chaos in the reform of American education. The genetic model enables educators to acquire and understand the necessary information to make informed decisions regarding how their schools could become internationally competitive and world-class.

To develop a theory of action, we presented and discussed current research expressly designed to shape the readers' thinking about issues, content, and practices for the 21st century. We modeled for the reader an approach to studying research that would lead to world-class practices. Beyond the research, however, we provided the means for districts to articulate and analyze their fundamental principles, core values, and practices that result in their current way of operating and to determine if they do reflect world-class practices. This was done through the Chromosome Worksheet activities in chapters 4 and 5. It is our hope that from building these chromosomes, districts have identified those areas that are highly effective and those that need further development and integration. Each district has the opportunity to shape its own future using the genetic model.

Four themes cross the boundaries of the six chromosomes. First, continuous improvement is the cornerstone upon which the chromosomes are built. The capacity-building chromosomes enable the district to create and sustain an environment to become a learning organization. These chromosomes define the district's vision and the focus and process by which continuous improvement can become a cultural norm. The teaching-learning process chromosomes articulate the substance of teaching and learning. The interaction of curriculum, instructional practice, and assessment enables the district to improve its instructional programs and delivery systems so that world-class performance can be achieved.

Second, each chromosome is rooted in current research. As we mentioned from the outset, research must be thoroughly studied and applied. Educators must not be afraid of the findings if they contradict their current views of schooling. To the contrary, they must embrace them as the seeds of improvement, just as a doctor uses an accurate medical diagnosis to provide the beginning point for determining a sound medical treatment.

Third, each chromosome requires a commitment to professional development. Teachers need the opportunity to learn new content, process, and skills. In each chromosome there are new concepts to learn, and we recognize that as districts begin to tackle these six areas, their staffs will need to gain new knowledge and methods to implement that learning. As we have stated throughout the book, professional development is a necessary, ongoing process, but often it is under-emphasized. It is our hope that districts will view professional development as an indispensable activity as they work with each of the six chromosomes.

Finally, each chromosome requires a self-evaluation component for the recommended processes and frameworks. For example, when a school district implements a new program, it must evaluate how effectively the program is accomplishing its intended purposes. Therefore, if a new curriculum is implemented, there must be an evaluation component in the program to determine if it is as coherent and rigorous as expected. If a new model of professional development is implemented, evaluate it to see if it really is making a difference in changing teachers' beliefs and values so that their classroom instruction is different. It will also be important to see if the new approaches are, in fact, improving student achievement. It is always important to remember that a new program does not guarantee positive change or that a new process will be effective. It is essential to evaluate processes. If you take a different approach to implement change, is that approach making a difference? Self-evaluation of all new initiatives and approaches is critical, and you must use quantifiable measures to determine their effectiveness.

It is at this juncture that we return to the notion that education needs to become a more mature profession. Douglas Carnine, professor at the University of Oregon, argues that the education field relies heavily on qualitative research and virtually avoids statistical research methods. He contends that practitioners need to be influenced more by evidence rather than philosophy, and that they must not reject the evidence because it does not fit their ideological preferences.[73] We agree with Carnine that quantitative studies are desperately needed; yet we do not discount the value that sound qualitative reviews of educational practices can help teachers improve.

School districts must begin to adopt practices that demonstrate their efficacy. Pressure is already being brought to bear from the outside with local, state, and national demands for accountability. As we mentioned in the Assessment Chromosome, the public is seeking more information than ever and they trust quantified data because it reduces subjective decision-making. The genetic model attempts to move to this level of accountability.

The time has come for education to begin its metamorphosis into a mature profession. Carnine writes "Only when the profession embraces scientific methods of determining efficacy and accepts accountability for results will education acquire the status – and the rewards – of a mature profession."[74]

In summary, the genetic model puts the spotlight squarely on those values, beliefs and practices that will bring about higher student achievement and improved teaching. While the genetic model allows for local control, it utilizes research-based, data-driven decision-making with both a sound qualitative review of education practices in schools and countries that have high student achievement and effective teaching practices. It emphasizes the need to use quantitative findings to make objective decisions. The ultimate outcome is to improve performance that results in the students becoming members of a WORLDWIDE COMMUNITY OF EXCELLENCE.

We hope that by using a scientific metaphor for school improvement that the wider American community will gain a better understanding of the complexities and challenges inherent in school systems and in the teaching-learning process. We have attempted to describe a vision that a more sophisticated conceptualization of school systems is necessary to meet the challenges of the 21st century society, just as we see it in both business and medical professions. It is our hope that districts will recognize the necessity to invest the time, energy, passion, patience, and resources to develop a community of high-performers who can compete with the best-achieving students in the world and be productive citizens in an ever-changing global society.

Endnotes

72. Theodore M. Porter, *Trust in numbers: the pursuit of objectivity in science and public life* (Princeton, NJ: Princeton University Press, 1996).

73. Douglas Carnine, "Why education experts resist effective practices (and what it would take to make education more like medicine)," Thomas B. Fordham Foundation (April 2000), pp. 9-10.

74. Carnine, "Why education experts resist effective practices (and what it would take to make education more like medicine)," p. 10.

Appendix A

Guest Essays

World-Class Education Concepts

Why We Need a World-Class Education System— One Governor's Perspective
by James Geringer
Governor of Wyoming

Mention the "new economy" and most people think it has something to do with a Dot-Com company or the makers of the latest high-tech gadget.

Yes, that's part of it, but the new economy isn't just about the creation or use of new technology. It's also about how we use information in every part of our lives, from school to the workplace to entertainment to the delivery of government services. Nearly everything we do has been changed by the better use of information and understanding interrelationships. We are overwhelmed by information and data. What we need is the ability to make better decisions. Today's economy, whether in Old Economy businesses or New Economy startups, depends upon how value is added through people, through knowledge, and through ideas.

In the New Economy, the competition is relentless, people are the most important resource, and there's no such thing as a smooth ride. Increasing a person's capability depends on understanding how knowledge builds wealth. Technology is here to stay. Alliances or partnerships are the way to get things done. Connectivity and networking are not just nice to have, they are essential. The old economy had workers moving to where industry and jobs were, located near material sources and transportation hubs. In the new economy business comes to the worker, not vice versa, and value today is added through people more than ever before.

Today's workers in the new economy aren't just focused on economic goals. Equally important are personal and societal goals, which clearly requires access to education that enriches the person and society as much as it enriches our economic pursuits.

I regularly speak with people in education about the exciting possibilities that technology can bring to the education experience. I speak of how technology properly applied, can enable students to discover information, learn concepts and explore issues in ways that would have never been possible without technology. "Don't just automate old processes, transform them!" Develop the whole person with the whole world as the learning place!

Learning that comes through discovery is the most exciting and enduring way to learn. Technology enables discovery learning. Technology, properly applied, enables most students to become self-initiated and self-directed in the learning process, thereby giving their teachers the gift of more time to spend with other students who may not be moving as quickly along the path of learning. Later in life, the self-motivated students will have the confidence to be self-initiated and self-directed in their jobs, just what our employers want and certainly a key ingredient for success in the new economy.

I tell school administrators that if they carry technology as a separate line item in their budgets, they don't really know how to use it. The same applies to our businesses. Technology should be embedded in every part of education and business, enabling us in ways that would otherwise be impossible. Technology enables us to focus on results, not on inputs and processes. Education can and should be measured in terms of student competence or achievement, not just in terms of class attendance and seat time. Business must be focused on delivering the best service or product possible. Enhanced productivity is the key, and technology-enriched education can make that happen.

Access to university-based cutting edge research and pools of highly skilled workers are essential to sustain and grow businesses. Both require conventional and unconventional access to and delivery of education. Technology will be used, not only to leverage the production of products and services, but also to deliver instruction and skill training independently of time and place.

We will have to invest more than ever in human capital to attract and keep today's workers motivated and competitive. Today's news is filled with statistics about our nation's very low unemployment rate. Business can't find enough workers. Government can't find enough workers. Our schools can't find enough teachers. In times past, workers had to go to where businesses were. Today, businesses come to where the workers are, and where the workers would rather stay. Employees no longer have to relocate or take whatever job is available. They can be selective and be employed on their terms and those terms are more focused than ever on quality of life.

The need for higher quality, better-educated employees implies a smaller pool from which to choose. Counter to that implication is the realization that the pool from which to recruit is shrinking daily for other reasons. That requires us to deliver more and better education to our kids and to our citizens overall, in order for our businesses and our society to remain competitive and sustainable.

Education is the foundation upon which everything else is built. Lifelong learning isn't a luxury; it's a necessity. The day you stop learning is the day you start losing.

We need education reform in the public schools that comes through improvements in teacher quality and student assessments. We need investments in higher education that encourage more awareness of today's markets and responsiveness to where the new economy should be, not just where we are today. We need livable communities that understand civic responsibility. Hockey's great Wayne Gretzky made it clear that he never skated to where the puck was. He always skated to where the puck was going to be. Likewise, we need to realize that success means keeping our citizens, young or old, in front of where they need to be.

Education isn't the silver bullet that gives each person a one-time shot at success in life. Rather, education is the silver lining that lets us discover new paths to success all through life.

World-Class Education Concepts

Why Have World-Class Schools?
by Richard Haynes
co-author of *World-Class Schools*

Two presidents, the U.S. Secretary of Education, and a myriad of governors have called for world-class schools. What would happen if the United States dedicated itself to making U.S. schools world-class? Why bother?

Anyone who has asked foreign exchange students from Western Europe about their year in U.S. schools could answer the question. Graduate students in my Comparative Education course interview international students and frequently hear: "As an exchange student, I was told to have a wonderful time in the United States and to work on my English, but my year in a U.S. high school wouldn't count at home." One of my students remarked, "That's embarrassing! Why aren't our schools good enough for them?"

Why doesn't the U.S. have world-class schools? In part, the education reform movement of the past two decades has failed to ask the right questions, choosing to guide reform with political agendas rather than reason. The U.S. rejects, sans reasoning, the idea of a national curriculum, national assessment, and a longer school year. Americans simply assume such changes can't happen in the United States. Yet they happen in other countries. Great Britain moved from a curriculum as chaotic as that in the United States to a national curriculum in 1988. France lengthened the school year. It was all based on sound reasoning. Can't the United States do the same thing?

If the United States were to move to world-class schools, what good might come from those changes? Here are a few examples:

1. If there were a national curriculum and assessment, textbooks would meet one standard, thus becoming smaller, automatically aligned, and cheaper (at least, they should be). Better home support materials would be cheaper and available for parents to buy (as they are in Japan) while waiting in grocery store lines. Children who move from state to state (often lower achievers), wouldn't be thrown

further behind by moving from one curriculum to another. An intelligently designed national curriculum would substantially raise U.S. international rankings on comparative test scores.

2. If the school year were world-class, teachers should see salaries rise as they work more days. Students would have the same learning time as their higher-producing counterparts in other countries. A long summer break wouldn't assure lost learning, which impacts most of the slowest, lowest SES students. School days could be used creatively like other countries do—offering weekly staff development on Wednesday afternoons when students go home early as is found in Germany.

3. If sports programs were world-class, towns and communities would continue to turn out in droves for the big game. But they wouldn't draw money from school funds. Students wouldn't leave school for sports events. How? In most countries sports are municipal activities, supported by towns, not by schools. That may explain why so many students from world-class schools answer the question "what does it take to be really popular in school?" with: "being a really good student!"

4. If special education programs were world-class, U.S. special educators wouldn't have 50% of their time spent doing paperwork. Because many world-class schools start special educators at ten percent higher salaries for their extra year of teacher preparation, there might not be a shortage of special education teachers. Also, there would only be one set of behavior rules and punishments for all students.

5. If our students were world-class, there would be an incredible difference in their lives. Far fewer students would come from divorced families. The suicide and homicide rates of students would drop by over 80%. Teacher assaults would be virtually nonexistent. Students would do homework, start driving at a later age, and watch less TV.

Why have world-class schools? Why not? The best teachers have always "stolen" the best ideas from other teachers to improve their own teaching. Why shouldn't school systems "steal" the best ideas from each other to create better-educated students globally? Our students deserve nothing less than the best because they are the "only next generation" we have.

Creating world-class schools will take flexibility and creativity. During the change to them, there will be controversy and challenges. But engineers joke that the glass is neither half empty nor half full because to them, it is the wrong size! U.S. leaders need such creative and intelligent assessment of good schools that can get better with the right leadership and world-class ideas.

Capacity-Building: Professional Development

Teaching to World-Class Standards Requires Powerful Professional Development
by Dennis Sparks
(Executive Director of the National Staff Development Council)

Student learning is directly linked to the quality of teaching that occurs in classrooms, numerous studies and national reports tell us. And a significant influence on the quality of teaching is the quality of the ongoing professional learning experiences districts and schools provide teachers, administrators, support staff, and school board members.

To play its vital role in standards-based reform, staff development must be results-driven, standards-based, and job embedded. In addition, it must focus on providing all teachers with a deep knowledge of the content they teach, the most effective methods for teaching that content, and frequent opportunities to learn and work with their colleagues to improve student learning.

The type of staff development that is most powerful:

- Deepens teachers' knowledge of the content they teach. Deeper understanding of academic content and its application in real-world settings requires sustained, intellectually rigorous study. While occasional awareness sessions about content standards or after-school make-and-take workshops may be appropriate as part of a comprehensive staff development plan, they alone are insufficient. It is also critical that teachers are taught with methods that are consistent with those they are expected to use in their own classrooms.

- Expands teachers' repertoire of research-based instructional skills to teach that content. Some strategies are more effective than others in particular subject areas. NSDC's report, "What Works in the Middle: Results-Based Staff Development," provides descriptions of staff development programs in the core content areas that have demonstrated their effectiveness in improving student learning in the middle grades. *The Handbook of Research on Improving Student Achievement,* edited by Gordon Cawelti, is also an excellent resource for such practices.

- Provides ongoing classroom assistance in implementing new skills. Teachers need generous amounts of "at-the-elbow" assistance in implementing many new instructional strategies. This assistance can come from other teachers, trainers, or the school's principal.

- Has at its core a small team of teachers who meet several times a week to plan lessons together, critique student work, and assist in problem solving. To increase collaboration and to provide the practical assistance and emotional support they receive, all teachers need to be members of teams in which participants support one another in teaching all students to high standards. These teams should meet for a hour or more several times a week.

- Provides teachers with the classroom assessment skills that allow them to regularly monitor gains in student learning resulting from improved classroom practices. In addition to data on student learning provided by the school district, teachers need efficient, practical ways to monitor weekly and monthly improvements in student learning. Not only will the acquisition of these assessment skills improve teaching, they also will enable teachers and staff development leaders to determine the effectiveness of their efforts.

- Is surrounded by a culture and supported by structures that encourage innovation, experimentation, and the collegial sharing of new ideas and practices. Because school cultures exert a powerful force on performance, teachers must be surrounded by norms, symbols, and stories that support high expectations and create an environment in which continuous improvement thrives. School calendars and schedules, labor contracts, incentive systems, and other structural elements must also support continuous learning on the part of all teachers.

- Connects teachers to teachers within and beyond their schools and connects reform-oriented schools to one another. Teacher networks (face to face and electronic) can serve as important sources of information, materials, and support. Networks enable teachers to connect to the latest research and advances in their fields and to have interpersonal connections that enrich their work. Networks of schools also enable teachers and administrators to learn and receive support.

Quality professional development for everyone who affects student learning is not optional if the goal is high levels of learning for all students. World-class standards require world-class professional development.

Teaching-Learning Process: Curriculum

A World-Class Curriculum in Mathematics: What Does It Mean?

by Ramesh Gangolli

Professor Emeritus, Department of Mathematics, University of Washington

The poet A. E. Housman was once asked to define the qualities of a good poem. He is said to have replied, jokingly, "Asking a poet to define a good poem is like asking a terrier to define a rat. A terrier can't describe a rat, but he knows one when he sees one." (I do not vouch for the exact words of this quote. The event is widely recounted, although probably apocryphal.) One runs into somewhat similar difficulties when asked to define what one means by the phrase "world-class". One can choose to respond with an epigram, but that is not very helpful as a basis for further discussion. It may be useful for us to have at least few structural criteria by which we can gauge what we mean by this phrase. This can be important especially because policy might be formulated on some informal understanding of that phrase.

I think that the phrase "world-class curriculum," as commonly used, has both relative and absolute connotations. On the one hand it implies that the curriculum referred to can creditably withstand a comparison (based on some unspecified set of criteria) with other curricula in use around the world. On the other hand, there is also an expectation that it meets an absolute standard that is very often left unspecified. To clarify this point let us imagine that we are speaking about curriculum in an emerging subject or issue to which most nations in the world are paying no attention. It would be easy to be a leader in such a field, with a curriculum that has little content. (The current state of the issue of environmental policy might give us a rough parallel: most countries in the world, for inevitable economic reasons, are unwilling to address this issue at any level in their educational system.) Although such a curriculum would withstand comparison with other curricula, one would hesitate to point to it with pride as a "world-class" curriculum. Clearly, the term "world-class" assumes an unspecified absolute standard.

Our specific concern is to think about what we might mean by a "world-class mathematics curriculum." Here we have a fair amount of information that one can use for relative as well as absolute judgments. Mathematics is an ancient discipline, whose long history cuts across all nations and cultures, and it has been universally considered to be a basic building block of the educational system. The accumulated experience of different cultures and nations has shaped a large number of curricular models that might serve as benchmarks for relative judgments. On the other hand, mathematics as a discipline is essentially culture-free. Its verities are abstract, and do not depend on cultural prerequisites in order to be accepted. The beauty and utility of mathematics has been appreciated and valued by every human culture, over many centuries. As a result, a disciplinary consensus about the central ideas of the subject is possible, to a far greater extent than it would be in most other disciplines. This gives an absolute standard of sorts. A curriculum that does not adequately address the assimilation of those central ideas would clearly not be "world-class" when held to this internal disciplinary standard.

In what follows, I am going to argue that basing the notion of a "world-class curriculum" (a term that makes me squirm) largely on international performance comparisons is not a sound or fruitful course to follow. This view probably runs counter to the tendencies ingrained in our national culture. Conditioned largely by models of competition appropriate to the Olympic games, the popular expectation is that the same model applies in all fields. We want to be "first" in everything, and our hearts swell to the strains of the national anthem occasioned by the gold medal, irrespective of what field of endeavor we might be considering. I want to argue that specifically in our case (that is, concerning mathematics curricula), there can perhaps be other ways to proceed. My view is that we need to rely much more on a consensual disciplinary standard in the task of designing excellent curricula. Moreover, we need to realize that the design of curricula alone does not ensure their effectiveness. They need to be implemented in conjunction with systemic programs of support and development for teachers. I emphasize that I will not argue that all testing against international benchmarks is irrelevant. Such tests can provide us with information about how specific groups in our system perform when held to the standard of such tests. We need to aspire to doing well on them, but, even though the results of such comparisons might be discouraging to us, I feel that it would be a mistake to make our system responsive solely to the desire to excel in such comparisons.

Relative international judgments about the effectiveness of various facets of educational systems are not easily made. Indeed, fifty years ago the idea of trying to engage in such a comparison for mathematics curricula might have been considered unnecessary and impractical. It is only relatively recently that the idea of international comparisons has taken root, and efforts have been made to mount relatively ambitious international comparisons, the most notable of these being the Third International Mathematics and Science Study (TIMSS) in 1995, and a repetition of a similar study (with somewhat different participating nations, and somewhat more restricted coverage) made this year (2000) designated as TIMSS-R. The TIMSS study was based on assessments of student learning at ages that roughly correspond to our grades 4, 8 and 11. The TIMSS-R is an assessment at grade level 8 only, with tests similar to the tests given in TIMSS, but with somewhat different participating nations. One can anticipate on a priori grounds that such studies are necessarily circumscribed in scope, for a tremendous variety of reasons. For one thing, the diversity of the educational systems makes the task of designing a test that would allow valid comparisons very difficult. Besides, the interpretation of results from such studies is rather complex, especially if one wants to draw inferences about the effectiveness of a particular aspect of a nation's educational system (such as curriculum) from the result of such studies. We know that many other socio-economic and cultural factors (such as: expectations imposed on students and parents by the culture, disparities in economic infrastructure, availability of texts in the local language) have an impact on student learning, and it is hard to abstract away from so many variables to focus on any single one. Moreover, such assessments cannot be regarded as assessments of the entire system, since they examine the system through a tiny aperture focused on student performance on a test at a few grade levels. (This point is particularly relevant to our present situation. The U.S. has fared rather badly in TIMSS except in grade 4. However, U.S. achievements in scientific research and technological innovation are at very high levels, and our higher (especially) graduate educational system seems very effective, and envied by many nations (such as Japan) that come out very well in TIMSS but who are concerned about the effectiveness of their total educational system judged by the standard of scientific research and innovation.)

What are some of the features that we might reasonably set up as an absolute standard for excellence in designing mathematics curricula for our schools? In my view, an excellent (a.k.a. "world-class") curriculum needs to be:

a) Coherent: The curriculum should lead students to understand and appreciate connections between different strands in the curriculum; moreover, treatment of the various strands should be compatibly paced.

b) Comprehensive: The curriculum should offer opportunities for the assimilation (by students) of the major concepts regarded as central to mathematics study at their level.

c) Effective: The curriculum should enhance students' comprehension of concepts as well as techniques, treating these two aspects as complementary (rather than competing) elements in their education.

A great amount of effort has gone into the study of standards (such as the NCTM standards and the large number of studies that they have stimulated) that could be helpful in this regard. The effort has focused on largely on ideas that would help our curricula achieve the first two of the desired criteria listed above. Such efforts need to be continued and extended, with an even greater collaboration between K–12 educators, mathematics educators in higher education, and the mathematical sciences community in higher education. As a nation we have tremendous disciplinary resources in research in the mathematical sciences. The insights about the process of mathematical discovery (and not just technical expertise) that they can provide in designing curricula that address comprehensive and coherent curricula can be very valuable, and we need to use that expertise much more effectively than we have in the past. Undoubtedly there will a period of disagreements and (acrimonious?) debate when this is attempted. (We have already seen examples of this recently.) But it seems to me that there is no alternative but to continue to build wider bridges between these communities, so that a deeper comprehension of the realities of K–12 education results.

The last item in our list is perhaps the most crucial item, and certainly the most difficult item to get a grip on. I think that there is widespread appreciation that no matter how carefully it is designed, a curriculum by itself does not constitute a guarantee of effectiveness. In its pristine form, a curriculum might start off as a list of desirable topics of study. This list might be augmented by careful discussion of interconnections between strands, and appropriate pacing. We might even have exemplary curricular materials that conform to these standards. Even if we assume that all these ingredients are available, we surely know that in order for a curriculum to be effective, many other conditions are necessary. The most obvious among them is a systemic and ongoing set of practices of professional development for teachers that will continually enhance their knowledge of the mathematics they teach and also support them in the day-to-day implementation of curricular materials that militate towards the achievement of these standards of excellence. In this regard I particularly like the Japanese idea of inculcating in teachers a view of themselves as professionals whose primary task is to improve their own effectiveness as teachers, and viewing their own professional development efforts (via many routes, combining lesson study, seminars, conferences, and further formal work) as a lifelong process. This self-image is then continually reinforced by adequate support in terms of preparation time for thinking about teaching.

Of course, there are many other aspects of our educational system that constitute major barriers to effectiveness. Unless we address them, no curriculum can be fully effective. Thus, in the final analysis, we might say that there are no "world-class" curricula, just "excellent" systems. We can aspire to keep working towards an excellent educational system that incorporates disciplinary and pedagogical standards that are widely accepted as appropriate by mathematical educators and professional mathematicians—a system in which teachers are adequately trained, supported, and acknowledged for the important job they do for the future of the nation. We can hope that as we keep working towards such a systemic transformation, our students will improve their performance in international comparisons, and will be regarded as "world-class" by any reasonable standard.

Teaching-Learning Process

Performance-Driven Schools:
Why Rigorous Academic Standards Matter
by Denis P. Doyle
Vice-Chairman and Chief Academic officer, SchoolNet LLC

What are performance-driven schools? They are institutions that set goals and measure their accomplishment. Why are rigorous academic standards essential? Rigorous standards are a school's intellectual armature. They define the school's purpose and what it expects of its students. Rigorous academic standards describe what the value added of schooling is: what difference going to school makes. What has a student mastered because he or she attended school? Standards tell us what students should know and be able to do as a condition of graduation. The student can explain the causes and results of the Revolutionary War. The student can multiply fractions. The student understands photosynthesis. The student can play a musical instrument. They also define how good is good enough: if the physical education standard is the student runs a measured mile, the performance standard is the time it takes to run the mile. If the standard is the student can sight read and interpret French prose the performance standard is the degree of difficulty of the prose, the accuracy of the translation, and the student's speed and facility.

In their earliest incarnation, standards come from the French etandard, the pennant around which the King's soldiers rallied. So long as the etandard flies, the cause of King and Crown is being successfully pursued. If the pennant falls, so too the cause fails. Schools are no different. Standards distinguish them and define them. High standards are a badge of honor, high accomplishment evidence of success.

But there is more to standards than simply setting them. They must be set by the right people in the right place at the right time. Who should set them? The answer is found in the oldest question of political science: quis custodiet, ipsos custodiet? Who shall guard the guardians? The short answer is we shall. Whoever uses the standards—teachers, parents, citizens-at-large and students—should set them. They should do so for several reasons, the most important being ownership. Whoever sets the standards owns them. The principle behind this is at once economic and political: subsidiarity is the term of art. By it political scientists mean that the individual closest to the problem, the worker closest to the work, should address it and solve it. The issue is more than one of simple equity, or even justice. Subsidiarity is important both because it is democratic (with a small "d") but because it works. Indeed, it works better than the alternative.

As important as setting standards is meeting them requires sensitive and sensible measurement. And the decision as to how to measure standards should also be locally owned. If everyone is expected to meet high standards, the tests that measure mastery must be criterion referenced; that is, they must measure the extent to which the student has mastered the standards. Criterion referenced tests benchmark student knowledge against standards; norm referenced tests simply compare one student to another. A criterion referenced tests reveals whether or not you can multiply fractions or run titrations; a norm referenced test reveals whether you have a bigger or smaller vocabulary than other test takers.

Finally, there is the question of consequences: does mastery matter? In what way? To whom? To the student, mastery of a demanding curriculum should be one condition of earning a diploma. Citizenship, deportment, school and community service may be required as well. So too, teachers should be able to demonstrate mastery of their craft, both content and delivery. And administrators must be able to demonstrate that they are more than merely competent: they too must be masters of their craft. But if individuals are held to high and real consequences, organizations must be as well. If significant numbers of students are not "getting it," instructional practice must change; if teachers are not "getting it," pre-service and in-service activities must change; if administrators are not "getting it," rewards (and penalties) as well as incentives must change.

Standards set, standards met, and consequences—this triptych describes the performance-driven school of the 21st century. How do we make this a reality? There is one more piece to the puzzle. The key is the strategic use of data. All schools are awash in data, but few schools know how to use it constructively. Typically, school data is gathered, stored and reported for compliance purposes—as a consequence, most schools view data as a burden, not an opportunity. By way of contrast, the modern firm sees data as an asset, one to be thoughtfully exploited. When schools make this transition, and use data to solve problems and seize opportunities, they will be on the high road to reform. Performance-driven schools use data to improve performance, to fine-tune policy, and improve practice.

Finally, modern IT (information technology) makes it all possible. A Web-based data warehouse (organized as a relational data base), standards, curriculum and testing alignment, and a district-wide Extranet are the key. With them the modern school can be run as efficiently as a contemporary high-tech firm and as humanely as a liberal arts college. The road from standards to mastery may be long, but in the modern world at least, it is direct.

Teaching-Learning Process: Curriculum and Standards

Globalization and Standards

Christopher T. Cross, (President) and M. Rene Islas, (Policy Analyst)
Council for Basic Education

Ever since Sputnik I orbited the earth in October 1957, education in the United States has felt the impact of the shrinking globe. Sputnik not only signaled the start of the space race, but the education race too. The Cold War competitors saw education as strategic ammunition having the potential to be the deciding factor in winning the war. Despite the fall of the Berlin Wall and the dissolution of the USSR in December 1991, the education race persists. It persists, however, in a new atmosphere that continues to value comparison and competition, but is more welcoming of an international exchange of ideas.

The new environment that supports exchange is one that will impact education greatly, especially in the United States. By now, 49 out of 50 states in the U.S. have adopted standards-based reform as the predominant framework to raise student achievement. The standards movement, borrowed from business models of reform, has given students, parents, teachers, and policymakers a clear roadmap of expectations. Research shows that when students understand what they are supposed to learn, when teachers know what to teach, when parents know what to expect of their students and teachers, and when policymakers are able to gauge what is going on in schools, student achievement rises. When expectations are clear, aligned assessments appraise progress, and systems of accountability are fair, standards-based reform supports a positive educational environment.

The success of the standards movement in the United States, as indicated by large achievement gains in states such as Texas and North Carolina, suggests that similar strategies may be useful in an international context. The U.S., specifically, can use international comparisons to rate itself against its economic competitors. Beginning with international comparisons of expectations, student work and performance, and teaching methods; participants will expose themselves to new perspectives on education. Data, such as acquired in the Third International Mathematics and Science Study (TIMSS), mark the strengths and weaknesses in education across the world. The benchmarks reveal what the international level of student achievement is and how close students are to attaining it. More specifically, the data is useful in focusing effort and resources on areas that have the potential to raise student performance.

Collecting, analyzing, and benchmarking international student work through the Internet is a valuable process for gaining an understanding of student performance as well as teaching effectiveness and style. Programs, such the Council for Basic Education's Students Around the World (SAW), offer teachers across the world the opportunity to compare student performance based on work samples. Programs such as SAW's that encourage international collaboration are extremely valuable because they create an environment where perspectives are broadened and effective instructional practices are shared. When SAW teachers benchmark work they are actually engaging in a powerful form of professional development. They learn to evaluate and use student work to improve student learning and achievement by investigating, evaluating, and deliberating strategies used to implement curricula in their classrooms. In addition, teachers in the SAW network share assignments and rubrics and receive feedback from other teachers about the quality of their students' work.

International cooperation can result in a set of "world-class standards" that may guide educators to build a curriculum that prepares students to succeed in a competitive global environment. The experiences gained by international cooperation through programs like Students Around the World and research such as the Third International Mathematics and Science Study have the potential to drive a system where world-class standards can exist to guide education and student achievement to reach high levels in every nation on the globe.

Teaching-Learning Process: Instructional Practice

Reading and Learning
by Marie Carbo
Reading Styles Institute

> James, August 1995: "I hate to read. You will never make me read and I <u>will never read</u>!"
>
> James, May 1996: "I read every night before I go to bed. I especially like to read Sports Illustrated. Before this class, I hated reading. Now I want to read everything that interests me, especially sports."
> by Marie Carbo

Like so many of our nation's struggling readers, James had been taught through his weakness for most of his school career. Finally, in ninth grade he was taught through his natural reading style and interests. In that school year, James moved from a fifth- to an eighth-grade reading level. His class of 42 struggling readers from the poor, delta region of Mississippi, averaged reading gains of 2.6 years, with some students gaining six grade levels in reading.

Critical Importance of Reading Styles and Interests
It's our job as educators to make the <u>process</u> of learning to read easy and enjoyable, so that learning is accelerated, especially for struggling readers like James. Twenty years of data indicate that high gains occur in reading achievement, motivation, and self-concept in short periods of time when students' reading styles are accommodated.[1]

In our staff development program, teachers use the *Reading Style Inventory*, or RSI to identify students' reading styles (their strongest learning pathway for reading). The RSI is a questionnaire that provides information about students' reading styles and describes compatible reading strategies to use for optimum progress. In addition to the use of the RSI by teachers, a great deal is known about the reading style *pattern* of struggling readers. Accommodation of this pattern is an excellent first step.

Our data, and those of others, strongly suggest that the predominant reading style of struggling readers is global, tactile, and kinesthetic.[2] Global learners are emotional, intuitive, and spontaneous. Above all, to do their best they <u>must be vitally interested</u> in what they are reading. Tactile and kinesthetic learners need to touch, move, and experience to learn easily. Struggling readers also generally have high mobility needs, prefer to work in groups, concentrate best in environments with some soft light and comfortable furniture available, and work well with structured choices. They learn skills most easily with small amounts of direct instruction, combined with larger amounts of modeling methods (that is, recordings, choral reading, echo reading), and hands-on, experiential activities like games and role-playing.

Like all readers, below-level readers have a variety of reading interests. In our trainings, we emphasize the need for a range of reading choices for these youngsters that include large amounts of <u>high-interest short-stories</u> with excitement, mystery, adventure, surprise, humor, and/or action. Very often, we provide special, slow-paced, word-by-word recordings of these stories, read with good expression.

The accommodation of students' reading styles has produced such high gains in reading, particularly with struggling readers, that the Kentucky Department of Education recommended the Carbo Reading Styles Program for "its consistently high student performance results." Later, the U.S. Department of Education named the Carbo Reading Styles Program as one of seven national, research-based school-reform programs in reading.[3]

The Web address of the National Reading Styles Institute is NRSI.com.

References

1.   Barber, L., Carbo, M., & Thomasson, R. (1998). *A comparative study of the reading styles program to extant programs of teaching reading.* Bloomington, IN: Phi Delta Kappa; *Carbo Reading Styles Program: Research Update.* (2000). Syosset, NY: National Reading Styles Institute; Oglesby, F., & Suter, W.N. (1995). Matching reading styles and reading instruction. *Research in the Schools* (Mid-South Educational Research Association, 2(1), 11-15; Skip-

per, B. (1997). Reading with style. *American School Board Journal, 184(2), 36-37.*

2.   Duhaney, L.M. G., & Ewing N.J. (1998). An investigation of the reading styles of urban Jamaican middle-grade students with learning disabilities. *Reading Improvement, 35(3), 114-119;* Sudzina, M. (1993). *An investigation of the relationship between the reading styles of second-graders and their achievement in three basal reader treatments.* ERIC Document Reproduction Service No. ED 353 569.

3.   *Catalog of School Reform Models.* (1st ed., 1998). Produced by the Northwest Regional Educational Laboratory and the National Clearinghouse for Comprehensive School Reform. URL: *http://www.nwrel.org/scpd/catalog/index.shtml/;* Results-based practices showcase (1997–1998). Louisville, KY: Kentucky Department of Education, Division of School Improvement.

Teaching-Learning Process: Instructional Practice

Improving Teaching
by James Stigler and James Hiebert
Authors of *The Teaching Gap: Best Ideas from the World's Teachers*
for Improving Education in the Classroom

As the reform movement continues it becomes ever clearer that standards and assessments alone will not lead to higher levels of student achievement. To improve achievement, the process of teaching that occurs inside classrooms must be carefully examined. This is the process most closely connected with what students learn and, if the new standards are to be reached, teaching must be improved.

How can teaching be improved? The most obvious solution is to recruit more capable teachers. This is the focus of many well-meaning efforts and it is a strategy endorsed by many policy makers and by a large percentage of the public. Set higher certification standards to weed out the weak candidates and increase salaries and signing bonuses to attract the more talented prospects, and teaching will improve. This sounds plausible, and we certainly applaud the efforts to raise teachers' pay and improve the capabilities of the teacher corps.

But the belief that teaching will improve when more qualified individuals enter the classroom is largely a myth. Even if all current teachers could be replaced with new teachers who score high on all measures of academic success, teaching would change very little and students would learn about the same. Why? Because the effectiveness of teachers depends mostly on the methods they use. And the methods U.S. teachers use have changed little over the past hundred years. Cross-cultural research has shown that even in a country as diverse as the United States, the variability in teaching methods is rather small. The vast majority of teachers, regardless of their qualifications, teach the way they were taught, using the methods that have been passed down from generation to generation.

In our research on teaching, we see many examples of teachers implementing competently limited methods of teaching. They are doing a good job of teaching in the way they were taught. It's not the competence of teachers that lies at the heart of the problem; it's the inability to improve on the methods of teaching that most teachers use. Real, long-lasting, and widespread improvement of teaching methods requires building a knowledge base of teaching. Indeed, a true profession is defined by its knowledge base, which determines, in part, the standard practices used by its members. These standard practices of teaching are what need to be improved, over time, if we are to improve the average student's learning in the average classroom.

Improving teaching, as opposed to teachers, will require giving teachers the opportunity to examine their practices, study them, evaluate them, and figure out ways to improve them. They will need to read the research literature and observe their own students to learn about how students learn. They will need to observe their colleagues—whether in other classrooms, other schools, or other cultures to find alternative ways of teaching that can improve the learning of their students. And they will need the courage and the opportunity to experiment with new techniques in their classrooms, as well as the common sense to judge whether the new techniques are more effective than the old.

Each day, three million teachers go to work, and they no doubt learn something from their experiences. But we have no mechanism to accumulate or share what they learn with other teachers, so each new generation must start all over again. We waste the collective experience of our teachers. Our society can do better. New ways must be devised to accumulate professional knowledge so that it can be shared with each new generation of teachers. Perhaps new technologies can create digital libraries of effective teaching practices, organized around the learning goals and standards that increasingly guide society's efforts to improve. Whatever mechanism is developed, educators must work to change the school culture in which each teacher labors alone, unable to take advantage of what others before have learned. Let's change the culture and enlist teachers to work together on improving teaching. Let's start now.

Teaching-Learning Process: Assessment

World Class Math Education
Through Classroom Assessment
by Jan deLange
Freudenthal Institute, Netherlands

Paul lives five miles from school, and Annie three miles from the same school. How far apart do Annie and Paul live from each other? (Hint: the answer is not: 2)

The distance between ideal and reality is almost maximal in classroom assessment. The reason is simple: there is almost no culture to speak of in classroom assessment in part because of the identification of assessment with standardized tests. A literature study by Black and William (1998) shows that many innovative efforts have failed because they did not address properly the most important variable—classroom assessment. A proper classroom assessment system forces curriculum designers, teachers, administrators, parents, and students to reflect on what constitutes "high quality mathematics education." A variety of instruments, varying from discourse and observations via extended open-ended tasks to presentations can help us to bring the best out of our students and teachers and make assessment an integral part of the teaching learning process.

North, South, East, West—the cardinal directions. There is a North Pole and a South Pole but no East Pole or West Pole. How is that possible?

We should not expect teachers to conquer both North Pole and South Pole; we expect teachers already to excel in just about everything. But, as numerous examples of published items of standardized tests show: even experts quite often design items with very high reliability and validity but ridiculous mathematical content. Teachers should become a "passive" assessment expert that is that they can judge the quality of published items and are able to "design" a complete assessment instrument that is fair to the curriculum and fair to the students. This is a reasonable and reachable goal as our research shows.

If a mathematician looks in the mirror he sees that top remains top, bottom remains bottom, but left and right are changing places. How come?

A change of perspective is needed: we need to look in the mirror: do we just want higher scores on multiple choice items and short open-ended questions? Move to states that have made education into test preparation, and stop thinking. Just like the students. Or you can go to California which has a framework that is "mathematically correct" and is being operationalized with multiple-choice items. Multiple choice—now we are speaking assessment. Therefore, we propose that we not only make teachers passive experts but politicians, administrators, parents, and superintendents, not to forget mathematicians as well.

A plane flies on a windless day from A to B in 30 minutes and from B to A in the same time. The next day the same trip is made under windy conditions. What do you need to know about the wind in order to be able to judge whether the trip from A to B and return will take longer, shorter, or the same time?

If you don't know the answer within a couple of seconds your reasoning skills need some training. This deficiency should have been caught during the classroom assessment at your school, and if so, you would never forget. Don't worry—you will pass most standardized tests without any problem. But if you are serious about mathematics education, look in the mirror and realize that education is meant for kids. And they deserve the best—not higher scores on meaningless multiple-choice tests. And indeed, the trip toward that goal will be windy; expect strong headwinds en route.

Teaching-Learning Process: Assessment

World Class Tests©
The development of tests of mathematics and problem solving for pupils aged 9 and 13
by Martin Ripley
World Class Tests Programme Director, Qualifications and
Curriculum Authority, England

In March 1999, the UK government published a policy statement, *Excellence in Cities*. Among many initiatives designed to improve inner city schools and the performance of their pupils, new "World Class" tests were proposed.

The major elements underpinning the idea of these new tests are simply expressed.

- There should be tests of mathematics and problem solving.
- The tests should be aimed primarily at pupils of 9 and 13 years of age.
- The tests should, where educationally viable, be computer-based.
- The tests should be aimed at the top 10% (in ability terms) of pupils.
- The tests should be internationally calibrated to provide teachers with comparative information in relation to the performance of pupils in other countries.
- The tests should be widely available, should be available for pupils to take whenever they are ready, and should be available throughout the world.
- The tests should be supported by other learning, teaching, and assessment materials designed to aid teachers and parents in preparing pupils for the tests.

The philosophy and educational politics reflected by the tests embrace a number of considerations. First, these tests represent a significant development in educational policy in England: Schools are expected to identify the needs of their most able pupils and to provide for the needs of those pupils. Second, the launch of World Class Tests reflects a wish to improve England's relative international performance (as exemplified through the TIMSS and TIMSS-R studies). Third, it is also intended that the tests, together with the teaching and learning underpinning them, will be a means of measuring the extent to which the performance of our most able pupils is improving over time. Fourth, the tests reflect a view that computer technology can be harnessed to design and develop worthwhile and valuable assessment activities at the same time as delivering other benefits, such as speed of marking and improved accessibility.

Work on developing these tests commenced in late 1999, with the New Projects Team at the Qualification and Curriculum Authority (QCA) in England taking the role of project leadership. This has involved a number of external teams working under contract to QCA.

- The Assessment and Evaluation Unit (AEU) at the University of Leeds is developing the mathematics tests content.
- The Mathematics Assessment Resource Service (MARS) team at the Shell Centre in the University of Nottingham and Durham University is developing the problem solving tests content.
- NCS Pearson is programming the computer-based test questions developed by MARS and AEU.
- AQA (a major provider of examinations and qualifications based in England) and Doublestruck, a software provider, will be working with QCA to provide the test administration, marking and reporting service to pupils taking the tests.

World Class Tests will be available beginning late 2001.

The Test Model

World Class Tests will ultimately be provided as online tests. However, the current model of the tests involves pupils taking two components for each test. One of these is computer-based; the second is a paper-based test, as set out in the following diagram of the mathematics tests. (A similar structure applies to the problem solving tests.)

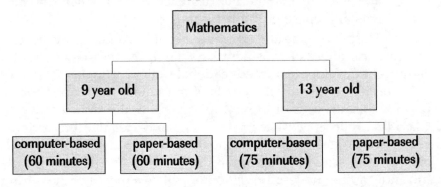

A model for developing the tests has been established, involving the teams indicated above, a range of teachers and random samples of schools from England.

- The teams construct early drafts of test questions.
- They try out these ideas in one or two schools.
- Expert groups review questions.
- Questions are refined and informally piloted in schools with about 20 pupils.
- A Teacher Review Group (a group of about 35 teachers from England) critiques the draft questions.
- Questions are formally pretested with a larger sample of pupils (about 200).
- Questions are evaluated and, where appropriate, approved.
- Balanced tests are constructed.

A first international pretest, based in Chicago USA, has also been completed. This included a systematic review of the content and difficulty of the tests by teachers from about 30 schools.

Purposes of the Tests

Working from the vision for the tests, four purposes of the World Class Tests can be defined.

1. **To identify and recognize the achievements of pupils.**
    This reflects the intrinsic value to the pupil (and parents) of his or her achievement in the tests.

2. **To provide guidance to schools and teachers on the standards to be expected of the most able pupils.**

    It is intended that there will be teaching and learning materials to support the tests. In addition, the tests themselves will help schools understand the sorts of skills, understanding and knowledge that their most able pupils should be taught as well as the standards of performance that can be expected of them.

3. **To provide schools with guidance about the standards expected of the most able pupils in other countries.**

    The tests will reflect standards and expectations of the top 10% of pupils internationally. The domains for the tests and the content of the tests are designed to reflect this vision—

test questions, question contexts, assumed and tested knowledge and standards of performance are designed to reflect this international context.

4. **To provide schools with information about how well their pupils are performing in relation to other countries.**

Building on purposes 2 and 3, the final purpose is that of providing test results information to schools in such a form that teachers (and parents) can readily make internationally comparable judgments about their pupils' performance.

Test Content

Problem solving in World Class Tests encompasses those mental activities that may be brought into play when there is a demand to apply existing knowledge, skill and experience to unfamiliar situations. Pupils are rewarded for their success in arriving at a solution and for being able to reveal understanding of the patterns and structure revealed. All stages of problem solving will be assessed: planning, carrying out strategy, reviewing, and presentation. The problems are set in mathematical, scientific, and design contexts.

The problem solving tests will contain a range of task types, drawing from the following categories:

Select   The task is to select and analyze information bearing on a decision in order to select a best solution. This might include optimising one or more continuous or discontinuous variables.

Invent   The task is to create a procedure or design an artifact to meet design constraints. This might include the planning of scientific investigations.

Discover   The task is to find (and justify) relationships or generalizations, uncover underlying structure and extrapolate or predict.

Model   The task is to invent, interpret, and explain models that represent reality. This might include estimating.

Translate   The task is to take data from one form and to represent in another

Critique The task is to review an artifact, an argument, or a pro-
          cedure and suggest improvements.

Deduce   The task is to make deductions from data.

The mathematics tests sample from the following skills:

SKILL	EXAMPLE
Procedural – application of known procedures in a difficult form	Solving equations involving decimals
Applying knowledge to new situations	How many 6-digit square numbers are there?
Transferring knowledge across areas	Applying percentages in a geometrical context
Using effective mental strategies to deal with chains of operations	Where efficient strategies involve mental manipulation and retention
Translating linguistic forms into mathematical symbolism	Solving a word problem
Making deductions	Calculating a missing angle
Drawing inferences and making judgments	Predicting a number in a sequence

The mathematical content of the tests will be drawn from a number of areas of mathematics, including: numbers and number sense; fractional number and proportionality; algebra; geometrical reasoning; measurement; and data representation, analysis, and probability.

Test Examples

QCA's Web site (*http://www.worldclassarena.org*) contains many examples of test questions, taken from both the paper-based and the computer-based components. The following three questions are examples of the sorts of questions being developed.

Example One: Mean Change

Mean Change is a computer-based question, taken from a mathematics test for children at the age of 13 or younger.

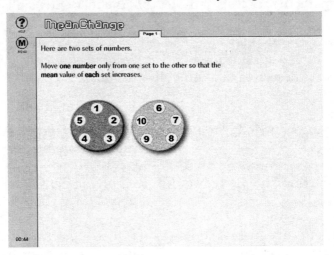

Example Two: Sunflower

Sunflower is a computer-based question taken from a problem-solving test for children at the age of 9 or younger.

Example Three
The third example question, below, is taken from a paper-based test of mathematics designed for children at the age of 9 or younger.

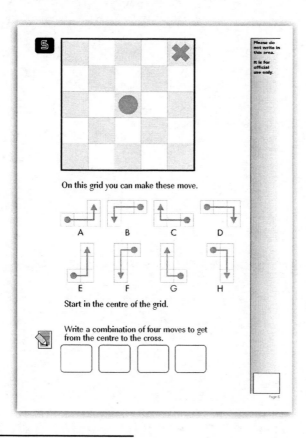

Appendix B

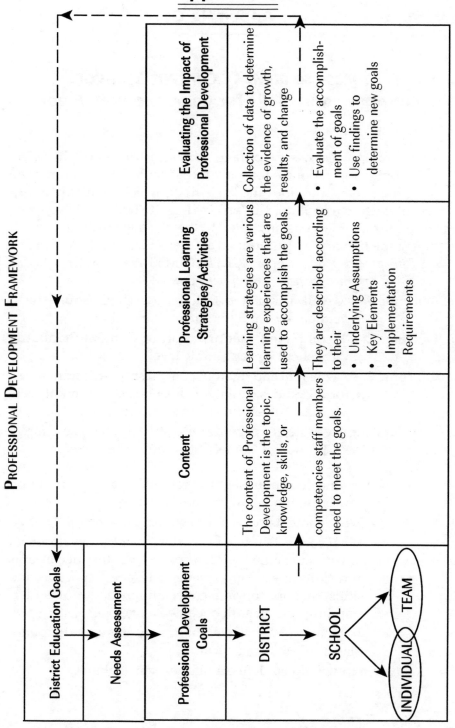

PROFESSIONAL DEVELOPMENT FRAMEWORK

District Education Goals	Needs Assessment	Professional Development Goals	DISTRICT	SCHOOL	INDIVIDUAL · TEAM

Content

The content of Professional Development is the topic, knowledge, skills, or competencies staff members need to meet the goals.

Professional Learning Strategies/Activities

Learning strategies are various learning experiences that are used to accomplish the goals.

They are described according to their

- Underlying Assumptions
- Key Elements
- Implementation Requirements

Evaluating the Impact of Professional Development

Collection of data to determine the evidence of growth, results, and change

- Evaluate the accomplishment of goals
- Use findings to determine new goals

Appendix C

A Process to Identify Content Standards, Concepts, and Skills for Coherence and Rigor©

In this process we encourage school districts to identify the philosophy and rationale for why the curriculum is structured the way that it is. It provides the basis upon which to justify and to articulate the curriculum. This process helps to build the DNA-gene strand for the roles of standards. We then lead the district through the completion of the Identification of Content Standards Worksheet.

This process is taken from NCREL's TIMSS-1999 Guidebook. *The process is designed to yield three specific outcomes:*

Outcome 1: A well articulated rationale and philosophy for a mathematics and/or science curriculum

Outcome 2: A completed Identification of Content Standards Worksheet for each grade level

Outcome 3: A coherent and rigorous content standards framework for all grades upon which to build and modify lessons, and determine instructional materials

The following seven steps will guide the district through the completion of the Identification of Content Standards Worksheet.

1. Determine your philosophical rationale for the curriculum by answering the following four questions:
    a. What content areas should students learn?
    b. What core beliefs will be a priority for the development of your curriculum with respect to mastery of concepts and skills at each grade level, reteaching concepts and skills, age appropriate expectations, depth of understanding and breadth of content coverage?
    c. To what extent will integrating concepts and disciplines play a role in the curriculum?
    d. How will you define a rigorous curriculum?

By answering these four questions you should be able to complete the following statement:

Our curriculum is based on the belief that:

and, therefore, is designed to:

2. Identify the standards document that will serve as a basis for the development of the content standards, concepts, and skills.

3. Using the standards documents, determine the content areas and topics that you will address in the curriculum from kindergarten through Grade 12 and write them on the Content Standards Identification Worksheet.

4. Using the same standards documents, complete the grade level Content Standards Identification Worksheet for each grade level by identifying the concepts and skills to be emphasized. Use verbs to describe all concepts and skills.

    Note: These descriptors will likely have a performance expectation characteristic to them. Remember a "pure" content standard will typically say *knows* or *understands*. We suggest more of a performance flavor since you will likely be thinking in those terms anyway.

5. As you build content standards, keep in mind the total number of concepts and skills you are emphasizing and the time that will be needed to provide in-depth instruction. In addition, give thought to how the concepts will build on each other through the grade levels. (This is the breadth, duration, and flow issue.) You will want to total the number of topics, concepts and skills to ensure that you have a reasonable and appropriate number at each grade level.

6. Align all concepts to the your state Learning Standards. Code them in the column provided on the Content Standards Identification Sheet. Recognize that you may include categories, concepts, and skills that are not addressed in the your state Learning Standards.

7. Finally, consider contacting the Mid-Continent Research in Educational Learning (MCREL) to seek a review of your content standards document if you want validation on its coherence and rigor.

Having completed all seven steps you should have a clearly defined rationale that provides the philosophical underpinnings of your curricular area. Second, the completed Content Standards Identification Sheets provide you with a content framework that articulates the exact grade level a typical student in your district should learn concepts and skills. These documents define the core curricular standards of your program. Using these standards you can build specific lessons, activities, and tasks. You are then in a position to align your standards with these lessons and/or your instructional materials, and determine any adjustments in your instructional practice and assessments.

Grade Level Content Standards Identification Sheet

(Concepts and Skills)

Subject _____

Grade Level _____

Standards Document(s) _____

used to build content standards _____

Category	Topic	State Learning Standards	Concept/Skill to be learned

References

Aumiller, E., Kimmelman, P., Kroeza D., Masini, B. (2002) *Learning from TIMSS 1999: A guidebook for using TIMSS 1999 data for local school improvement*. North Central Regional Educational Laboratory, Naperville, IL.

Barber, M. (1999, September 27). Citation drawn from a speech delivered at the Skol Tema Conference Stockholm, Sweden.

Before it's too late. (2000) National Commission on Mathematics and Science Teaching for the 21st Century. Washington, DC: U.S. Department of Education.

Bennis, W. (1997). *Managing people is like herding cats.* Provo, Utah: Executive Excellence Publishing.

Carnine, D. (2000). Why education experts resist effective practices (and what it would take to make education more like medicine). Thomas B. Fordham Foundation.

Chalker, D., and Haynes, R. (1994). *World class elementary schools: agenda for action.* Lancaster, PA: Technomic Publishing.

Chalker, D., and Haynes, R. (1997). *World class schools: new standards for education.* Lancaster, PA: Technomic Publishing.

Checkley, K. (1997, June) Assessment that serves instruction. *Education Update*, Vol. 39.

Christiansen, D. (2000, Fall). *Research to practice: a framework for closing the gap* (policy paper), pp. 1–4.

Crockett, R. (2001, July 16). Motorola: can Chris Galvin save his family's legacy, *BusinessWeek*.

Doyle, D., and Pimentel, S. (1993, March). *Kappan*.

Dunn, R., and Dunn, K. (1978). *Teaching students through their individual learning styles.* Reston: VA: Reston Publishing.

Effective professional development systems. (1998). Paper prepared for the Council of Chief State School Officers Annual Meeting. Consortium for Policy Research in Education.

Elmore, R. (1996, Spring) Getting to scale with good educational practice. *Harvard Educational Review, 66*, 1–2.

Fox, D. (2001, Spring) Three kinds of data for decisions about reading. *Using data for educational decision making*, Vol. 6, Comprehensive Assistance Center, Region VI.

Fullan, M. (1993). *Change forces: probing the depths of educational reform.* London: Falmer Press.

Fullan, M. (1999, March). Seminar on Educational Change. Urbana, IL.

Fullan, M., and Hargreaves, A. (1998). *What's worth fighting for out there.* New York: Teachers College Press.

Goldhaber, D., and Brewer, D. (1996). Evaluating the effect of teacher degree level on educational performance. *Development in School Finance*, p. 199.

Greenspan, A. (2000, September 21). Statement before the Committee on Education and the Workforce, U.S. House of Representatives.

Kennedy, M. (1997, October). The connection between research and practice. *Educational Researcher*, pp. 4–14.

Kotter, J. (1996). *Leading change.* Boston: Harvard Business Press.

Linn, R. (2000, March). Assessments and accountability. *Educational Researcher*, Vol. 29, pp. 4–16.

Marshall, E. (2000). *Building trust at the speed of change.* New York: Amacom Books.

McWalters, P. (1999, September). A collaborative approach to educational research: what will it take? Policy paper by the National Education Research Policy and Priorities Board Forum. Washington, DC: U.S. Department of Education.

National Research Council. (2000). *How people learn: Mind, brain, experience, and school (expanded edition).*

Pascale, R. T. (1990) *Managing on the edge.* New York: Touchstone.

Patterson, J. (1997). *Coming clean about organizational change: leadership in the real world.* Arlington, VA: American Association of School Administrators.

Porter, A., et al. (2000). Does professional development change teaching practice? Results from a three-year study. Washington, DC: U.S. Department of Education.

Porter, T. (1996). *Trust in numbers: the pursuit of objectivity in science and public life.* Princeton: Princeton University Press.

Powell, C. (No Date). *Lessons on leadership.* (Online). Available: *http//blaisdell.com/powell*

Principles and indicators for student assessment systems. (1995, August). Washington, DC: National Forum on Assessment.

Quinn, Robert, E. (1996). *Deep change: Discovering the leader within.* San Francisco: Jossey-Bass Publishers.

Report of the National Reading Panel. (2000, April). National Institute of Child Health and Human Development.

Sagor, R. (2001). *Guiding school improvement with action research.* Alexandria, VA: Association for Supervision and Curriculum Development.

Sarason, S. (1999). *Teaching as a performing art.* New York: Teachers College Press.

Schmidt, W.H., McKnight, C.C., and Raizen, S.A. (1997). *A splintered vision: an investigation of U. S. science and mathematics education.* Dordrecht, the Netherlands: Kluwer Academic.

Senge, P. (1990). *The fifth discipline.* New York: Doubleday.

Simmons, R. (1994, February) The horse before the cart: assessing for understanding. *Educational Leadership,* Vol. 51. No. 5.

Sparks, D., and Hirsh, S. (1997). *A new vision for staff development* Alexandria, VA: Association for Supervision and Curriculum Development.

Stake, R. (1999, May). The goals on American education. *Phi Delta Kappan,* pp. 668–672.

Steffy, B., and English, F. (1997). *Curriculum and assessment for world-class schools.* Lancaster, PA: Corwin Press.

Testing, teaching and learning: a guide for states and school districts, (1999). National Research Council. Washington, DC: Washington Academy Press.

Traub, J. (1999, December). *Better by design, a consumer's guide to schoolwide reform.* Thomas B. Fordham Foundation.

Tucker, M., and Codding, J. (1998). *Standards for our schools: how to set them, measure them, and reach them.* San Francisco: Jossey-Bass Publishers.

White House Press Release. (1999, October 22). Remarks by the President of the United States to the National Board for Professional Teaching Standards, Hyatt Regency: Washington, DC.

Index

Introductory note: All pages in **bold** indicate charts, figures or tables

About the Authors

Paul Kimmelman, Ed.D.

Paul L. Kimmelman is Special Advisor to the Executive Director at the North Central Regional Education Laboratory and serves as a consultant to the Qualifications and Curriculum Authority for the British Department of Education. He has also served as Senior Consultant to Project 2061 Professional Development Programs of the American Association for the Advancement of Science and as an adjunct professor at several colleges and universities. He worked in K-12 education for over 30 years as a teacher, assistant principal, principal, assistant superintendent, and superintendent. Mr. Kimmelman has authored numerous articles and publications on education and presented at national and state education meetings. He was appointed by former Secretary of Education Richard Riley to the National Commission on Mathematics and Science Teaching chaired by former Senator and astronaut John Glenn and served on the TIMSS Technical Review Panel.

David J. Kroeze, Ph.D.

David J. Kroeze is superintendent of Northbrook School District 27, in Northbrook, Illinois. For more than two decades he has presented at national education forums and conferences, published articles, co-authored numerous publications with the Department of Education and the North central regional Education Laboratory, and consulted educators across the nation on world class schools and school improvement. Dr. Kroeze co-founded the First in the World Consortium where he serves as the Consortium's Chairperson for Research.

Mr. Kroeze received his doctorate in educational administration from the University of Chicago. While at the university, he was mentored by Dan C. Lortie. Mr. Lortie taught him the value and impact that dynamic leadership can have on schools and the teaching-learning process.